The Invisible Workers of the U.S.–Mexico Bracero Program

The Invisible Workers of the U.S.–Mexico Bracero Program

Obreros Olvidados

Ronald L. Mize

LEXINGTON BOOKS
Lanham • Boulder • New York • London

Published by Lexington Books
An imprint of The Rowman & Littlefield Publishing Group, Inc.
4501 Forbes Boulevard, Suite 200, Lanham, Maryland 20706
www.rowman.com

Unit A, Whitacre Mews, 26-34 Stannary Street, London SE11 4AB, United Kingdom

British Library Cataloguing in Publication Information Available

Library of Congress Cataloging-in-Publication Data

Includes bibliographical references and index.
ISBN 978-1-4985-1780-5 (cloth : alk. paper)
ISBN 978-1-4985-1781-2 (electronic)

∞™ The paper used in this publication meets the minimum requirements of American National Standard for Information Sciences Permanence of Paper for Printed Library Materials, ANSI/NISO Z39.48-1992.

Printed in the United States of America

Contents

Preface

In 1956, Don Jorge left his small village (*pueblo*) in Colima, Mexico, where he had lived for the first eighteen years of his life. He embarked on a journey that shaped not only the next three years but also the rest of his life. As the eldest son, he started the first leg of his trip, approximately 150 miles, from the *milpa* (agricultural lands) in West Central Mexico his family had occupied for generations producing *maíz* for subsistence. He traveled to the recruitment center in Irapuato, Guanajuato. He knew that as a young man, his hands sufficiently calloused as evidence of prior agricultural experience, he had bought the necessary papers from the local government official (in his case about 300 pesos or US$25 in 1950), and he met all requirements that enabled him to register for a temporary worker contract. He waited in Irapuato until his number was called. He was lucky this trip as he was contracted quickly, but in the ensuing years, he would not be so lucky. From Irapuato, he was bused nearly 1,600 miles to Calexico, California, and there he was given his necessary papers and identification card. He did not like to talk about this portion of the journey as it was here that he was subjected to mass medical examinations, delousing with DDT, and a dehumanizing process that marked the beginning of how he will be subsequently treated as a Mexican Bracero in the United States. When discussing his experiences with me, he confirms the examination of his hands because he had big balls of callouses from wielding agricultural implements like *el cortito*, or the short-handled hoe, that is later banned from U.S. agriculture due to its deleterious health effects. He nods to confirm the mass examination where he is stripped naked in front of a hundred compatriots and subjected to an anal exam for hernias, and an examination for sexually transmitted diseases, and acknowledges his private parts and the private parts of all would-be Braceros were on public display for the U.S. doctors to determine whether they were fit to work and not a public hygiene threat. Just in case the doctors missed anything, the men are then herded *en masse* to an outdoor facility where they are sprayed with DDT to mark them as disease-free, clean, and fully deloused. Wanting to skip over these unpleasant details, Don Jorge mentions he still carries in his wallet the original Bracero identification card that was issued on that day. He tells me he holds onto it for *recuerdos* (memories), and every subsequent Bracero I interview has the card in his wallet.

In the years following his first sojourn, subsequent trips to secure contracts become much more difficult. One year, he waited on the streets of Monterrey for three months with no food, shelter, money, or hope he would actually receive a contract. An amendment to the agreement between the federal governments of Mexico and the United States relocated the recruitment centers from central Mexico (where the majority of would-be Braceros reside) to the U.S.-Mexico border in order for the U.S. government to cut their transportation costs. This time, his approximately seven-hundred-mile trip to the border is an expense he must shoulder. Upon arriving in the closest recruitment center in Monterrey, he sees men starving to death around him. Don Jorge suffers too but he holds out for a contract until he can wait no longer. After the third month, he wires his parents in Colima to ask for money to survive and return home. Fortuitously, the very next day he is told that work is available.

But his luck often runs out when it comes to the living conditions in the United States. In terms of housing, the forty other Braceros he works with stay in army barracks that the company converted. On subsequent trips to Michigan, Ohio, and Texas he works with *el cortito* (short-handled hoe) that most likely led to his current unemployment due to chronic back problems. The work was hard but "he endured" as he often states it. He witnessed a few strikes over wages, deductions, or rotten food but was never an instigator. He notes that the rabble rousers were noticeably absent after a food or wage strike and assumes they were deported.

Yet, Don Jorge prefers to detail the happier aspects of his life as a Bracero. He speaks at length about his Sunday "day-on-the-town" stories, the good bosses, the contracts that went well, and his pride about how his children never had to work in the fields. Even though he is residing in Fresno, California as of 1997, where most of his sons and daughters are working in factories, his home is Colima, his heart and loyalty are *Puro Mexicano*.

The story of the U.S.-Mexico Bracero Program is rarely told from the perspective of the workers, if it is told at all, even though their life stories are a testament to the truism that government policies are rarely enacted in accordance with the spirit, intent, or letter of the law. From 1942 to 1964, the federal governments of the United States and Mexico arranged a set of accords that supplied U.S. agricultural growers, and for a brief time the railroad industry, with a steady stream of Mexican labor. Initially intended to serve as a war-time relief measure, the temporary-worker arrangements were allowed to continue until 1964. The vast majority of workers were sent to three states (California, Arizona, and Texas) but a total of thirty states participated in the program.[1] Don Jorge de Colima's life story attests to both the desperation in Mexico that forced people to migrate and how he personally paid the consequences of binational governance decisions.

The ex-Braceros and their families who shared their experiences for this book were asked to recall their experiences in what is referred to as the life story approach. Life stories are the accounts of a person's own lived experiences as orally communicated by that person. Life histories are life stories and the supplementary materials to the person's own story like written documents, other biographies, and other sources of history (Bertaux 1981, 7). This approach enables respondents in marginalized positions to tell the stories about important events that have shaped their lives and fit into my overall methodological approach I refer to as archival ethnography. The intersubjectivity of all sources of history can be critically explored by focusing on the formal characteristics of each textual source. The potential applications of the approach are varied but it is suited for both the study of lived social relations and the subjective recollections of those relations. Life stories were collected in two waves and locales and the memories of the ex-Braceros interviewed in 1997 Fresno differed significantly from the ex-Braceros interviewed by Dr. Sergio Chavez (at the time a graduate research assistant) in 2005 on the Mexico-U.S. border.

The men, seventeen ex-Braceros, interviewed for the book had a wealth of shared experiences to draw from, yet they were unique from each other in many ways. They hailed from their Mexican home states of Chihuahua, Coahuila, Colima, Durango, Guanajuato, Michoacán, Nayarit, Oaxaca, Sinaloa, Sonora, and Zacatecas. The U.S. states in which they were contracted to work were just as varied. They were employed in Arizona, Arkansas, California, Colorado, Michigan, Ohio, North Carolina, Pennsylvania, Texas, and Utah. They experienced incredibly difficult working conditions by toiling in the following crops: grapes, strawberries, celery, lettuce, asparagus, spinach, tomatoes, carrots, cotton, squash, chiles, lemons, oranges, avocados, cantaloupe, cucumber, beans, sugar beets, green beans, potatoes, broccoli, grapefruit, peaches, and wheat. One former Bracero interviewed was a track worker on the railroads. Their work time as Braceros spanned from 1945 to 1964, though most of the men worked in the late 1950s and early 1960s. In addition to the life stories of former Braceros, I interviewed forty-five informants impacted by the program, including family members, a food provider, a money order processor, a crew boss, a housing inspector, residents, a migrant service provider, and Chicano activists. The unique approach I took to investigating the experiences of the men who received contracts to work as Braceros was a result of twenty years of archival and field research in four locales

(Central Valley of California, Colorado, Oregon, and Mexican border towns). I conducted an extensive archival analysis of the Ernesto Galarza papers at Stanford University (the foremost public intellectual who documented the abuses Braceros endured), Oregon State University Bracero and Extension archives, state archives in Colorado and California, and a media textual analysis (print and electronic) during both the program and the contemporary redress campaign. I also interviewed, with the research assistance of Rice University Professor Sergio Chavez, Braceros before and during the social justice movement that successfully sought redress from the Mexican government for the ten percent of wages that were automatically deducted from paychecks as an enticement to return after temporary contracts ended. The men rarely received the ten percent wage withholdings that they were guaranteed.

Even though the men came from all over Mexico and traveled all over the United States to tend a variety of crops, they were very similarly situated in terms of their time spent as Braceros and their treatment by crew bosses, farm labor contractors, growers, and U.S and Mexican state officials. The men had to navigate a racial and class terrain that relegated them to the bottom of the U.S. agricultural ladder with attendant Jim Crow-, Anglo-style enforcement of racial lines of segregation. The Bracero Program, with its express support from the U.S. and Mexican states, was organized precisely to quell discontent and allow for despotic labor regimes that transcended the boundaries of the fields. Nearly every aspect of the Braceros' behavior was under surveillance and a rigid set of role expectations was imposed from above at nearly every turn in the lived experiences of Braceros. Rather than assuming that class and racial factors are analytically distinct or practically autonomous,[2] I treat the relationship as a historically produced question as to the *degree* of articulation between race and class. Bracero men were conjointly raced and classed upon entering the United States. The high degree of articulation between racial oppression and class exploitation created the marginal conditions I define as the "Bracero total institution" (see Mize 2006a, 2004). The social relations that Braceros were inserted into demanded a set of grower-based role expectations that assumed Braceros would accept the conditions of employment without complaint, regardless of the deplorable conditions.

Some workers found the conditions unbearable and their forms of resistance consisted of two main responses: Braceros either openly demanded better conditions and as a result were swiftly deported, or they quit coming back altogether and found jobs outside the U.S. agricultural sector. The two options—deportation or exit—were most often the sole means of actively resisting oppression. Otherwise, one survived by meeting the expectations as to conduct, work productivity, and acceptance of the existing conditions placed upon one by the dictates of the Bracero Program. The life stories, which provide the main materials for this study, are the stories of those who endured. The life stories represent those men who saw no other options available but to subject themselves to these sets of conditions so thoroughly constructed by racial and class inequality.

Prior versions of this manuscript have been published as *The Invisible Workers: Articulations of Race and Class in the Life Histories of Braceros* (author copyright 2000). Doctoral dissertation on file with UMI Abstracts, Department of Sociology and Rural Sociology, University of Wisconsin–Madison (2004). “The Persistence of Workplace Identities: Living the Effects of the Bracero Total Institution,” pp. 155–175 in *Immigrant Life in the US: Multidisciplinary Perspectives* Donna R. Gabaccia and Colin W. Leach editors, New York: Routledge Press, (2006). “Power (In)-Action: State and Agribusiness in the Making of the Bracero Total Institution.” *Berkeley Journal of Sociology* 50 (1): 76–119 (2006). “Mexican Contract Workers and the U.S. Capitalist Agricultural Labor Process: The Formative Era, 1942–1964,” *Rural Sociology* 71(1): 85–107 (2005). “Reparations for Mexican Braceros? Lessons Learned from Japanese and African American Attempts at Redress.” *Cleveland State Law Review, LatCrit VIII Symposium Issue*, 52 (1/2): 273–295.

NOTES

1. From 1942–47, the following states contracted the following number of Mexican Braceros: Arizona: 5,975, California: 124,305, Colorado: 7,643, Idaho: 11,088, Illinois: 1,083, Indiana: 382, Iowa: 3,033, Kansas: 796, Michigan: 7,516, Minnesota: 5,288, Montana: 12,767, Nebraska: 4,039, Nevada: 2,577, New Mexico: 151, North Carolina: 410, North Dakota: 3,094, Oregon: 13,007, South Dakota: 1,577, Utah: 3,361, Washington: 15,029, Wisconsin: 4,817, Wyoming: 2,732 (adapted from Rasmussen 1951, 226). In addition, Arkansas, Georgia, Mississippi, Texas, Ohio, Missouri, Tennessee, and Louisiana participated in the later years of the program (Lyon 1954, 225). One respondent I interviewed stated that her father worked in the agricultural fields of New York but I have found no official record of Braceros working in New York agriculture. However, Driscoll (1999) identifies railroad Braceros employed in New York.

2. The sociological specialization or subdiscipline of “migration studies” is indicative of the larger problems in the discipline of sociology. The dominant trend is to operationalize theories into distinct, measurable categories, isolate those variables, and treat complex overlapping processes as mutually exclusive. This process gains legitimacy in the name of the scientific pursuit of parsimonious, operational definitions to be statistically manipulated. Each subdiscipline limits its scope of analysis and conducts studies based on the isolated variables within the distinct area of study. This goal of moving the discipline toward increased specialization and boundary-policing is inhibiting the study of the experiential in sociology. One of the few areas left in sociology to study the experiential is the work conducted from the margins (often by academics who are themselves marginalized in some manner) on inclusive studies of the interconnections of race, class, gender, sexuality, and other mutually experienced forms of oppression.

which provide the main materials for this study are the stories of those who endured. The life stories represent those men who saw no other options available but to subject themselves to these sets of conditions so thoroughly constructed by racial and class inequality.

Prior versions of this manuscript have been published as: *The Invisible Hands: The Formation of Race and Class in the Life Histories of Braceros* (author copyright 2000), Doctoral dissertation on file with UMI Abstracts, Department of Sociology and Rural Sociology, University of Wisconsin–Madison (2004). "The Persistence of Workplace Identities, Living the Effects of the Bracero Total Institution," pp. 155–173 in *Immigrant Life in the US: Multidisciplinary Perspectives*, Donna R. Gabaccia and Colin W. Leach editors, New York: Routledge Press, (2003). "Power, (In)-Action, State and Agribusiness in the Making of the Bracero Total Institution," *Berkeley Journal of Sociology* 50 (1): 76–110 (2006). "Mexican Contract Workers and the U.S. Capitalist Agricultural Labor Process: The Formative Era, 1942–1964," *Rural Sociology* 71(1): 84–107 (2006). "Reparations for Mexican Braceros? Lessons Learned from Japanese and African American Attempts at Redress," *Cleveland State Law Review, Law of Redress Symposium Issue*, 52 (1-2): 273–295.

NOTES

1. From 1942–47 the following states contracted the following number of Mexican Braceros: Arizona, 5,975; California, 124,505; Colorado, 1,843; Idaho, 11,088; Illinois, 1,743; Indiana, 382; Iowa, 3,065; Kansas, 796; Michigan, 2,516; Minnesota, 5,248; Montana, 12,367; Nebraska, 4,037; Nevada, 2,572; New Mexico, 151; North Carolina, 431; North Dakota, 3,094; Oregon, 15,002; South Dakota, 1,377; Utah, 5,865; Washington, 15,029; Wisconsin, 4,817; Wyoming, 2,722 (adapted from Rasmussen 1951, 226). In addition, Arkansas, Georgia, Mississippi, Texas, Ohio, Missouri, Tennessee, and Louisiana participated in the later years of the program (Lyon 1954, 277). One respondent I interviewed stated that her father worked in the agricultural fields of New York, but I have found no evidence of Braceros working in New York agriculture. However, Driscoll (1999) identifies railroad Braceros employed in New York.

2. The sociological specialization or subdiscipline of "migration studies" is indicative of the larger problems in the discipline of sociology. The dominant trend is to operationalize theories into distinct measurable categories, isolate those variables and treat complex or overlapping processes as mutually exclusive. This process gains legitimacy in the name of the scientific pursuit of parsimonious, operational definitions to be statistically manipulated. Each subdiscipline limits its scope of analysis and so remains studies based on the isolated variables within the distinct area of study. This tool of dividing the discipline has increased specialization and boundary policing in defining the study of the Bracero Program in sociology. One of the few texts left in sociology to study the experiential is the work conducted from the margins by academics who are themselves marginalized in some manner on inclusive studies of the intersections of race, class, gender, sexuality, and other mutually experienced forms of oppression.

Acknowledgments

Most acknowledgments pages are ordered, whether intentionally or not, starting with those deemed most important to the successful publication of the book and ending with the least important. Invariably, it is spouses, family, and close relatives that find themselves on the bottom of the list. For me, there is no question that the project I envisioned and cultivated to fruition was first and foremost a product of my family, their unconditional support, and our family history. It is for every preceding generation who sacrificed that I am truly grateful to be in the position I am now to contribute to the intellectual discussion on the plight of the Mexican population residing in the United States. It is also at the top of my list that I recognize the men who were interviewed for this book and I hope that their *testimonios* are read with true compassion, understanding, indignation, and a felt need for societal transformation. All Braceros' names are pseudonyms designed to connote their Mexican state of origin as well as protect their anonymity. U.S.-born respondents' names are pseudonyms as well. Partial funding for this project was provided by the Social Science Research Council Committee on International Migration, the Department of Sociology and Rural Sociology at the University of Wisconsin–Madison, Cornell University's Latino Studies Program, and Oregon State University. Major funding was provided at usurious interest rates by Mastercard and Visa, the federal student loan lifetime payoff program, and a loving partner that made it possible to conduct my research while she honed her social work skills at Dodge County (Wisconsin) Social Services, a Fresno methadone clinic, San Diego Job Corps, and San Diego Juvenile Probation Department (and many more positions since then). Books are rarely written in a vacuum even though the process feels quite alienating. The emotional support of my family, both nuclear and extended, made this project possible and my eternal gratitude starts first and foremost with my family: Chris Batman-Mize, Tori and Theo Mize, Ron Mize Sr., Veronica Mize, Nena Herrera, Anna Herrera, Trinidad and Cindy Herrera, Theresa and John Martinez, Michele Harvey, Rhonda and Todd Anderson, Emily, Rachel, John Jr., Jessica, Amelia, Andrew, Chelsea, and their hijo/as. This book is dedicated posthumously to my late cousin Zachary Herrera (1984-2002) who successfully battled childhood diabetes only to be senselessly taken from our family before he was able to truly begin his adulthood.

In the process of my research, a number of informants and guides were essential in translating, locating participants, sharing knowledge, and providing general support. In Colorado, I would especially like to thank Victor Lara, Carmen Atilano, Jorge Amaya of Rocky Mountain SER, Michael Welsh at University of Northern Colorado, and Father Kyle Fisher, pastor at *La Nuestra Señora de la Paz* Catholic Church in Greeley. With the provision of documents, Roman Ramos and Marinda van Dalen of Texas RioGrande Legal Aid were instrumental in the initial and final stages of this project. In California, Catalino "Cat" Jaquez, Gloria Hernandez, the United Farm Workers headquarters in Parlier, and Andy Alvarado (CSU Fresno) were a few of the many people who helped the project through to fruition. The Stanford Library Department of Special Collections staff were extremely helpful with the papers of Ernesto Galarza. Trying to locate Don Ernesto's relatives to secure permissions, Richard Chabrán and Carlos Muñoz were very helpful.

At Oregon State University, I am grateful to Natalia Fernandez and the Oregon Bracero archive she oversees. My colleagues in the School of Language, Culture, and Society have given me a welcoming home I feel we have all truly earned. I am deeply grateful to be part of the Women, Gender, and Sexuality and Ethnic Studies programs as my colleagues have weathered similar storms and are truly committed to building a better institution with a foundation of love, support, understanding, compassion, collaboration, and mutual betterment (anathemas to way too much of my disciplinary training and at too many research intensive universities).

This project began as a doctoral dissertation under the tutelage of Jess Gilbert in Rural Sociology at UW–Madison. His willingness to allow me to do exactly what I wanted to do was unbelievable, looking back at it all now, but his commitment to see me through when I prematurely left Wisconsin to pursue post-graduate life with no dissertation in hand is a testament to his willingness to go above and beyond the call of duty as an advisor. My committee members—Jane Collins, Michael Apple, Paul Lichterman, and Jack Kloppenburg—were instrumental in making me a better scholar and all five stand out in my memory as the educators who influenced my thinking by challenging my presuppositions and giving me the latitude to make intellectual mistakes and learn from them. They have read various versions of the present manuscript and all improvements are to their credit, the mistakes lie with me. Doris Slesinger, John Fiske, Bill Freudenburg, Kevin Boyle, Roberto Ibarra, and Victor Lares also provided substantive comments, research opportunities, and support at Wisconsin.

Viewing myself as the academic equivalent of a pro basketball "journeyman," I have a number of people at several academic institutions to thank for assisting me along the way. By teaching and researching at ten universities, spending one year with the Navy College Office-Naval Air Station North Island, and working more temporary jobs than I care to count—all since 1994—I apologize to those whom I forget to mention. The Sociology Department at Colorado State University has been a constant source of positive mentorship and was the first to take a chance and actually give me money to study with them. All of the faculty and graduate students, current and former, are too numerous to identify and my debts to them also too numerous to single out, but the passing of Professor Ronny Turner (1942–2003) stands out as one of the single saddest moments in my and my partner's lives so our sincerest public condolences go out to the Turner family and all of the students he influenced throughout his career. Ronny is sorely missed.

At University of California San Diego, the Ethnic Studies Department, and then-chair George Lipsitz, rescued me from a stint as a Navy contractor and a decidedly non-academic life. I'd like to give a shout out to George, Ramon Gutierrez, Yen Espiritu, Denise da Silva, Ross Frank, Charles Briggs, Leland Saito, and Jane Rhodes for giving me a temporary institutional home and my first shot at making it to "the show." George and Ramon have been crucial to making sure I stepped into a permanent starter's role—*mil gracias*. Ricardo Griswold del Castillo and Jorge Mariscal gave key words of advice and support at exactly the right time so my thanks to them as well.

At California State University San Marcos, Silverio Haro, Patricia Rivas-McCrae, Claudia Huiza, Anthony Navarrete, Andre Vasquez, Sharon Elise, Garry Rolison, Richard Serpe, Vivienne Bennett, Bonnie Bade, Peter Arnade, Gerardo Gonzalez, Marti Gray, and Pat Worden helped me weather a storm that no young scholar should ever have to confront and I particularly thank both sets of staff members at the National Latino Research Center for their support and allegiance during some of the most difficult times of our collective professional careers. I'd like to say more but the gag order precludes me from doing so.

Next stop: University of Saint Francis, Fort Wayne, Indiana, where I was the only full-time sociologist who shared a department with the two historians and a government program with no political scientists. Under these circumstances, the serious academic environment was truly unexpected but so welcoming. I have to thank Phyllis Gernhardt, Paul Buckingham, Jackie Feller, and Art Leighton who allowed me to serve as the black sheep (there always has to be one) in their Catholic college family. Being in a department with first-rate scholars, I am so thankful for their presence and hopefully the university will one day recognize the importance of having scholars with active research agendas as an asset. Additional collegial support from Matt Smith, Dan Torlone, Emily Guerrero, Barb O'Connor, Sister Felicity Dorsett, Stacy Adkinson, and the entire Scholars-In-Formation-Colloquia was most appreciated and I applaud their continued efforts at making the university an academically respectable one.

At a time when I needed external support to complete this work, I heeded the advice of those without my best interests at heart for reasons rendered spurious at best. This did not need to be a twenty-year project but in the end I am deeply grateful for the good people, with good intentions, who supported me while I persevered. The Latino Studies Program at Cornell University I am so very thankful for. The Fall Creek neighborhood provided a safe haven in an island of certifiable insanity. I am thankful to Mary Jordan for her editing and formatting assistance. To Sergio Chavez I am particularly indebted as he took on the research project of former Braceros who settled on the Mexican side of *la frontera*. Additional words of praise and appreciation go out to Alicia Swords who took on the task of translating and transcribing in the eleventh hour. *Mil gracias a todos*. My year in the Department of Sociology at Humboldt State University renewed my faith that there are indeed good sociologists in the world.

My current academic home in the School of Language, Culture, and Society at Oregon State University has been greatly enriched by a group of colleagues who truly enjoy working with one another. From the Portland faculty carpool that starts our seventy-five-mile commute each morning at Exit 290 to the Friday Rain OR Shine writing group that nourishes all of us and provided the space and support to complete this book, I am deeply thankful to my colleagues and friends Lucy Arellano, Natchee Barnd, Bradley Boovy, Kathryn Ciechanowski, Qwo-Li Driskill, Patti Duncan, Kryn Freehling-Burton, Juan Herrera, Janet Lee, Christina León, Aaron Lewis, Marta Maldonado, Nana Osei-Kofi, Todd Pugatch, Patti Sakurai, Dana Sanchez, Adam Schwartz, Susan Shaw, Mehra Shirazi, Karen Thompson, Robert Thompson, Tara Williams, and too many colleagues to name here that have deeply impacted me. I'm grateful to Cynthia Gomez Norzagaray for key last minute translations and enduring support. The entire Latino Network Unid@s Cohort IV have deeply inspired me and this work.

In its various formulations, this work has been greatly improved by its readers and reviewers. I would like to thank Ramon Gutierrez, Mary Romero, Donna Gabaccia, Josh DeWind, George Sanchez, George Lipsitz, Nancy Foner, Jess Gilbert, Jane Collins, Mike Apple, John Fiske, Paul Lichterman, Phil McMichael, Mary Pat Brady, Maria Cristina Garcia, Helena Viramontes, Deborah Cohen, Gilbert Gonzalez, Derek Chang, Clem Lai, and Michael Jones-Correa for their constructive comments and criticisms. Any mistakes herein lie with me.

My story of academic department migration is so irrelevant when compared to the lived experiences of former Braceros who are the main focus of this monograph. It is in the end I hope a collaborative project that I share with the reader the experiences of those who were willing to talk with me and share their recollections. Given the lives they have led, it is fully to their credit that they were willing to talk with me at all. Their testimony is something that cannot be lost because the written record on the Bracero Program has developed without truly listening to those who were directly affected by the program—the workers themselves.

Chapter One

The Invisible Workers of the U.S.–Mexican Bracero Program

The San Luis Valley of Colorado is comprised of agricultural towns that arose from the headwaters of the Rio Grande. The semi-fertile valley in southern Colorado is historically recognized as one of the farthest northern interior outposts of Spanish colonialism and small towns like Alamosa, Monte Vista, Del Norte, Blanca, Antonito, and Conejos have maintained their Mexican connections far preceding the times when they hosted a portion of the Braceros recruited to work the fields of Colorado during the 1950s and 1960s—once the state was removed from the blacklist that barred them from employing Bracero laborers. In 1997, I interviewed Señor Palmas,[1] who was charged with providing tortillas to the labor camps that housed Braceros. As the sole tortilla vendor in the San Luis Valley, his vantage point is quite illuminating in comprehending why Braceros entered the United States in search of temporary work that was bound to be difficult, dirty, dangerous, and poorly paid.

> Why are those guys willing to leave their families, their culture, their language, everything that they've ever known? I can't imagine waking up in the morning and saying, "I'm tired of all this bullshit. I'm tired of the Spanish. I'm tired of my religion. I'm tired of my culture, I'm tired of my family. I'm going to the United States." . . . What happens is that his level of existence, the economic level, is somewhere in the neighborhood of flat-ass desperation for him to make this move.

Señor Palmas describes the dire straits that many in Mexico grappled with in their decision to migrate to the United States between the 1940s and 1960s. In 1958, the streets of Monterrey, Mexico, are filled with would-be Braceros waiting for their numbers to be called to secure a contract that would allow them to enter the United States as temporary agricultural workers. In the crowd, we return to Don Jorge from Colima. It is his third trip as a prospective Bracero, and clearly ends up being his most difficult. Don Jorge recollects that he spent three months on the streets waiting for his number to be called. He witnessed scenes of horror in a group of like-situated men: young, starving, impoverished, hailing from the Mexican countryside, far from home and desperate for an opportunity to work. Men who rarely entered cities, like Monterrey, were reduced to living homeless on the streets with no money and literally starving to death.

> Don Jorge: That's where the contracting was. There we were for like three months.
>
> Interviewer (Int): Oh, working [in Monterrey]?
>
> Don Jorge: No, man! In the street! We came and we were there and we couldn't [find work] . . . it was full of people. Lots of people then they would go by lists. It's "*fulano*'s" [so-and-so's] turn. He gets sent to such and such a state.
>
> Int: How did you live . . . ?
>
> Don Jorge: It seems at that time I sent a telegram to my house. [I asked them to] send for me to come back because it was a long time already and they couldn't contract me, right? They sent me money, but then it was my turn to be lucky and they called us. So instead of going home, I got contracted. We went through Piedras Negras. And we went to Texas.

Recounting the events of living on the streets of Monterrey for three months visibly upset Don Jorge. He was lucky, he tells us, because he had a little cash with him but all of the hotels were full so he found himself without shelter. His desperation and call to return home was a result of running out of money and seeing the starvation and death that surrounded him, but in interview he did not feel comfortable talking about that. The belief in "luck" or "*buena suerte*" would be a common trope deployed by those Braceros who endured the hardships in order to secure a contract. In Monterrey, Don Jorge and his compatriots would often struggle in silence and outside the purview of the public, even the mass media—their struggles were invisible. However, two years later, the plight of migrant farmworkers was for the first time nationally televised to the U.S. public.

On Thanksgiving Day (November 25) 1960, the U.S. television-viewing audience received its first glimpse of a population rarely, if ever, seen by most Americans. The name of the documentary, "Harvest of Shame," was seen on acclaimed journalist Edward R. Murrow's *CBS Reports*. It chronicled the lives of migrant farm workers in the United States and exposed the dire living conditions and abject poverty to which they were subjected. The documentary wove interviews of growers in California and Florida, Secretary of Labor James Mitchell, President of the American Farm Bureau, Congressman Harrison Williams (D-NJ), a journalist, a teacher of migrant children, a crew boss, a reverend who lived with migrants, and several White and Black migrant families were interspersed with images of migrant camps, shakedowns, unsafe transportation practices, an Agricultural Workers Organizing Committee (AWOC) union rally for striking cherry pickers, and approximately twenty-eight seconds of Mexican Braceros crossing the border into the United States for agricultural work.

The voice-over that accompanied the first shot of Braceros, suitcases in hand, walking across the Mexico-California border in front of a "United States Customs and Immigration" sign says:

> Another complication of the migrant stream is the constant flow of foreign workers into the available pool of domestic workers.

Second Shot: Panning across a number of Braceros—shirtless, expressionless, and most wearing white-straw cowboy hats—the voice-over continues:

> Hundreds of thousands of Mexican Braceros, and thousands of offshore laborers from the Caribbean area, hired by contract, depress the wage scale of domestic migrants. This controversy is most bitter on the West Coast. [pause] Joseph Woods, a Marine combat veteran of the Pacific, competes against the Braceros . . .

Third Shot: A close up of Mr. Woods, a White migrant, in front of a tree that suffices for shelter for him, his wife, his father-in-law, and three young children. After detailing the Woods' living conditions and dismal prognosis for the future interspersed with cut-aways to the Woods' daughter staring into the camera and the father-in-law smoking a cigarette, the scene ends with Murrow's last quip.

> Throughout the United States there are others like the Woods family who are not able to enjoy the luxury of living in a labor camp (Murrow et al., 2005 [1960]).

The documentary then returns to the plight of Black migrants on the East Coast to expose their deplorable living conditions in substandard labor camps.

This scene, a later one that takes place in the union rally,[2] and two background shots of workers in the fields and canneries[3] are the only references to Mexican farm workers in the documentary. As abruptly as the Mexican Braceros are thrust onto the scene to further deepen the plight of citizen workers and, at that, even war veterans, they fade again into the background to be rarely seen and never heard. Briefly characterized as a complication, an unwelcome source of competition, and here to take jobs from Americans or undercut wage advances for native workers, the Mexican Braceros are framed as villains stealing jobs from good, hard-working Americans.[4] The only discussion of the approximately 316,000 Braceros contracted to work in the U.S. fields in 1960 was to cast them off as undesirables (see Table 1 for the total number of Braceros contracted).

It is ironic to consider that this documentary, purported to shed light on the forgotten people, excludes the "hundreds of thousands" of Mexican-origin agricultural laborers from its portrayal. The stated purpose of "Harvest of Shame" was to introduce those forgotten, or invisible, workers who harvested the food that found its way to the Thanksgiving dinner tables in the United States. As Murrow states,

> These are the forgotten people. Were it not for the labor of the people you are going to meet, your table would not be laden with the luxuries that we have all come to regard as essential. We should like you to meet some of your fellow citizens who harvest the food for the best-fed nation on earth. (1960)

Murrow's focus on "citizens" is laden with assumptions that persist in the United States about the Mexican-origin population that resides within U.S. boundaries. Rather than even mentioning the U.S. citizens of Mexican descent who worked in the fields or extensively dealing with the issues surrounding the immigrant population from Mexico, all Mexicans are deemed non-citizens in the twenty-eight second portrayal and referred to as an "unwelcome source of competition" for White citizens.

"Harvest of Shame" succeeded in shedding light on the Black and White citizens whose labor put food on the table for the U.S. public. At the same time, it relegated the Mexican population residing in the United States even further into obscurity, despite the fact that their labor was equally responsible for feeding the best-fed nation on earth. Rendering Braceros invisible arises again when we critically analyze the academic literature of the Bracero Program.

When I began my research around 1995, the Bracero Program was not on the radar screen of most Chicano historians (who ended their histories at World War II) nor by migration scholars (who had already moved on to post-1965 new "new immigrants" from Latin America and Asia). Several studies were conducted both during the Bracero Program (Anderson 1963, Galarza 1964, 1956) and thereafter by social scientists and state theorists (Bach 1978, Calavita 1992, Craig 1971, Hawley 1966, Scruggs 1988, 1960) but my concern was the voices and perspectives of Braceros were by and large absent in standard accounts of the program. An emerging interest in the Bracero Pro-

Table 1.1. Mexican Nationals Contracted during Bracero Program, 1942–1964

Year	# Admitted	Year	# Admitted
1942	4,203	1954	309,033
1943	52,098	1955	398,650
1944	62,170	1956	445,197
1945	49,454	1957	436,049
1946	32,043	1958	432,857
1947[1]	19,632	1959	437,643
1948	35,345	1960	315,846
1949	107,000	1961	291,420
1950	67,500	1962	194,978
1951	192,000	1963	186,865
1952	197,100	1964	177,736
1953	201,380	Total	4,646,199

1. From 1947 to 1950, these figures seriously underestimate the number of Braceros. Calculations do not include those who entered the United States as undocumented workers and were subsequently legalized on site and given Bracero contracts. In 1947, the number of Mexican workers legalized was approximately 55,000 (Calavita 1992, 218).

gram is particularly heartening as questions of political economy and landscapes (Mitchell 2012), masculinity and modernity (Cohen 2011), gender and family relations (Rosas 2014), and overviews of the state of research (Johnson Gonzalez and Loza 2016, López 2010) are collectively recognizing the central role that the Bracero Program played in codifying existing migrant streams that connected Mexican sending communities to established U.S. agricultural regions and state-sanctioning new streams to thirty states employing Bracero laborers.

The Bracero Program has been analyzed and scrutinized by a number of academics from economics, political science, ethnic (Chicano) studies, history, and sociology.[5] The major shortcoming of the existing literature on the Bracero Program is that the Mexican workers who were directly involved are relegated to the margins in favor of accounts interested solely on state decision-making, interest group politics, or U.S.-Mexican foreign relations.[6] Academic accounts of the Bracero Program tend to focus exclusively on the U.S. state and its *official* political channels that are open to U.S. citizens (in this case, U.S. growers) for influencing government policy.

The majority of the academic literature on the program has focused mainly on the state as the unit of analysis. One would be hard-pressed to find a historical case more dominated by state-centered approaches to policy formation and implementation. Regardless of the state theory purported to best explain the origins and modifications of the policy (pluralist/interest group theory, instrumentalist, structuralist, or institutional approaches), most authors note that growers obviously had a vested interest in securing labor from Mexico.

Though the author claims to address the issues of policy formation, interest group politics, foreign relations, and labor issues, Craig's (1971) *The Bracero Program: Interest Groups and Foreign Policy* is the best source to date on the specific topic of interest groups and exemplar of the pluralist approach. Craig (1971, xii) purports to utilize a "macro perspective" to employ "the more restricted interest-group approach in a detailed analysis of the group struggle at national and subnational levels." But his analysis relies solely on secondary sources written by U.S. academics, U.S. legislative hearings, and U.S. (and a few Mexico City) newspapers. These sources significantly narrow the study to, at its best, an application of pluralist theory to the Bracero Program and, at its worst, a very surface and often stereotypical characterization of the Mexican people and their political system.[7]

Other state theories have been advanced in order to account for factors, other than interest group politics, which influence decision-making at the level of the U.S. state. As Calavita (1992, 172) notes in her summation of the literature on the Bracero Program:

> Ellis Hawley [1966], adopting an essentially instrumentalist position to explain the dominance of growers in defining "labor shortages" and "prevailing wages" in the bracero era, argues that the local branches of the Farm Placement Service in California were puppets of grower associations. Harry Anderson [1963] was more specific, describing details of the economic and personal connections between the largest bracero users in the state and the California Farm Placement Service.

Instrumentalist discussions on the Bracero Program have focused on the fact the growers had their interests met by the U.S. state and were able to continue a war-time labor relief measure for twenty-two years (Anderson 1976, 1963, Craig 1971, Galarza 1964, 1956, Grove 1996, Hawley 1966, Kirstein 1977, Scruggs 1960).

A structural analysis of the Bracero Program, offered by Bach (1978, 64), details the U.S. state's role vis-à-vis Mexican migration as ". . . the basic contradictory relations between global accumulation and political intervention on the relations of exchange; and, state intervention to rationalize the resulting conflict by regulating commodity flows and stabilizing working class struggles." This theory is applied exclusively to the U.S. state and assumes that there are no relevant internal struggles within the state that precludes the basic contradiction of capital accumulation and legitimation.

Going against the conventional wisdom of agribusiness dominance in politics, Calavita (1992) examines the interests of state bureaucrats in continuing the "war-time" relief measure. Following the lead of García y Griego (1996, 1983, 1980) and Rasmussen (1951),[8] she posits that the program was continued by the Immigration and Naturalization Service (INS) because it temporarily "solved" the basic contradiction facing the agency. On the one hand, a strong stance had to be taken to remedy the illegal immigration problem. On the other hand, there was mounting pressure by grower interest groups for assistance in recruiting foreign labor to do jobs domestic workers were not willing or unable to do. The INS dealt with the illegal immigration problem by officially sanctioning and recruiting cheap, captive labor for southwestern agriculture (Calavita 1992, 181).

What we see in the resurgent literature on the Bracero Program is a growing awareness that the internal differentiation of a bureaucratic structure, specifically the U.S. state and pressures within the Immigration and Naturalization Service, have a major impact on the shaping and implementation of policies. Also noteworthy is the acknowledgment that the Bracero Program was in fact a binational arrangement that significantly impacted both the United States and Mexico. Though both insights are important, they have not been extended to all of the important actors in the formation, implementation and termination of the Bracero Program. In the conclusion, we will consider each set of actors' role in perpetuating the abuses endemic to the program and assess their levels of culpability in perpetuating peonage conditions for Braceros.[9]

Since the vast majority of research on the program is state-centered, a direct result of this focus is that the experiences of workers are deemed irrelevant or at the very least not considered as a valid source of information. The history of Anglo-Mexicano relations of race, class, and nation is discounted in most accounts (for two exceptions, see Gamboa 1990 and Kirstein 1977, chap. 1). When the experiences of the Braceros receive attention, they tend to be treated homogeneously as if they constitute a unitary experience. The different circumstances that Braceros met upon entering thirty states of the United States at specific times during the program's operation has not been scrutinized. The works of three authors, Herrera-Sobek (1979), Gamboa (1990), and Galarza (1964, 1956), are the main published works that place the experiences of Braceros as central for understanding the story of the Bracero Program. The best example is Herrera-Sobek's (1979, 39–74) oral history that culminates in an extended discussion of "the composite bracero." The author uses the term "bracero" to refer to all Mexican migrant farmworkers, not those specifically recruited for the Bracero Program, but the sixteen respondents she spoke with in Mexico all came to the United States in the 1950s. This would lead one to assume that a significant portion were under contract. Those sixteen experiences are presented as "Pedro's Story" and all of the variations in subjective evaluations about the program as well as what each respondent experienced is lumped together into a "representative" composite of *the* Bracero experience (Herrera-Sobek 1979, 42).

Gamboa (1990) eloquently places the experiences of Braceros within the context of Chicano history. He focuses on the Pacific Northwest and on Bracero resistance in the form of strikes and work stoppages. The sources of his materials are archive-based, so a serious limitation of the study is that it purports to uncover the experiences of Braceros without directly consulting those who actually experienced the effects of the program.

The most ambitious study to date is interwoven with the scholarly lifetime of Mexican-American, scholar-activist Ernesto Galarza. The major findings are published in *Strangers in our Fields* (1956) and *Merchants of Labor* (1964) and are a culmination of a number of interviews conducted between 1953 to 1958 with Braceros who were at that time under contract. Most often, Galarza located men walking from labor camps to town to pick up supplies and subsequently interviewed them (Galarza Papers, Stanford University Libraries, "Field Notes, 1952–1957," Box 3, Folder 1). As a labor organizer, Galarza had a great deal of difficulty gaining access to the labor camps located on growers' property so his interviews were conducted when workers were beyond the confines of the fields or the labor camps. His studies were predominately limited to the Salinas, Central, and Imperial Valleys of California. His research notes, housed at the Stanford University Libraries Department of Special Collections, do not consist of interview transcripts or even a large number of direct quotes from interviews with Braceros. They consist of confirmations of conditions that Galarza was already aware of. For instance, Galarza collected hundreds of pay stubs that detailed shifting pay rates, illegal deductions for blankets and carrot ties, exorbitant deductions for insurance and food, and a substantial number of instances where workers did not receive their guaranteed wage (Galarza Papers, "Braceros [Conditions]," Box 19, Folders 3–4).

I am particularly indebted to the work of the three authors since without their attention to the workers who comprised the program, this study would not have been conceivable. Without the scholarly interventions of Galarza, Herrera-Sobek, and Gamboa, the story of the Bracero Program would be told exclusively by, for, and about elites. The present study is designed, first and foremost, to pay attention to those voices that have been excluded from discussions about the Bracero Program. Using the life stories of former Braceros as the main source materials for this investigation, one can shed light onto the conditions they faced during their contracted time spent in the United States as well as analyze the bases for their perceptions of those conditions.

The present account centers the experiences of Braceros through their recollections and in the process, highlights the centrality of race and class in shaping the contours of the Bracero Program. I explicitly challenge the state-centered view that belies an understanding of how the program operated to shape the experiences of Braceros. My dual intention is to avoid the privileging of the state as the sole focus of analysis, while avoiding the limitation of the study to how the Bracero Program impacted the United States. Two conjoined processes, class exploitation and racism, are central to defining the way in which Braceros were systematically mistreated and abused. My intention is to understand how the invisible workers persevered under circumstances that have profoundly influenced their subjective evaluations about their experiences rendered invisible by U.S. society.

The Bracero Program began on August 4, 1942, in Stockton, California, as a result of the U.S. government responding to requests by southwestern agricultural growers for the recruitment of foreign labor. The agreement, negotiated between the federal governments of Mexico and the United States, stated the following general provisions that would come to define the program's twenty-two-year existence.[10] The first provision barred racial discrimination targeted at Braceros: "The Mexicans entering the U.S. under provisions of the agreement would not be subjected to discriminatory acts." The second provision guaranteed the costs of migration and temporary settlement would be shouldered by U.S. growers: "Workers would be guaranteed transportation, living expenses, and repatriation along the lines established under Article 29 of Mexican labor laws." The third provision concerned the displacement of U.S. workers to guarantee that Braceros would not undercut native wages or be used as strikebreakers: "Mexicans entering under the agreement would not be employed either to displace domestic workers or to reduce their wages" (Garcia 1980, 24, *op cit.*). Under much of the same agreement guidelines, though utilizing different administrative channels, nine months later the railroad industry secured the importation of Mexican laborers to meet war-time shortages (Driscoll 1999, Jones 1945).[11]

The first provision was designed to explicitly ban discrimination against Mexican nationals and served as the key bargaining chip by the Mexican government to promote safeguards of Braceros' treatment by Anglo growers. The arrangements of the First Bracero Program, during World War I, were conducted without the input of the Mexican government (Kiser and Kiser 1979, Scruggs 1988, 1960). As a result, Mexican nationals worked in the United States without protections and subsequently, workers were subject to a number of discriminatory acts. The protections from discriminatory treatment stemmed from Executive Order 8802, signed by President Franklin D. Roosevelt on June 25, 1941, which stated, "that there shall be no discrimination in the employment of workers in defense industries or government because of race, creed, color, or national origin, and I do hereby declare that it is the duty of employers and of labor organizations, in furtherance of said policy and of this order, to provide for the full and equitable participation of all workers in defense industries, without discrimination because of race, creed, color, or national origin." In relation to E.O. 8802, the Bracero Program was couched as a government-sponsored program in the larger service of national defense and it recognized the reality that Mexicans were subject to discrimination, whether as a result of race, color, and/or national origin.

From 1942–1947, no Braceros were sent to Texas because of the documented mistreatment of Mexican workers by Texan growers and other citizens. A series of assurances by the Texas state government were secured before growers were allowed to import labor from Mexico. Texas was infamous for the Jim Crow-style segregation and racial violence practices that defined the post-bellum South and the state was responsible for more lynching of Mexicans than any other state. The states of Colorado, Illinois, Indiana, Michigan, Montana, Minnesota, Wisconsin, and Wyoming were also blacklisted by the Mexican government, up until the 1950s, due to discriminatory practices documented in each of the states. The central source of contention was a prevalent practice in the sugar beet industry that paid Mexican workers considerably less than the wages paid to Anglo workers for the same work. The discriminatory wage structure illustrated a second-class citizenship that Mexican laborers were subjected to throughout the Midwest and Rocky Mountain states.

The second provision was designed to guarantee workers safe passage to and from the United States as well as decent living conditions while working in the United States. The costs associated with transportation, room, and board would be covered by someone other than the workers if the article was followed to its exact wording. But these costs were subject to negotiation by the Mexican government and as a result, workers had a number of these expenses deducted from their paychecks. Individual work contracts signed by Braceros and representatives of both the Mexican and U.S. governments set standards on how much could be deducted for room and board (see Appendix III).

Transportation costs were shouldered by different groups depending on which time period and place the Braceros were migrating to and from. Based on the life stories collected, transportation costs were not paid by Braceros from the recruitment centers in Mexico to the U.S. processing centers and eventual job sites. But the costs associated with getting to the Mexican cities where the Braceros were recruited was shouldered by them and the costs varied depending on where the recruitment centers were located. Throughout the duration of the program, the U.S. and Mexican governments struggled over where recruitment centers would be located because the United States was responsible for paying the transportation costs. The U.S. government wanted recruitment centers near the U.S.-Mexican border to reduce costs whereas the Mexican government wanted recruitment centers in the interior of Mexico where the major sending states were located. These struggles had major impacts on the Braceros who had to secure the funds to afford to pay their way to the recruitment centers.

The final provision was designed to reduce competition between domestic and contracted labor and the U.S. government played two roles in assuring that competition would not arise. The first role was the determination of the "prevailing wage" in each region of the country. To ensure that Braceros were receiving the same wage as domestics, the prevailing wage was determined prior to the harvest season in each locale and Braceros were to receive that wage. Galarza (1964) notes that the prevailing wage was approved by the Department of Labor but it was in fact growers who got together prior to the harvest and fixed the pay rates in order to determine the "prevailing wage" they were willing to pay.

It was also the responsibility of the Department of Labor to designate when a certain region had a labor shortage of available domestic workers. Again, growers were the key to this determination because they were responsible for notifying the Department when they expected labor shortages to occur. Most often, growers would set a prevailing wage rate so low as to effectively discourage domestics by requiring them to work at wage levels below the cost of living in the United States.

In regard to each of the provisions, the Bracero Program was lived out much differently by the workers than how the program was designed to work on paper. Unfortunately, the majority of the established literature on the Bracero Program assumes that the program operated according to the guidelines put forth by both governments.[12] Rather than critically examining the experiences of workers, the majority of the published research slights the former Braceros as sources of information and takes for granted that the four general guidelines were enforced and actualized. The history of the Braceros documents how the safeguards "guaranteed" by the governments were rarely put into practice or poorly enforced. Workers were severely disempowered in their attempts to request those issues guaranteed to them in the standard labor contracts and the agreements made between both governments.

Outline of *Obreros Olvidados*

Chapter 2, "Braceros and the Social Formation of Anglo Racial Frames," provides an analysis of both the institutional bases of racism as well as the practices and logics that comprise interpersonal racism. The analysis is specific to how Mexican Braceros were treated and viewed in the United States. Institutional and interpersonal racism are interrelated as evidenced in the specific case of the blacklisting of Texas. From 1942–1947, the government of Mexico did not allow Braceros to be used in Texas due to the racial discrimination that was prevalent in the state during that time. At the structural level, the repatriation measures of 1954, collectively dubbed "Operation

Wetback," served as a particularly strong reminder to the citizens of Mexico residing in the United States of their second-class citizenship.

In chapter 3, "The Bracero Working Day and Contested Terrain of Class Relations," I examine how the actions and, to a certain extent, the thoughts of Braceros were actively managed through a web of labor controls that were the pre-condition for employment. I discuss the central components of labor process that served as the basis for the despotic labor regimes that Braceros were inserted into based on the terms of their contracts. In addition, I specifically examine the issues of wages, deductions, and remittances because the direct testimony by former Braceros seriously challenges the established academic literature on the program that relies upon official sources for its information. The Bracero Program is most often discussed by scholars in terms of "guaranteed wages" and "protections above and beyond those given to the domestic worker" yet the conditions experienced by the Braceros interviewed belie any notion of the Braceros' privileged status in these regards. Finally, the chapter concludes with a suggestive analysis of class reproduction by documenting the class positions of the offspring of former Braceros. The results are not encouraging if one views the process of immigrant adaptation in terms of intergenerational upward mobility.

Chapter 4, "The Making of the Bracero Total Institution," reconstructs the history of the Bracero Program as experienced by the men who shared their life stories for this project. Their recollections are supplemented with an archival analysis of the Galarza papers, a critical examination of the secondary literature, and supplementary interviews with those who had firsthand knowledge of the workings of the program. From the point that Braceros made the decision to migrate, the dictates of the institution placed a number of external and internal controls over the worker. After discussing the conditions in Mexico that impelled the choice to sojourn, every shared aspect of the Bracero experience is detailed to capture the experiences of former Braceros. The way in which race and class articulated in the making of the Bracero total institution points to the efforts in the post-war era to render invisible those deemed unworthy: particularly those marked as noncitizens, racially inferior, and subject to unfettered economic exploitation.

The conclusion discusses the recent events involving ex-Braceros that resulted in a successful redress campaign that partially rectified past wrongs Braceros endured. In 2002, I was contacted by legal counsel representing former Braceros in a class action lawsuit claiming peonage. In preparing an affidavit on behalf of the Braceros' claim, I was introduced to the popular mobilization around the mandatory saving program that Braceros were never able to recoup upon return to Mexico. This burgeoning social movement became a crucial catalyst for former-Bracero social movement organizations and a call on the Mexican government to redress past injustices. These grassroots mobilizations are still taking place, with qualified successes, in the major sending and border states in Mexico. The current relevancy of the Bracero Program is twofold: both in the way that the past injustices are galvanizing former Braceros, now in at least their sixties, to make claims on their citizenship rights and just as importantly the way that current U.S. and Mexican government elites are renewing calls for a reinstatement of the Bracero Program.

In the 2000s, former braceros met weekly in Ciudad Juarez, Tijuana, Mexico City, and Zacatelco (Tlaxcala) to name a few locales, and publicly shared how they were cheated out of wages by schemes such as the mandatory savings program. At the time, the Mexico Solidarity Network sponsored speaking tours of ex-Braceros to introduce U.S. audiences to the atrocities committed from 1942 to 1964. The ex-Braceros are beginning to collectively place blame where it squarely belongs: on the actors who made the decisions from above to construct the Bracero Program in a way that systematically denied the rights and dignities of contracted workers. *Alianza Braceroproa*, National Assembly of Ex-Braceros/*La Asamblea Nacional de Ex-Braceros*, and the Binational Union of Former Braceros are the more prominently recognized of the social movement organizations placing pressure on the Mexican government for monetary redress. In the process or organizing for restitution, the men are beginning to share their experiences of the most repressed and humiliating aspects of the medical examinations, how growers and their intermediaries treated them, and the deleterious health effects of stoop labor. In the final chapter, I discuss the Bracero reparations movement and its prognosis for success in the face of resurgent clamoring for a new Bracero Program by U.S. politicians.

A theoretical appendix, "The Articulation of Race and Class in the Making of the Bracero Total Institution," discusses the problematic prior applications of Goffman's (1961) "total institution" and how the post-war timeframe of social theorizing provides an important context for elite attempts at instituting mechanisms of total control. Criticizing Elkins' appropriation of the total institution to explain the social psychological effects of slavery, I engage sociological theories from the post-war period to the 1960s protest movements, that took its cues from U.S. society in assuming that those deemed marginal or undesirable were best kept out of sight, in large monolithic institutions beyond the public's purview. The total institution framework, as introduced by Erving Goffman (1961), applied this attempt at total social control to the mental asylums of the era. However, the way Goffman analyzes power seems to exclude some of the central forms of marginalization during that period: particularly along the lines of gender, race, and class. To address those shortcomings, I turn to Foucault's various attempts at theorizing disciplinary power as an alternative route to viewing the relationship between total control and bodies. During the time of Goffman's writing, the U.S.-Mexico Bracero Program was underway and deploying many forms of social control both he and later Foucault mentioned to secure the optimal workforce for U.S. agribusiness. In this appendix, I analyze how the Bracero total institution operated within this power matrix of state-sponsored migration, second-class citizenship, and dominated class relations—all within a thoroughly racialized context.

A second appendix, "Working in the Field: Historial Memory, Archival Ethnography, and Direct Accounts of Agricultural Migrant Labor," discusses the collection of life stories and how the archival ethnography approach serves as an alternative framework for understanding the recollection, forgetting, and silencing of memories. Though the life stories of individual Braceros are the centerpiece of this work, the life history method necessitates a context to understand these stories. The context provided is based in ethnographic, participant observation, and historical archival analysis. The methodological investigation of life histories has a long, yet sporadic, tradition in the study of migration. From Thomas and Znaniecki's *The Polish Peasant* (1918–1920), American sociology has been particularly indebted to this methodological approach. While the life history approach has recently been resurrected, it has rarely been applied to the study of migration (see Bertaux 1981).[13] The study of lived social relations and the effects of class and racial oppression are of critical relevance to this study. As a leading contemporary exponent of the method argues: "It is one thing to reestablish the structure of power relations, the laws and customs governing some sector of social life in the past, another to imagine its consequences on the lives of people. Direct testimonies help chart the consequences" (Bertaux 1982, 102).

NOTES

1. All Braceros' names are pseudonyms designed to connote their Mexican state of origin as well as protect their anonymity. U.S.-born respondents' names are pseudonyms as well.

2. Giving testimony to other striking workers, a rank-and-file man of Mexican descent but presumably an U.S. citizen (since the AFL-CIO's AWOC—Agricultural Workers Organizing Committee—did not attempt to unionize immigrant workers) states in English with a thick Spanish accent that: "You make about five or ten dollars today and tomorrow you just a looking for job and staying out on the street. Looking for job. You ain't got no job to do another day. What do the local people supposed to do?"

3. Behind a California grower, Mexican workers tend to fields with hoes as the grower tells us "the industrial type of union has no place in agriculture." Finally, viewers watch a Mexican man operating a machine that moves canned vegetables while we are told that "some of the major canneries do pay fair wages and provide adequate housing."

4. The only other group that rivals such a negative characterization in the news report are those growers interviewed. But even the growers were allowed air-time to represent themselves and in effect, give themselves their well-deserved negative portrayal. This is what one Florida grower had to say about his African-American workers in "Harvest of Shame" when asked, are the people happy? "Well I guess they got a little gypsy in their blood. They just like it. A lot of them wouldn't do anything else. Lot of them don't know any different. That's all they want to do. They love it. They love to go from place to place. They don't have a worry in the world.

They're happier than we are. Today they eat, tomorrow, they don't worry about [*sic*]. They are the happiest race of people on earth."

5. See Anderson 1963, Calavita 1992, Cohen 2011, 2001, Craig 1971, Crisler 1968, Driscoll 1980, 1999, García y Griego 1980, 1983, 1996, Gonzalez 2006, Grove 1996, Hadley 1956, Hancock 1959, Hawley 1966, Jones 1945, Kirstein 1977, Kiser and Kiser 1979, Lessard 1984, López 2010, Lyon 1954, Mitchell 2012, Rasmussen 1951, Rosas 2014, Scruggs 1960, 1962, 1988.

6. Of the sources cited in this paragraph, there is not a single direct testimony from a Bracero. All references, in the abstract, to "Braceros" or "laborers" are attributed to the findings of Ernesto Galarza, whose work we will return to later in this section.

7. Craig's characterization of "the typical Mexican Bracero" will be addressed fully in chapter 2.

8. Long-time USDA historian, Wayne Rasmussen, provided the historical documentation that would enable later researchers to realize that the bureaucratic departments within the U.S. state apparatus had their own agendas and the power to enact and enforce policies that served the interests of the department.

9. A very interesting course of study would examine the internal differences among U.S. growers who employed Bracero contract laborers. Growers have not been analyzed in terms of the differences between large-scale grower associations (by far the biggest beneficiaries of the Bracero Program) and small growers who were not integrated into the agribusiness network. Small growers often complained that the rules for employing contract labor were cumbersome, nettlesome, impossible to comply with, and all at a cost too high for an individual to rationalize the use of the system. Though a study of grower differences is beyond the confines of the present study, I utilize the same rationale for conducting a study of the life histories of the former workers of the Bracero Program.

10. See Appendix IV for the full details of the arrangement. The initial provision stated "Mexican contract workers would not engage in U.S. military service." Beyond the focus of this present analysis, it was designed to quell Mexican popular discontent and apprehensions about how earlier uses (during World War I) of Mexican labor were thought to have occurred during, what Kiser and Kiser (1979) refer to as, the First Bracero Program. Without government interference, U.S. growers directly recruited laborers from Mexico to meet war-time labor shortages. After the First World War, the citizens of Mexico heard a number of rumors that Mexican laborers, brought to the United States to work in the agricultural fields, were forced into the military to fight in the war effort. My attempt to research this contention revealed, to the best of my knowledge, no evidence of this practice. Both the governments of the United States and Mexico denied that the practice ever occurred. Nevertheless, to quell Mexican popular apprehensiveness and allay fears, the first article was agreed upon by both governments.

11. The claim of a shortage of domestic labor is a source of contention in the literature. Those who disagree with this prognosis and see Braceros as used by growers to undercut domestic wages include Anderson (1976, 1963), Galarza (1964, 1956), Copp (1971), Hadley (1956).

12. Exceptions to scholarly hegemony identify that the historical record of the treatment of Braceros developed contrary to the guidelines put forth by the Mexican government. Galarza (1956) documented the lack of adequate housing, substandard wages, exorbitant prices for inedible food, illegal deductions for food, insurance, health care, inadequate transportation, and a lack of legal rights. Gamboa (1990, 129) found in his study of Braceros working in the Pacific Northwest that "although the workers had contracts guaranteeing minimum job standards, their employers unilaterally established rock bottom and discriminatory wage rates. In doing so, growers reduced the workers to a state of peonage. . . . In addition, the farmers' reckless abandon of human considerations was shocking and led to numerous job-related accidents." Both the works of Galarza (1964, 1956) and Gamboa (1990) represent exceptions to the established literature on the Bracero Program by placing more of a focus on how the program was actually lived out in the experiences of workers.

13. Contemporary mainstream approaches in the sociology of immigration have been apprehensive about the use of "soft" qualitative methods as a source of scientific knowledge. The

dominant trope in the field is generalizability so accordingly, qualitative methods are designed to emulate this goal or abandoned altogether in favor of survey methods and statistical replicability.

Chapter Two

Braceros and the Social Formation of Anglo Racial Frames

The song, "Deportees,"[1] by Woody Guthrie offered a brief glimpse into the precarious living conditions that Mexican immigrants recruited to work in U.S. agriculture were forced to endure. Artists ranging from Arlo Guthrie, The Byrds, Judy Collins, Joan Baez, Bruce Springsteen, Ben Harper, Sweet Honey in the Rock, Dolly Parton, to the Highwaymen have covered the Woody Guthrie/Martin Hoffman tune. Guthrie wrote the lyrics in response to national news coverage of a plane wreck in 1948, near Los Gatos, Fresno County, California, that was carrying twenty-eight recently deported Mexican agricultural workers. The news reports never mentioned the dead by name but only *en masse* as "the deportees."

Little did Guthrie know at the time how his prescient words would resonate again in 1954 when the derisively coined "Operation Wetback" would forcibly repatriate over one million Mexicans.[2] The racialization of Mexican-origin residents of the United States is the common theme that unites the mass deportation practice across time and Guthrie's recognition of how the essentialism associated with only recognizing people as labels (such as deportees, wetbacks, or illegal aliens) and not individual human beings with names. As one of Ernesto Galarza's respondents stated, while working for the San Joaquin Farm Production Association, "we have no names—we are known by numbers" (Galarza Papers 3:1).

The Bracero Program was not created in a vacuum and the history of Anglo-Chicano race relations had a tremendous impact on the eventual formation of the World War II-era Bracero Program. Mexicans had historically, and persistently, been denied the fruits of their labor and the full rights accorded with citizenship or even temporary guest worker status. A cyclical history of Mexican immigrants feeling the pulls for their labor and the repulsions as potential citizens or settlers informs the dialectical manner in which Braceros were treated.

A growing attention to the racialization processes and institutions that transcend the U.S.-centered Black-White binary of race relations can be located in the work of Bonilla-Silva (2014, 2001), Cobas, Duany, and Feagin (2009), Feagin (2010), Lipsitz (2011, 2006, 1998), Mize (2013), and Omi and Winant (2014). As Lipsitz (1998, 4–5) succinctly notes, "there has always been racism in the United States, but it has not always been the same racism. Political and cultural struggles over power have shaped the contours and dimensions of racism differently in different eras."

For Mexican Americans and Mexican immigrants, their racial status has been a source of contestation since the signing of the Treaty of Guadalupe-Hidalgo that ended the U.S.-Mexico War in 1848 (Goméz 2007).[3] As citizens, Mexicans were deemed *de jure* White even though their *de facto* racialized treatment proved much to the contrary. It was not until the *Hernandez v. Texas* (1954) Supreme Court case that Mexican Americans were clearly established as a legally cognizable class, deemed non-White, and thus subject to civil rights protections (Delgado and Palacios 1975, 395–96, Martinez 1997, 328).[4] The case noted that the Texas county of Jackson (and at least seventy other Texas counties) had never allowed a Mexican American to sit on a jury. By law—*prima facie* White, by practice—patently non-White became the complex limbo that many Mexicans found themselves residing in the United States.

In the sociology of race and ethnicity, the singular focus on explaining Black-White racial differences has precluded the intellectual space to explore the racialization of non-White, non-Black groups in the United States. This space has been opened up significantly by Omi and Winant's racial formation theory, Lipsitz's comparative ethnic studies, Bonilla-Silva's racialized social systems,[5] and Feagin's white racial frame. Ideological frames of racialization are central analytical frameworks to both Bonilla-Silva (2014, 74) and Feagin (2010, 10–11), and are best defined by Feagin's analysis of "the white racial frame," as "an organized set of racialized ideas, stereotypes, emotions, and inclinations to discriminate . . . Critical to the white racial frame is an interrelated set of cognitive notions, understandings, and metaphors that whites have used to rationalize and legitimate systemic racism" (Feagin 2006, 25, 28; Cobas, Duany, and Feagin 2009, 3, *op. cit.*). Both sociologists are explaining race relations specific to the Black-White binary and both use frame analysis to link systems with ideologies, but it is clear from the case of the Bracero Program that there is no singular white racial frame and *the* white racial frame is not fully transposable to Anglo-Latino relations. For this reason, I refer to Anglo racial frames (in this case particular to Anglo-Chicano-Mexicano relations) to explain the specific actors who deployed Anglo racial frames and the varied Mexican American, Bracero, and Mexican national responses.

> Racism in its interpersonal form is no less insidious or damaging than institutionalized racism to those who are its direct target. Institutional racism has a major impact on the life chances of the subordinate group as a whole, but interpersonal racism is how race is felt: the words, thoughts, and actions that make clear to both actors (the racist and the racialized) their respective places in society. . . . Racism is both a matter of interpersonal relations governing daily interactions and an institutional process that shapes the boundaries on large-scale social relations (Mize 2013, 342, 359).

At the institutional level, there developed an increasing social isolation of Mexican immigrant contract workers from Chicanos and the remaining U.S. citizenry. I discuss the racialized aspects of this social isolation in relation to large-scale agribusiness's desire to maintain a controlled labor force. Racist logics and practices at the interpersonal level are key justifications of these systemic inequalities and they figure into shaping the lived experiences of Braceros. The Mexican government's position on the treatment of Mexicans residing in the United States is first addressed. Grower attitudes, government reports, life stories by former Braceros and an academic account by a former farm labor contractor also provide the materials for analyzing the interpersonal racing of Braceros. The analysis focuses on the structural basis of institutionalized racism that put Mexican laborers into the fields in the first place. Using the state of Texas and the repatriation measures collectively known as "Operation Wetback" as case studies, this chapter delineates how institutionalized racism accounts for the ways Braceros were raced depending on the encompassing social conditions of Anglo-Chicano relations. These tensions were further exacerbated by the mass repatriation campaigns that between 1929 and 1954 removed an estimated two million-plus Mexicans residing in the United States. In addition, the chapter will cover the U.S. government's attempts to deal with illegal immigration and its relationship to undermining the status of would-be Bracero contract laborers.

AGRIBUSINESS AND THE INSTITUTIONAL RACE-ING OF MEXICAN BRACEROS

Mexicans entering the United States during the 1942–1964 period were following the migrant streams established during the preceding four decades and as a result, they were disproportionately found in agricultural and railroad industries. The predominance of Mexican immigrants working in these two sectors was codified by the state-enforced rules and regulations of the Bracero Program. In the case of Texas, the piecemeal gains, as documented by Montejano (1987), by Mexican Americans in terms of political incorporation (extended voting rights and more representation in political office), integrated schools, and expanded economic opportunities as a direct result of war-time industrialization were not shared by all Mexicans.[6] The expanded opportunities for Mexican Americans enabled the domestic farm worker population to move out of the rural areas in order to pursue industrial options in the urban areas. In other words, the gradual breakdown of the racial segregationist framework for Americans of Mexican descent was accompanied by the further segregation of Mexican nationals who migrated to rural areas often vacated by Mexican Americans.

One of the key means of securing a high degree of social isolation and racial segregation was the institutionalized practice of housing Braceros in labor camps. The labor camps were often located on growers' private property but there were other means of housing workers away from local communities or nearby small towns. During the Great Depression, labor camps were built and maintained by the federal government under the aegis of the New Deal unemployment-alleviation measures. Of these fifty-four camps put to use by growers to house contracted workers in 1948, twenty-three were located in California (see Figure 2.1).[7] Galarza found Braceros housed in other public spaces such as county fairgrounds. In the course of my research in Colorado, labor camps consisted of converted schools and gymnasiums. Galarza's field notes refer to the Stockton county fairgrounds he visited in October 1951 (see Figure 2.2 for a photograph of the interior):

> 300 circa in labor pool, cots 2 feet apart, one blanket per bed—temp 50 degrees in early a.m., dormitory in pavilion "4-H Dairy and Beef" sign, no partitions—"all provisional," no locker space provided-no other facilities, Dining room festooned with fly papers, Cokes 10 cents etc. under a concession—1 dr[inking] fountain (Galarza Papers 17:11).

The Bracero Program was implemented in such a way that the grower associations were best suited to employ Bracero labor in the most cost-effective manner. The federal labor camps housed labor for grower associations or even larger agribusiness entities. In northern Colorado, the Fort Lupton (Granada) labor camp was the first stop for all Braceros who would eventually harvest the sugar beets for the Great Western Sugar Company. Those farmers who had contracts with Great Western received their labor from the company and most often the costs associated with housing, board, and transportation were not covered by farmers. Approximately 50 percent of all Braceros brought to Colorado were recruited by Great Western Sugar (Crisler 1968, 88).

Batch-handling was more "efficient" than expecting each individual farmer to secure his own labor force for the one to two months needed to harvest the sugar beets. All aspects of the recruitment process were centralized in the hands of the association or processor. Interstate transportation only had to be arranged to bring one large group of workers to and from the U.S. border processing center. Since individual crops do not necessarily ripen at the exact same time, Braceros could be working at one farm for a short period and shift to other association members' farms on an as-needed basis. Room and board was provided in an institutional manner which reduced costs per worker. Small farmers could not compete with large-scale agribusiness and effectively use Braceros since they had to cover the expenses of housing, board, transportation, and downtime. Of course, the Bracero Program was not designed with the small farmer in mind. Large-scale contracting complemented large-scale agriculture and as long as the workers did not place a burden on the surrounding communities by becoming a visible presence, grower associations and agribusiness were allowed by the state to continue their use of Mexican labor.

But at the same time that Mexican Braceros were increasingly recruited to fill the bottom rungs of the agricultural ladder, Mexican American and other marginalized U.S.-born groups were finding ways to escape agricultural production altogether. Citing 1930 census data, 33.6 percent of the Spanish-origin population in Texas were employed as farmworkers and that percentage steady declined until 1980 when 3.8 percent of Hispanics were farm-

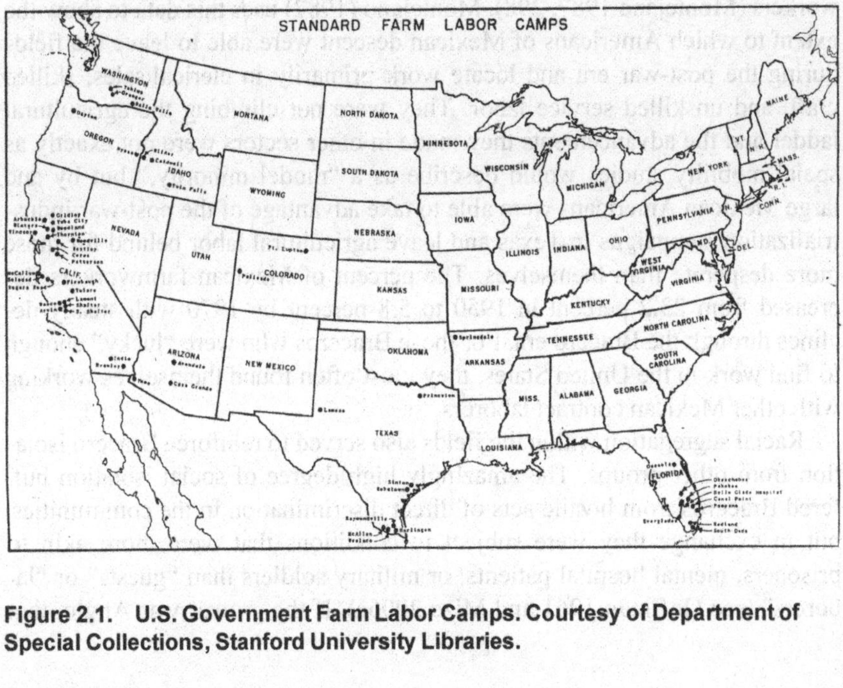

Figure 2.1. U.S. Government Farm Labor Camps. Courtesy of Department of Special Collections, Stanford University Libraries.

Figure 2.2. Stockton, California, Fairgrounds: Stock Pavilion where Braceros were Housed. Courtesy of Department of Special Collections, Stanford University Libraries.

workers (Montejano 1987, 298). Montejano (1987) uses this data to show the extent to which Americans of Mexican descent were able to leave the fields during the post-war era and locate work primarily in clerical/sales, skilled craft, and unskilled service labor. They were not climbing the agricultural ladder and the advancements they made in other sectors were not exactly as social mobility studies would describe as a "model minority," but by and large Mexican Americans were able to take advantage of the post-war industrialization campaigns in Texas and leave agricultural labor behind for those more desperate than themselves. The percent of Mexican farmworkers decreased from 23.2 percent in 1950 to 5.8 percent by 1970 with steady declines through the Bracero era. For those Braceros who were "lucky" enough to find work in the United States, they most often found themselves working with other Mexican contract laborers.

Racial segregation within the fields also served to reinforce Bracero isolation from other groups. The amazingly high degree of social isolation buffered Braceros from hostile acts of direct discrimination in the communities, but in exchange they were subject to conditions that were more akin to prisoners, mental hospital patients, or military soldiers than "guests" or "laborers" (see Goffman 1961 and Mize 2006a). If the grower was Anglo, that was the Braceros' primary, if not only, source of contact with the Anglo community. Many workers never knew the growers who owned the crops they harvested. Growers worked together to form associations in order to cut the costs of recruitment and set prevailing wages prior to the growing season. Intermediaries, or farm labor contractors (FLCs) and crew bosses, conducted all of the business for growers and this became the only connection to Anglos for some workers. For the respondents I interviewed, FLCs and crew bosses were all of Mexican descent (usually Mexican American) even though their work took them to places as far from the Southwest as Michigan, Ohio, and North Carolina.

Some workers stated that they worked in the same fields with other ethnic groups but as one respondent stated:

> Don Daniel: We worked with others: Chinese, other Mexicans, Blacks.
>
> Int: Did you ever talk with them or get to know them?
>
> Don Daniel: No, they worked together and we worked together, no mixing. They lived away from us too. We did not talk with them.

Other Braceros worked in the fields with Mexican Americans but even those Braceros were isolated from native workers. "Where I was I only saw Mexicans, I only worked with other Braceros and I was all over California" (Life Story of Don Francisco 1997). In the San Luis Valley, attempts to contract the Native American reservations of Northern New Mexico and Arizona reservations were made in the same manner as the Bracero Program. "The government tried to do the same thing with Navajo Indians, but it didn't work because the Indians would come to work drunk or didn't show up for work" (Interview with Señor Paulo 1997). I was unable to locate any documentation that corroborated this labor contract scheme nor did I find verification as to why the labor experiment with Navajos did not work, but it is noteworthy that the experiment's failure relied upon pre-existing racial stereotypes of Native Americans to justify the program's demise.

The organizing feature of the institutionalized racism that Braceros faced was the marked degree of segregation that they experienced. Whether the locale be the fields, the labor camp, or the community, the common theme of the life stories collected was the high degree of social isolation that they felt. Coupled with the interpersonal acts of racism, which are detailed in the following section, these two forms of racism provided an effective system for subjugating Braceros into the most menial and low-status job tasks available in the agricultural industry.

INTERPERSONAL RACISM: PRACTICING DELIBERATE ACTS OF HATRED AND BIGOTRY

Racism in its interpersonal form is no less insidious or damaging than institutionalized racism to those who are the direct targets of it. Institutional racism has a major impact on the life chances of the subordinate group as a whole but interpersonal racism is how race is felt: the words, thoughts, and actions that make clear to both actors (the racist and the oppressed) of their respective places in society. The attitudes and actions that comprise interpersonal racism against Mexican Braceros have received scant attention from scholars of the program. This in spite of the fact that one of the key agreements to the original accords was an anti-discrimination measure codified by U.S. and Mexican officials. A few scholars have paid some attention; the following section below will deal with how Lessard (1984) and Kirstein (1977) define race and discrimination and the limits of those definitions. In particular, the Mexican state deployed these definitions that informed the early critical scholarship so the official state position from protecting Braceros from discrimination to blaming them for their mistreatment demonstrates the limits of the individual-based discriminatory framework. I will also discuss the racist undercurrent that informs the authoritative source on the Bracero Program and interest group politics (Richard Craig's [1971] *The Bracero Program: Interest Groups and Foreign Policy*). Then, I will focus on grower attitudes that were given as part of the legislative testimony meant to set the terms of debate on the "Bracero problem." In addition, I will return to Hancock (1959) as prime example of the racialized thinking that permeates the dominant position in the Anglo grower-Mexican worker relationship. Finally, I will discuss how particular Mexican-American groups adopted these racialized logics and employed them to further the agendas of particular Mexican Americans at the expense of Mexican immigrants.

Mexican Government Frames of the Bracero Program

Based upon the stated positions of the Mexican government on the treatment of Mexicans residing in the United States (whether Mexican or U.S. born), it is clear that the second-class citizenship evident in the economic, cultural, political, and housing realms faced prior to 1940 were still in place.

> [Mexican officials] were also sensitive about the squalid and discriminatory conditions under which Mexicans continued to live in the United States. Indeed, so bitter had the Mexican people become on account of the abuses suffered by their compatriots north of the border, that no government in Mexico City dared to send workers to the United States without ample provision having first been made for their protection (Scruggs 1960, 142).

During the Second World War, Texan growers, facing a domestic labor shortage, turned to where they usually turned to meet their labor needs in times of short supply—Mexico. "In rural Texas, Jim Crow conditions remained virtually unaffected by the war against Hitler and race supremacy, a situation that prompted Mexico to exclude the state from its international agreement regarding guest workers" (Montejano 1987, 268). Instead of relying upon contracted labor due to Texas' blacklisted status (which I will detail shortly), growers utilized undocumented labor from Mexico.

Other regions of the United States that relied upon Mexican agricultural labor were also held responsible by the Mexican government for their mistreatment of Mexico's nationals. As USDA historian Wayne Rasmussen (1951, 210) noted, in 1946 Secretary of Agriculture Anderson sent a letter to Michigan U.S. Representative Fred Crawford detailing "Mexico's request that her nationals not to be used in Colorado, Illinois, Indiana, Michigan, Montana, Minnesota, Wisconsin, and Wyoming. This request was based upon reported discriminatory treatment and unsatisfactory earnings of Mexican nationals working in the cultivation and harvesting of sugar beets."

Discrimination, as it was referred to by the Mexican government, most often signified particular acts (racial threats, intimidations, and violence) or clearly visible practices such as restaurants and other public establishments that posted signs stating "No Mexicans Allowed" (see Foley 1997, "Illustration Plate 5"). These are all important components of the Anglo racial frame from 1942 to 1964 but it was the institutionalized force of segregation that put Mexican immigrants into the inferior set of social conditions that they had to endure. At the same time that the Mexican-American population was afforded piecemeal steps toward integration, as Montejano (1987) demonstrates, Mexican immigrants (whether undocumented or contracted) were further isolated from the rest of the U.S. population. Where Mexican immigrants migrated to (geographic segregation), what jobs they took upon entering the United States (occupational segregation), and who they worked with (intra-job segregation) were all determined by the increasing social isolation of Mexican nationals.

When the post-WWII mass deportations of undocumented immigrants began to be implemented, a Mexican public health officer named Xavier Castañeda addressed a group of undocumented workers who were being returned to Mexico via the Rio Grande Valley International Airport. Excerpts from his speech to the undocumented who were present are as follows:

> I am charged to tell you that you have committed a great sin in coming to this country without being asked for, without being needed here. The Government of Mexico is disgusted, fed up with this clandestine business of you, its citizens, going to the United States for the mirage of the dollar. But now it is all finished. . . . Now I beg you, in the name of our country, in the name of

> Mexico, I beg you not to return in this clandestine manner. In the name of Mexican Immigration, in the name of these American officers, I am charged with speaking to you in clear and simple Spanish, that you abstain. Your hands are needed in Mexico, and only the man who is worth nothing there, comes here in this manner. Do not continue to make yourselves warehouses full of cheap Indians. You should be ashamed of yourselves, abandoning your homes, traitors to your Mexico. Mexico is esteemed and loved in the world, you are making a bad example with this situation. . . . So I, a Mexican among the rest of you, with all my soul, as the shield of the University of Mexico says, "My spirit speaks for my race," I am speaking for my race. . . . So I want you to tell me, boys, are you going to come back illegally? (All answer "No, no.") Louder, are you going to come back? ("No.") May God help you and the Fatherland reward you. Above all, Mexico is our country. Later, if they start contracting, everyone of you who comes here legally contracted will be received with open arms. You will bear the name of a true Mexican citizen, rather than as a wetback, as you are now designated, a very sad thing for Mexico. . . . Finally, in the name of Mexico, I am going to repeat once more, are you going to come back without permits? (Answer: No.) We hope to God you don't. Go on back to your country. Your mothers, your daughters, the most precious treasures are awaiting you there. Viva Mexico! (Castañeda [1951] in Kiser and Kiser 1979, 164–166).

The messages sent by Castañeda were clear and unequivocal. First, undocumented immigrants were to blame for their situation. Second, a clear racial demarcation was present in the speaker's views of his segment of the Mexican race as acceptable and to be honored and the characterization of the Indian wetback as a source of embarrassment, easily exploitable by greedy Americans. Third, any form of social control would be utilized to deter further undocumented immigration (forced repatriation, calls to Mexican patriotism, a sense of pride in self, invocations of God and sin, the law of the land in both Mexico and the United States, intimidation, and a mix of guilt and patriarchy in the form of "precious treasures"). Finally, the Bracero Program would be viewed as the only viable means of migrating to the United States. Even though the reasons for migration would be the same ("mirage of the dollar") and the results would be the same (abandoning homes, hands needed in Mexico would be lost, families left behind, etc.), somehow that would all be acceptable as long as the would-be migrant subjected himself to the U.S. and Mexico state sanctioned contracting process. The way that the public health officer from Mexico denigrated the deported fits with both Mexico-based racializations of poor, indigenous, rural Mexicans and U.S. racializations of Mexican immigrants as "wetbacks." In one speech, these two differing racialized definitions are closely articulated into a unified means for denigration, intimidation, and social control.

Anglo Academic Frames of Racism as an Interpersonal Affair

The second provision that created the world's first binational guest worker program stated: "Mexicans entering the United States as result of this understanding shall not suffer discriminatory acts of any kind in accordance with the Executive Order No. 8802 issued at the White House June 25, 1941." The guideline specifically barred Braceros from being subjected to racially discriminatory treatment. The blacklisting of Texas represented the pinnacle of anti-discrimination enforcement but Texan growers consistently subverted the ban by recruiting undocumented labor along the border. The dual wage structure that marked the sugar beet industry, with Mexicans getting paid less than Anglos for doing the same tasks, led to the states of Colorado, Illinois, Indiana, Michigan, Montana, Minnesota, Wisconsin, and Wyoming also being blacklisted for the lesser Mexican wage. Both governments recognized the racism that Mexicans were subjected to yet race plays very little scholarly role in explaining how Braceros were treated.

Lessard (1984) devotes a chapter to the discrimination Braceros faced while working in the United States. But his explanation focuses on individual acts of discrimination (usually against the Mexican-American urban population), not on racism as an overall explanation for why Braceros were employed in the United States in the first place. Rather than capturing the general climate of hostile Anglo-Chicano-Mexicano relations, the chapter he devotes to racial discrimination reads more like a series of non-related, isolated incidents (the Zoot Suit Riots, the Texas blacklisting situation, the Mexican consuls' role in protecting Braceros from discrimination, and special interest groups in Mexico), even though his intentions are to the contrary.

Kirstein (1977) is better suited, with Mexican sources in hand, to see the institutional forms of racism in the formation of the lived experiences of Mexican immigrants in the United States. As the author quotes from the Mexico bi-monthly press, *Lectura*:

> In the United States, they despise us. They call us greasy and dirty and do not consider us worthy to associate with them. . . . It does not matter to the American that he (the Mexican) has money and that he has earned it with the sweat of his brow. . . . In some places he cannot even shop in the stores. . . . Racial discrimination . . . exists because there are North Americans who believe themselves . . . superior (Kirstein 1977, 54).

Kirstein states that the issue of Mexican immigration is rooted in the history of Chicano oppression but his brief discussion of racial discrimination relies on press reports that focus exclusively on the interpersonal acts of discrimination. Both Lessard and Kirstein attempt to document that Braceros were the subject of racial discrimination but neither author provides evidence specific to the program. It is another scholar's attempt to explain the suitability of Mexican peasants for U.S. agricultural migrant labor that unintentionally demonstrates how the interpersonal acts of racial discrimination relate to the institutionalized racism of the Bracero Program.

Richard Craig's (1971) *The Bracero Program: Interest Groups and Foreign Policy* is often acknowledged in the study of migration to be the central text for understanding the role of interest group politics in the unfolding of the various accords that comprise the Bracero Program. It is a work that had no intention of addressing the racial issues that Lessard (1984) and Kirstein (1977) attempt to detail. But it is from Craig's discussion of the "sociopsychological climate" of rural Mexico that we get a thorough attestation to the racist undercurrents that guide the views of the author. Considering the positive reception of the monograph, it is suggestive of the relative pervasiveness of Craig's viewpoint in scholarly circles and possibly wider audiences.

As Craig (1971, 14) states, "Again, in the mold of the model underdeveloped nation, Mexico suffers from overpopulation. It appears that religion and the cult of *machismo* ('virility' or 'masculinity') have combined during recent decades to produce a population explosion." Rather than seriously dealing with the issues of resource-for-use scarcity and economic dependence that articulate in the formation of the typical "underdeveloped" nation's demographic trends, Craig looks at the sociopsychological maladaptations of Mexicans and the "machismo" stereotype to explain away relations of dependency.

The machismo mindset is indicative, not only of essentialist characterizations, but of the argument that Craig is putting forward in terms of Mexicans' biological and mental predispositions for agricultural labor. "To toil endless hours in stifling heat and under generally adverse conditions demanded more than mere physical attributes. Granted, a unique and indeed remarkable physical specimen was required to successfully perform the arduous endless hours of stoop labor demanded of the field hand in southwestern agriculture. Such physical attributes alone, however, were not enough" (Craig 1971, 14). This apparent complement to the Mexican laborer for his remarkable physical prowess is more a means of claiming that the unique physical characteristics of Mexicans make them particularly suited for this type of work. Rather than questioning the labor practice of submitting workers to "endless hours of stoop labor," the task becomes explaining how bodies and minds of Mexicans predispose them to endure. The natural order of things is in balance, according to Craig, when racial groups, who are predisposed biologically to work in agriculture, are in fact employed in that industry.

But more than that, Craig takes biological essentialism one step further to claim that Mexicans also possess the requisite mental predispositions necessary to be used as agricultural labor (i.e., a mental acuity to being dominated). The Bracero is ". . . one accustomed to living, and indeed thriving, in a virtual state of physical and mental peonage. The Mexican peasant, by virtue of his rather unique sociopsychological background, was ideally suited for the task. The transition from *ejidatario* or *minifundista* to bracero was generally accomplished with utmost ease by the Mexican" (Craig 1971, 15). Again, rather than questioning why Mexican workers must submit to a state of peonage in order to be employed in the United States, the author looks for the racially inferior mental traits that Mexicans inherently possess that "ideally suit" them for thriving in a state of peonage. To claim that poor people thrive in conditions that compound their oppression is truly offensive when considered from the perspective of the laborers who had no other choice but to endure this hostile racial climate. "It would appear, in sum, that the sociopsychological milieu in which the average Mexican peasant was reared prepared him ideally for his role as the servile, hard-working, seldom complaining, perpetually polite bracero" (Craig 1971, 15).

Craig (see 15, *n.* 27) bases this assessment on Oscar Lewis' infamous culture of poverty studies of rural Mexico and a former farm labor contractor (FLC) turned academic's case study of the impact of the Bracero Program on Chihuahua, Mexico (Hancock 1959). In effect, Craig looks for pre-existent character traits, immutable racial and/or ethnic-based predispositions to serve as an apologia for the domination and oppression the Braceros faced as contract workers.[8]

Craig seemingly refutes his own argument of the "docile" Bracero by referring to: "[the s]eizure of haciendas, mass squatter movements, riots, and the occasional premeditated murders characterized Mexico's sporadically violent rural populace in the last quarter-century. . . . It is no exaggeration to surmise that many a potential rural agitator became, instead, a contented bracero" (18). Obviously, this historical context of active resistance runs completely contrary to the argument that Mexican *campesinos* are predisposed both mentally and physically to being oppressed and dominated. The role expectations of growers and their immediate representatives (FLCs and crew bosses) are much more plausible explanations of why Braceros acquiesced and acted subservient, rather than Craig's attributed backward predispositions of Mexican *campesinos*.

Grower Frames of the Bracero

Though it should be clear that not all growers viewed Braceros synonymously, those who took public stances unequivocally belittled and essentialized the labor force that they fully depended upon to harvest their crops and served as the source for their wealth and profit. In 1951, the U.S. President's Commission on Migratory Workers heard testimony from growers on the "Bracero Problem." The attitudes expressed by growers consisted of four general themes: Mexican workers and their natural inclination toward agricultural work, U.S. growers as rightfully entitled to Mexican labor, the Bracero Program providing the most desirable worker, and the program's provision for those workers at a cost too high for growers to pay.

As a grower from California characterized the Mexican agricultural labor force:

> Of all the groups tried, excepting the locals, the Mexican national is by all standards the best suited to this work. By temperament and aptitude, he seems especially adapted to farm employment. He, as a farmer, likes to work with living plants and trees. Mexico is one of the few remaining states which is largely agrarian (President's Commission 1951, 20).

The Mexican worker's "natural inclination" toward farm labor serves to justify why he was predominately found at the bottom layers of agricultural production. All of the factors referred to by the California grower posit the Mexican laborer as predisposed to the type of work he is subjected to in the United States. But Mexican laborers were employed as seasonal agricultural workers due to the historically constructed patterns that viewed Mexican immigrants as the ideal work force. There is a long history of agricultural labor recruitment agencies targeting Mexican workers to harvest the crops of the southwestern United States (see Deutsch 1987, Foley 1997, Kiser and Kiser 1979, Ngai 2005, Peck 2000, Sanchez 1993, and Takaki 1994).

In addition, growers often assumed that they were entitled to this labor force.

> The time has come when farmers along the southern border of the United States must stand up for their rights and demand that either the historic free movement of necessary seasonal labor from Mexico be permitted . . . [or] that farmers be given, not a "new deal" nor a "fair deal," but a good, honest "square deal" in the use of Mexican seasonal labor (U.S. President's Commission 1951, 20–21).

Again, the sentiments expressed by this grower from New Mexico are that the "historic free movement" is not a right of those who migrate but of growers who use this mobile labor force to pick their crops. Not only are the rights of growers circumvented with the "excessive rules and regulations" of the Bracero Program, but the labor they are rightfully entitled to is controlled by another source—in this case the U.S. federal government.

A Colorado grower specified what characteristics comprised the ideal agricultural worker. ". . . [A]ny nation is very fortunate if that nation can, from the sources near at hand, obtain the services on beck and call of labor, *adult male labor*, on condition that when the job is completed the laborer will return to his home. That is exactly the situation of this area" (U.S. President's

Commission 1951, 20). It is apparent who has the control in the employment relation and who is doing the beck and calling. The ideal laborer to U.S. growers is adult, male, Mexican, and willing to go back once his services are no longer needed. This was the exact arrangement codified by the state with the institution of the Bracero Program.

The duration of the contracts were pre-specified to coincide with the time necessary to harvest any particular crop. "In addition to bracero-employers and employers generally, communities preferred bracero employment to domestic migrants since Mexican contract workers returned to their homes south of the border when not employed and did not burden local social service agencies or the school system" (Grove 1996, 316). The "burden" is debatable but certainly, as pointed out by Burawoy (1976), the social costs of reproduction are bore by the Mexican communities who send adult, male laborers. The U.S. communities, which directly benefit from their labor, do not have to cover the costs of subsistence from the day-to-day level nor the reproduction of the labor force from generation to generation.

Even though the Bracero Program was designed to coincide with the interests of growers, the spokesmen who represented agribusiness voiced the complaints of growers to the Commission. In the summary of their position, the Commission stated that growers viewed the Bracero Program as "one-sided and does not represent the desires or needs and that it is discriminatory because it provides better conditions for the imported nationals of Mexico than those enjoyed by domestic farm labor" (U.S. President's Commission 1951, 50). The president of the Imperial Valley Farmer's Association of California elaborated upon this point.

> Negotiations with Mexico have always been settled with favor to the Mexican at the expense of the American farmer. The agencies negotiating for the farmer have given concessions to the Mexican above and beyond the conditions given to the American farm worker. These concessions are made under the excuse that Mexico will take no less. It seems to us that when these workers are coming over our borders to work regardless of agreements that common sense on the part of the United States agencies will show that we must have a program that is practical and workable without excessive red tape or the farmer is not going to use it (U.S. President's Commission 1951, 50).

As popular as "reverse discrimination" is in contemporary discourse, those responsible for the oppression of others have long used the counter-claim that they are in fact the victims who are discriminated against. The very notion that the grower is being discriminated against, by the same federal government that is securing the Mexican contract labor force for the grower, seems ludicrous. The invocation of the term "discrimination" to describe the situation of the grower belittles the serious nature of racism and its insidious effects. To make their point clear, the spokesmen state that the growers they represent will hire undocumented labor rather than meet the requirements of the Bracero Program.

These growers express their views toward "the Bracero," but it is specifically in how racism is manifested at *both* the interpersonal and institutional levels that explains the Braceros' subordinate status vis-à-vis the Anglo power structure. Unwittingly, Hancock (1959) demonstrates how these levels articulate with one another: attitudes designed to justify inferior social locations, which perpetuate negative interpersonal acts of discrimination and attempts at further segregation, and so the cycle perpetuates itself.

Richard Humphris Hancock was a former farm labor contractor and medical assistant for the screening of potential Braceros, and in his 1959 Hispanic American Society published thesis, he offers his "scholarly" analysis of grower-Bracero relations.

> Despite the occasional abuses which Mexican workers suffer at the hands of United States farmers, one of the happiest aspects of the bracero program is the personal relationship that develops between workers and farmers. The mutual pleasure and cordiality with which workers and their employers greet each other when the worker arrives with a new contract after a long absence in Mexico is unmistakable. It is a rewarding experience to witness the departure of braceros at the end of the season, to see a Spanish-speaking farmer say farewell to a group of his homeward-bound braceros, embracing each one individually and calling him by his first name. The well-fed, well-dressed, happy men who, wearing their inevitable new Stetson hats, depart for Mexico carrying shiny new trunks and great, clanking, canvas-wrapped bundles containing everything from plows to sewing machines, can hardly be recognized as the lean, ragged, worn-looking men who arrived in the United States in the spring with their possessions in small burlap bags. Although there is little in the attitudes of these returning workers or of their employers that suggests dissatisfaction, most of the printed reaction to the bracero program is unfavorable (Hancock 1959, iii–iv).

The social location of the author is extremely relevant in this case as it is from this position of power that the quote offers insight into, not simply his biases, but also the place from which he views the world. Characterizing grower-Bracero relations as the "happiest aspect," "personable," and "mutual pleasure and cordiality" should certainly heal the occasional abuses that workers had to deal with from time-to-time. In fact, I am sure it would be a rewarding experience to see such close, personal ties made with growers and workers, but this characterization does not capture the experiences of the Braceros that Herrera-Sobek, Galarza, Gamboa, Gonzalez, Cohen, Lopez, and I spoke with.

If Braceros seemed to exhibit dissatisfied attitudes, there certainly would be a strong basis for this belief. If the characterization that Hancock put forward had a stronger basis in workers' experiences, it might be more of a dilemma to explain why "the printed reaction to the Bracero Program is unfavorable." But Hancock never questions to whom the Braceros appear satisfied. As a FLC and medical assistant, he had a great deal to say in terms of who was contracted and who was allowed to work. Why would the Braceros complain to him? Why jeopardize their future dealings in the United States by presenting anything but a favorable disposition toward the entire experience as a contracted laborer?

As Hancock (1959, iii) tells us, "American doctors are amazed at the animal vitality with which the Mexican worker overcomes crushing physical injuries and illnesses which would ordinarily mean a lifetime disability for the average worker in the United States." From this perspective, it is clear that Mexicans are "naturally" suited for this type of work even with its everyday hazards and dangerous working conditions. If "American doctors" scientifically denote the Mexican's animal-like nature, then Hancock assumes it obviously must be true. What is missing is the level of economic desperation necessary to continually submit oneself to a job that inflicts so much physical harm.

"[Furthermore,] He will request leave to go home to participate in a blood feud with the same laconic composure as when he asks permission to go to Juarez for a night on the town" (Hancock 1959, iii). This statement gives us clues as to how the power relationship is manifested. For instance, why should an adult (barring those in jails, mental hospitals, or the military) have to ask for permission? This laconic manner of a request is a result, according to Hancock, of his "rural background" but there is also a set of assumptions about the "sociopsychological climate" of Mexicans feeding this stereotype.

> Most braceros are religious, serious-minded men who believe in authoritarian philosophy that man's natural state is to be found in a society in which the ability to command and the will to obey are both regarded as virtues. The willingness of these men to work is demonstrated in the eagerness with which a bracero frequently requests that he be assigned to a farm where he can work twelve hours a day, seven days a week . . . (Hancock 1959, iii).

The depiction (attitude or belief) that the Mexican laborer is better suited physically for agricultural labor provides a legitimation for the inferior social status of Mexican immigrants stuck in the lowest orders of U.S. agriculture. The depiction that Mexicans are naturally inclined to believe in societies that differentiate between those who rule and those who are ruled provides a justification for a labor process marked by coercion. The depiction of Braceros as eager and willing to subject themselves to exploitation, for substandard wages and in working conditions exceeding the threshold of human endurance, provides a rationale for superexploitation at the hands of growers.

"With increasing experience [working in the U.S.] the average bracero loses his almost childlike dependence on a superior and becomes a relatively decisive and self-reliant individual" (Hancock 120). Apparently, self-reliance is accepted as long as the Bracero *asks* if he can go visit his family or have a night out on the town. In actuality the grower-worker power relationship dictates that the Braceros submit to his superiors as if he is a child, completely dependent on their commands. The modern man, as embodied in Ralph Waldo Emerson's self-reliant individual, is exactly what U.S. growers were *not* looking for in a workforce designed to be subservient and used at their whim.

Mexican-American Frames of the Bracero Program

The Mexican-American population was not entirely innocent in its portrayal of Mexican immigrants during the Bracero Program. Though Hispanic academics and organizations certainly did not speak for the entire Chicano community, their words were given a prominent place whenever "the Spanish-American view" needed to be expressed in larger circles. In 1948, Mexican-American citizens banded together over what is now referred to as the Three Rivers Incident. A World War II soldier, killed in action, was refused burial in the cemetery of his hometown of Three Rivers, Texas, because the man, Felix Longoria, was Mexican American. After an interdiction by U.S. Senator Lyndon B. Johnson, the highly decorated soldier was eventually buried at Arlington National Cemetery. In the wake of Three Rivers, other Mexican-American veterans banded together to form the American GI Forum to voice their concerns over racism in Texas as well as provide additional representation to the Chicano population. The GI Forum of Texas took a leading role in blaming the Mexican immigrant for the generally poor conditions facing all Mexicans residing in the United States. As Hadley (1956, 335) quotes from the American GI Forum of Texas pamphlet, "What Price Wetbacks?":

> The vast majority of wetbacks are plain agricultural workers including women and children, mostly from the peasant class in Mexico. They are humble, amenable, easily dominated and controlled, and accept exploitation with the fatalism characteristic of their class. A common term applied to them is Guanajuato Joe, for the Mexican State of Guanajuato which supplies a large percentage of wetbacks apprehended in farm work. This type of wetback wants only to find work on a farm, mind his own business and be left alone by the Border Patrol. He accepts good or bad treatment, starvation wages, diarrhea and other sickness for his children from contaminated drinking water and unsanitary living conditions—all this he accepts stolidly and philosophically. He does not think in terms of native labor displacement, lowering the standards and the socio-economic effects of his presence in the U.S. Ideologies are beyond his comprehension. He understands only his way of life: to work, to suffer, and to pray to the Virgen de Guadalupe for a better life in the hereafter.

The Mexican immigrant is characterized as a peasant who, due to his feeble-mindedness, is prone to exploitation in the United States. To the GI Forum, the blame for the labor market positions that immigrants reside in is not a result of grower control but rooted squarely in the inferiorities and complacencies of the immigrants. A similar position, though much more explicit in its stereotyping of Mexican immigrants, was put forward by colleagues of University of Texas Professor George I. Sanchez (who I will discuss shortly).

> It is something of an understatement to point out that the wetback hardly represents the best in Mexican culture. Being poor, uneducated, unskilled, underfed, and frequently, unclean, he has little to endear him to a people who highly value material success, knowledge, skills, good health and cleanliness. And since he speaks Spanish, looks like the native Spanish-speaking population, and obviously has many things in common with them, it is quite natural for the Anglo to lump them all together in his thinking and to ascribe to all the characteristics of some (Saunders and Leonard 1951 [quoted in Gutiérrez 1995, 146]).

"Wetback" is a term of derision that often is applied to all people of Mexican descent, whether they are immigrants to the United States or they originally lived in the region of what became the United States. It is even more unfortunate to see Mexican Americans use the derogatory term to characterize Mexican immigrants who most often did not wade through the Rio Grande to illegally enter the United States. The main point is that the authors are trying to set themselves apart from the Mexicans they view as deserving of the negative Anglo-imposed stereotypes. By arguing that "those Mexicans" are an economic threat to the established Mexican-*American* population, immigrants are characterized as taking jobs from natives by working for lower wages and willing to accept negative treatment from employers because the immigrants feel that they deserve it.

One of the most prominent Mexican-American scholars during the Bracero Program, George I. Sanchez, was an extremely vehement opponent of Mexican immigration and, in his eyes, the Braceros' displacement of Mexican-American native workers. As Sanchez describes the situation: "As you know, the root of the evil as regards 'Mexicans' in the United States stems from the fact that, just across the border, there is a reservoir of cheap labor that growers in the United States can tap at will. The alien worker becomes, in effect, a strike-breaker or 'scab' who is a potent club to prevent the 'Mexican' already here from improving his lot" (Galarza Papers 1:3). This statement is found in a letter dated October 1948 to Ernesto Galarza. Other letters by Sanchez to Galarza reiterated the point that Mexican immigrants, Braceros in particular, were hampering the unionization of Mexican-American workers and guaranteeing that all Mexicans in the United States will be trapped in a surplus pool of cheap labor.

It is interesting to see how the negative characterizations often applied by Anglos to all Mexicans becomes focused on the Mexican immigrant in the hands of the relatively privileged Hispanic spokesmen of the time. Sanchez was not only making an argument about the economic threat that Mexican immigrants posed. He also was arguing that the large influx also threatened the cultural assimilation of Americans of Mexican descent.

> Quoted in a 1951 *New York Times* article provocatively entitled "Peons in West Lowering Culture," Sanchez averred that, "from a cultural standpoint, the influx of a million or more wetbacks a year transforms the Spanish-speaking people of the Southwest from an ethnic group which might be assimilated with reasonable facility into what I call a culturally indigestible peninsula of Mexico. The 'wet' migration tends to nullify processes of social integration going back 300 or 350 years, and I would say at the present time has set the whole assimilation process back at least twenty years" (Gutiérrez 1995, 145).

At the same time that Sanchez was speaking out against Mexican immigration, he was a vehement critic of Anglo racism.

> In a carefully documented article in *Common Ground* [Autumn 1943, 13-20] Dr. George I. Sanchez, of the University of Texas, former president of the League of United Latin-American Citizens, called attention to the pattern of discrimination in employment, in the schools, and in civic life throughout the borderlands. In the course of a hike, a Scoutmaster and his troop of Boy Scouts, all in uniform, were ordered out of a public park, where they had stopped to rest, because they were "Mexicans." Texas churches posted signs reading "For Coloreds and Mexicans" and refused Mexicans permission to attend the "white churches" on Sundays. "In many cemeteries, whether owned by county authorities, by private individuals or corporations, or by religious organizations . . . the bodies of 'Mexicans' are denied the right of burial. . . . In those cemeteries where such bodies are received they are assigned a separate plot of land, far enough from the plot destined for so-called 'whites' so as to be sure that the bodies of the 'whites' will not be contaminated by the presence of the bodies of the Mexicans." Toilets in many Texas courthouses have signs which read: "For Whites Only--Mexicans Keep Out" (McWilliams 1990 [1948], 243).

Correctly recognizing that the roots of these racist practices were in how Anglos perceived Mexicans, Sanchez was mistaken in his uncritical search for those elements of the Mexican population that (in his judgment) fit the negative stereotypes. Sanchez recommended that Mexican Americans pursue a course of action that would send Mexican immigrants back to the source of the problem—Mexico and its uncivilized, indigenous folkways. The repeated use of the term Mexican in quotation marks alludes to Sanchez's view on how Mexican Americans should be identified and trace their origins. Often, to refer to those U.S. citizens of Mexican descent, Sanchez uses the terms

"Spanish-speaking people" or "Spanish Americans" to divorce any associations with Mexicans from Mexico. Sanchez refers to his classic, *Forgotten Americans* (1967, 13), as a history of "the American of Spanish descent" in New Mexico. Being Spanish connotes European origins, even membership in the "white" race, or at least deserving of the association.

In the San Luis Valley of Colorado, finding a suitable location for housing Braceros became an important issue that demonstrates the strained relations between Mexican Americans, Mexican immigrants, and Anglos. Initial plans were to house contract workers in the largest city and county seat of the valley, on the south side of the town. This was the area where the majority of the Mexican-descent population resided and still does to this day. This plan met immediate opposition by the Mexican-American community (sometimes referring to themselves as Spanish) and Braceros were eventually housed outside the main town on the outskirts of the smaller towns near growers' properties.

This high degree of isolation was slightly tempered one day a week when Braceros entered the main "urban" center of Alamosa on Saturday afternoons. They limited their trips to purchasing money orders for remittances at the post office, purchasing small goods to take back to Mexico, and partaking in small *fiestas* they held at the town's city park in order to intermingle with other Braceros from surrounding farms. According to the postal worker who took money orders, these *fiestas* never included Anglos or the sizable Mexican-American population of the area. The remainder of the Braceros' time was spent in the fields or the farm labor camps which included a converted school in the town of Ft. Garland (twenty-five miles east of Alamosa) and former army barracks in Center (thirty miles north) and Antonito (thirty-five miles south).

In an interview, the provider of corn tortillas for the Bracero labor camps described how the San Luis Valley accepted the workers:

> Int: Were the Braceros accepted into the community? How would you characterize relations between Braceros, Anglos and Mexican-Americans in the Valley?
>
> Señor Palmas: They related real well. And I don't know if it was because of the type of people that they were or the particular controls that the contract had over them. Because of what they would do on like Saturday after work, I think they worked a half a day Saturday, so they were brought into town on buses. Then they did all their purchasing and sightseeing, and drinking if you will, and socializing amongst themselves. The community really took to them because they were so well, uh I don't want to say the word controlled, because I don't know if it was control that was in order, but they were just quite amenable to what they saw. Everything was new and everything was just awesome to them. And then they could buy certain things that they were allowed to transport back to Mexico. So they did a lot of shopping downtown and of

> course it was all cash. Of course, the merchants liked that. No haggling, no nothing, and everybody I communicated with commented that they were so polite and so friendly and so, uh, . . . Just great guys.

The other men I spoke with who were affiliated with the program focused more on the interactions with Braceros than attitudes toward them. The high degree of social isolation was corroborated by all three men's testimony (Interviews with Señor Freemont, Mr. Allen, and Señor Palmas 1997) that Saturday was the only day for community contact. In addition, all three men concurred about the general contours of intra-race relations in the valley.

> Our circles were basically Hispanics. Their circles were basically Braceros. Those guys that come in, groups and families and all that from transient agricultural workers. They pretty much everybody kinda gravitates toward their own. But there is a whole lot more interaction now. Among all of us. In other words, the circles have intersected but there still is we tend to gravitate to whatever sector we might come from (Interview with Señor Palmas 1997).

Other Braceros interviewed also corroborated this day-off practice, which was usually spent in the nearest town, as the only source of contact with local residents. For those Braceros who were granted the "privilege" of weekly visits, they were allowed to send money back to Mexico, buy groceries if they cooked their own meals, or purchase household items if storage space was allotted. Some respondents had all of these necessities handled for them, for a fee, by the FLCs and crew bosses. For these respondents, trips into the community were not allowed since transportation was not provided by growers. As one Bracero stated it, "We saw two buses: the one that brought us from Piedras Negras, and the one that took us back there" (Life Story of Don Antoñio 1997). The behavior of the Braceros in their Saturday afternoon community context is best explained by the Braceros' reading of the role expectations of the communities' views on how Mexican migrants should act in public. The quote from Señor Palmas about how well the Braceros related to the community in the San Luis Valley must be considered in relation to the social isolation that the other respondents noted. In addition, the indirect control of Braceros' actions ensured that they were to act polite and friendly in the local community context. Control cannot be *over*-emphasized in this explanation. If one was to go into town and raise a ruckus, it was quite likely the worker would be deported. In the end, it was not the community (Anglo or Mexican American) who the Braceros socialized with, it was other Mexican nationals from the valley's various farms and labor camps.

THE BLACKLISTING OF TEXAS: A CASE IN CONFRONTING RACISM

Racism, at both the interpersonal and institutional levels, reached such a fevered pitch in Texas that the Mexican government refused to allow Mexican Braceros to work in the state from 1942 to 1947. The U.S. railroad industry quickly attempted to circumvent the Texas blacklisting by contracting Braceros outside of the state and then transferring them to Monahans and Midland, Texas (McCain 1981, 58). The discrimination faced by the track-workers was detailed to a representative of the Mexican Foreign office in September 1943.

> The braceros in question complained bitterly of discrimination. They contended that they were denied entrance to public places of entertainment, were not permitted to sit at tables in refreshment parlors or to purchase items there except by using the service entrance, and could not patronize barbershops or other places of service except in areas almost inaccessible to them. On the matter of unequal treatment, they complained that they had straw mattresses while the Americans had cotton ones; they had no first-aid kits; they had inadequate bathing facilities, inadequate sanitation, and overcrowded conditions; and they were charged one dollar every two weeks for lodgings, which the employer refused to show on the payroll slips (McCain 1981, 59).

In this regard, the Mexican government held a more expansive view of what constituted racial discrimination and applied these definitions to completely bar the use of contracted workers in Texas by both the railroad and agricultural industries.

> The Mexican government also tended to view discrimination in economic as well as social terms, as connected with jobs and wages as well as schools, restaurants, and barbershops. In other words, its definition included the treatment of Mexicans as farm laborers. Because of the proximity of cheap labor in Mexico, discriminatory hiring practices of American labor and industry that restricted Mexicans to field work, and the workers' lack of non-agricultural skills, parts of Texas had long remained among the lowest farm wage areas in the country (Scruggs 1962, 124).

Texan growers began to formally request contract labor from the Mexican government as early as 1943 even though they strenuously objected to U.S. and Mexican government interference. During World War I, growers had directly contracted Mexican laborers. When the blacklisting continued beyond 1943, growers actively encouraged undocumented laborers to migrate to Texas through the same type of direct recruitment strategies that were implemented during World War I.

Throughout the Second World War, Texas Governor Coke Stevenson beseeched Mexican Foreign Labor Minister Ezequiel Padilla to permit the flow of recruited labor to Texas. Stevenson created a Texas Good Neighbor Commission in September 1943 and promised that State law officials would deal severely with Texans discriminating against Mexicans (Kirstein 1977, 54). The Texas Good Neighbor Commission would investigate charges of racial discrimination brought to their attention and promote a gradual education program of Anglo Texans about Latin America (Gutiérrez 1995, 140–141). Drawing upon President Franklin D. Roosevelt's 1933 inaugural address, that stated the U.S. intention to pursue a "Good Neighbor" policy toward the citizens of Latin America, the border state of Texas served as the focal point of this policy. This was ". . . due to the high percentage of Mexicans in its population, the correspondingly greater number of 'incidents,' and the application to Mexicans of many of the formal restrictions against Negroes throughout the state" (Scruggs 1962, 120). Mexican Foreign Minister Padilla stated that the Texas blacklist would continue because of the state's inability to solve its racist practices. As he stated toward the end of World War II:

> "In many parts of Texas, . . . Mexicans cannot attend public gatherings without being subject to vexations, complaints and protests. There are towns where my fellow countrymen are forced to live in separate districts. Just a week ago the daughter of a Mexican consul was refused service in a public establishment." The ban would not be lifted . . . until Texas had passed a law prohibiting such practices. A bill to this effect was introduced into the 1945 session of the Texas legislature but, needless to say, it did not pass (McWilliams 1990, 242).

Prior to this time, Texas had passed the so-called "Caucasian Race Resolution" in 1943 with the assumption that this law on the books would be sufficient to secure Braceros for Texan growers.

> Aware of the need to take action to improve a situation made more acute by acts of discrimination against Mexican-Americans in uniform and visiting Mexican dignitaries, Governor Coke Stevenson had induced the Texas legislature to pass the so-called "Caucasian Race" resolution, which he approved on May 6, 1943. The resolution affirmed the right of all Caucasians within the state to equal treatment in public places of business and amusement and denounced such privileges with 'violating the good neighbor policy of our state'. Doubtless, this manifesto of good intentions added to the surprise that greeted the Mexican announcement that braceros would not be allowed to go to Texas (Scruggs 1988, 88).

As historian Neil Foley perceptively notes of the resolution: "This clever resolution was intended to convince Mexico that discrimination against Caucasians would not be tolerated in Texas, the assumption being that Mexicans were, of course, members of the Caucasian race, which they were only in some legal, pseudo-scientific, and ethnographical sense; but practically no Texans regarded Mexicans, particularly bracero farm workers, as white" (Foley 1997, 206). And of course, this law was designed specifically to keep the system of racial discrimination against Blacks intact and really lays bare the intentions of the Texas state apparatus. The goal was neither to promote racial equality of treatment nor the eradication of racist beliefs. The Caucasian race resolution was promoted simply to ensure that Anglo growers in Texas had access to the labor pool they so desired. As the resolution stated:

> Our neighbors to the South were cooperating to stamp out Nazism and preserve democracy and to assist the national policy of hemispherical solidarity, the state of Texas resolves that all persons of the Caucasian Race . . . are entitled to the full and equal accommodations, advantages, facilities, and privileges of all public places or business or amusement. Whoever denied to any person these privileges shall be considered as violating the good neighbor policy of our State (Texas Caucasian Race Resolution 1943, [paraphrased in Foley 1997, 206]).

How ironic that in the effort to link the common agendas of Texas and Mexico in the eradication of the Nazi threat, the state promoted an agenda of equality for *Caucasians only* strictly in terms of access to public space. The state completely disregarded the economic issues surrounding race as well as its continued intolerance toward the Black population residing in Texas.

In response to the Good Neighbor policy, the Texas commission, and the Caucasian race resolution, people in Mexico developed their own organization, *Comite Mexicano Contra el Racismo* (Mexican Committee Against Racism) to document racial discrimination practices in the United States in the areas of education, labor and consumer establishments.

The Committee's publication, *Fraternidad*, included a column entitled "Texas, *Buen Vecino?*" ("Texas, Good Neighbor?"), which detailed the incidents of discrimination against Mexicans in Texas. *Fraternidad* documented a list of discriminatory practices that occurred in nearly 150 Texas communities. The committee had a strong impact on both the U.S. and Mexican state officials by pressuring them to deal with the racist practices of Anglo Texas.

In addition to the *Comite's Fraternidad*, the Mexican popular press documented the mistreatment of Mexicans residing in the United States. "Hardly a day passed, [U.S.] Ambassador Messersmith informed Washington in March, 1944, that some bitter article about discrimination against Mexicans in the United States did not appear in the press of Mexico City" (Scruggs 1962, 121). McCain (1981) briefly mentions the headlines of the major newspapers in Mexico during the 1942–1947 period that consistently referred to the continuing significance and persistence of racism in Texas.

The Texas situation clarifies how race is deployed as a power struggle to define the subordinate in ways that justify their unequal and limited access to resources and social institutions. Anglo growers used race as a line of division within class blocs to ensure themselves of a steady and cheap supply of Mexican immigrant labor. The hostile acts at the interpersonal level, documented by various sources in regard to Texas, articulate with institutional barriers to equality based on the demarcation of racial categories in the face of intentionally vacuous state resolutions. The Caucasian Race Resolution and the Texas Good Neighbor Commission failed in their stated goals because it was not the intention of its framers to promote social justice and anti-racist agendas. Quite simply, they represent attempts by the Texas state government to serve the interests of the most powerful in securing a cheap and controllable source of labor whose rights are always in question and easily amended to suit the needs of the employer. Texan growers (and other southwestern growers) circumvented the laborer safeguards, put in place by the Mexican government, by not contracting workers through the rules and regulations of the Bracero Program but directly recruiting undocumented workers from Mexico. U.S. state responses to these grower direct recruitment efforts are detailed in the next section.

BRACEROS Y LOS INDOCUMENTADOS: "GO BACK!" THE REPATRIATION CAMPAIGNS

During the Bracero Program, the influx of Mexican undocumented immigrants was dealt with in three ways. The most common means of dealing with growers using non-contracted labor on the part of U.S. state authorities was to ignore undocumented workers and allow them to seek work in the United States. These undocumented workers were usually directly recruited in Mexico by farm labor contractors or other intermediaries on behalf of growers. In particular, those growers near the border were able to directly recruit Mexican laborers and avoid the bureaucratic channels of the Bracero Program. The illegal status of undocumented farm workers was an advantage to growers since the rights guaranteed to Braceros did not have to be met. At no time were growers held responsible for directly recruiting "illegal" labor. It was not until *1986* that growers could be held legally responsible for hiring undocumented workers.

The second way of dealing with illegal immigration was to legalize undocumented workers by posthumously giving them Bracero contracts. From the period of 1947–1954, undocumented workers were contracted as Braceros at the U.S. work sites where they were already working. The bureaucratic regulations of the Bracero Program were then applied *ex post facto* to legalize illegal workers. As Garcia y Griego (1996, 57) describes the process:

"Legalization was a process by which deportable Mexicans who had been in the United States for a certain number of weeks were given bracero contracts, usually to work for the same employer, without the laborer having to return to Mexico and undergo the screening process in the interior, or the employer having to pay transportation to the United States."

The third way of dealing with illegal immigration was deportation. In 1954, Commissioner Joseph Swing of the Immigration and Naturalization Service mounted a mass repatriation campaign of illegal Mexican workers, dubbed "Operation Wetback," which resulted in an INS estimated return of 1.3 million workers to Mexico.[9] The means of repatriation varied—forced return migrants, voluntary leavers—but the effect was the same: "Operation Wetback did not bring an end to illegal immigration from Mexico. It did slow the influx for a short time but it brought no permanent solution to the problem. It was a stop-gap measure" (Garcia 1980, 232). Operation Wetback more importantly sent a strong message to the Mexican people about their rights to live and work in the United States. It also sent a strong message to Anglo growers. It stated that growers would not be held responsible for the mass migration that they initiated and perpetuated by actively recruiting and employing undocumented labor. This mass repatriation of Mexicans occurred at a time when the Bracero Program was running at its peak. At the same time, the contradictory message was sent to Mexican immigrants that they were not wanted in the United States yet their labor would be remunerated and rights acknowledged if they had a Bracero contract. Repatriation serves as a persistent reminder of the second-class citizenship status of Mexicans in the United States. Kiser and Kiser (1979) refer to two Bracero Programs: the first associated with World War I and the second associated with World War II. After both off these major invitations that the U.S. state extended to Mexican citizens to meet labor-shortage needs, each was accompanied by episodes of mass repatriations. During times of labor surpluses and/or economic downturns, a number of Mexican nationals and U.S. citizens of Mexican descent either voluntarily returned or were forced to return to Mexico. In Los Angeles alone during the 1930s, nearly one third of the Mexican population was returned to Mexico (Sanchez 1993, 123). The Mexican community in Detroit was totally displaced during the Depression-era repatriation movement. These episodes of mass repatriation, as witnessed by no other immigrant group in the United States, served as highly symbolic of the status of Mexicans in U.S. society.[10] Cardoso (1980) notes that after the U.S. officially state-sanctioned and growers recruited Mexican nationals during World War I, mass unemployment of the Great Depression was perceived to be "partially remedied" by the mass repatriation of Mexican citizens.

A CONCLUDING NOTE ON DEFINING "RACE"

The life history approach was crucial for understanding the way racism shaped the contours of Anglo-Bracero relations. The supplementary materials (government documents, interviews with non-Braceros, and secondary sources) served as the main materials for analysis because the life stories of Braceros were noticeably silent on these issues. Cohen's (2011, 10) field research encountered similar silences. Cohen states: "I had expected memories of racism and discrimination, yet that was not what I found. Or, more to the point, it was not what the men wanted to talk about. Instead, they described a range of mostly positive experiences." The high degree of segregation was evident in the life stories but mention of the racist acts they might have faced was largely absent. When asked specifically about the racism they experienced as an agricultural worker, respondents downplayed any negative experiences with Anglo society or they stated that they had little or no contact with the Anglo communities in which they were working. Contact with Anglos was extremely limited for most Braceros I interviewed.

An interesting discussion ensued when I asked two former Braceros, who were being interviewed together, about their exposure to racial discrimination.

> Int: So can you tell me about the racism your experienced during the program. You know, what were your [*ustedes*] experiences relating to the communities that you [*ustedes*] had gone into . . . that were predominately White?
>
> Don Francisco: I didn't have problems with them. When we went into the stores to buy things, they treated us fine. . . . I have always had good foremen. If you treat yourself bad, you will be treated bad.
>
> Int: And you?
>
> Don Jorge: When I see someone that has a Spanish face, And I say "You are Hispano" and they say, [in English] "Oh, no, no I don't speak Spanish," but they are Spanish.
>
> Don Francisco: But now they act like they are from here.

The discussion of the racism they might have dealt with was diverted into what the two gentlemen saw as racism within the Mexican American community. The respondents assumed that those workers who were the subjects of racism somehow deserved it because of their bad behavior. But within the Mexican community, those who assimilated were viewed as either internalizing racist views about what it was to be a Mexican by saying they don't speak Spanish or else they were acting quite presumptuous about their place in U.S. society. For both men, they knew their place in the United States and that was strictly as guests—poorly treated guests. Both men never acted "like they were from here" (i.e., the United States). This was the case even though both men were legal immigrants. In the ensuing discussion, race was interpreted as the second generation losing its culture and its language. Language was viewed by both men as crucial to their culture and one's denial of their Mexican roots, by acting more white (i.e., acting like a *pocho*), was their understanding of the racism they experienced. It is ironic that what these men determined was racism is what most migration scholars refer to as assimilation.

The majority of migration scholars assume that assimilation is both a normative ideal and an empirical inevitability. The assimilation and cultural pluralist positions both view American culture as a melting pot. In the first position, the melting pot produces a homogenous product much like a creamy soup. In other words, the differences are smoothed out to guarantee that each spoonful will taste the same. A cultural pluralist position would characterize the melting pot as the producer of chunky stews. Differences are allowed to coexist in the same stew because the different tastes tend to complement one another in the formation of one big stew. The assimilation position, which argues all immigrants will conform to the established (most often White, Anglo-Saxon, Protestant) or the "American middle class" ways of living, is precisely the cultural model that these two respondents abhor.

When members of particular groups subjectively assess their position as located completely outside of the melting pot, the issues of citizenship and racialization radically question the entire metaphor. The Braceros, who discussed the issue of racism as Mexican-American assimilation, were in effect questioning the notion of *an* American culture and the place of Mexicans in that culture. For these men, assimilation is the embodiment of the Anglo racism that is directed toward the Mexican population. According to the Braceros, to be American is to be White and European, not Mexican. Their place would always be as guests in the United States, regardless of their citizenship status.

The high degree of social isolation that the Braceros experienced stemmed directly from the racial segregation that predominated. Whether the Braceros were in labor camps, the fields, or local towns, they were in the exclusive company of other Braceros. Mingling and working with anyone other than Mexican contract workers was strictly prohibited. This high degree of social isolation also tended to shelter the Braceros from the interpersonal racism that also characterized the time period. But a survey of academic accounts, grower attitudes, and Mexican-American views of Braceros provides substantial evidence to the racist beliefs that shaped the debate on Mexican contract workers. Scholarly accounts spoke of the Braceros' "animal vitality" and "mental predispositions" toward back-breaking work and their "state of physical and mental peonage." Growers used Congressional hearings to express their "natural right" to use Mexican labor and document the biological predispositions that make Mexican laborers ideally suited for agricultural labor. Mexican-American scholars and voluntary associations sought to distance themselves from Mexican nationals by using the same rhetoric of growers and Anglo scholars to blame Mexican immigrants for the poor living conditions of all Mexicans residing in the United States.

The blacklisting of Texas from receiving Braceros between 1942 and 1947 demonstrates the deep-seeded racism that prevailed from growers and local community members to Texas state government managers. The formation of the Texas Good Neighbor Commission and the passage of the Caucasian Race Resolution did little to change racist attitudes and practices toward the Mexican population. These government initiatives were designed to ensure that Anglo growers had full access to Mexican immigrant labor. Also indicative of the racial climate were the repatriation campaigns that sent an estimated 1.3 million people of Mexican-origin to Mexico. These campaigns, dubbed Operation Wetback, served to solidify symbolically the definitions of citizenship, racial groups, and economic classes. The contradictory message that Mexicans received was that their labor was wanted but in no way were they welcome as citizens in the United States. The next chapter deals specifically with the labor that the Braceros were expected to perform, under conditions that they had very little control over.

NOTES

1. My sincerest thanks to H. L. T. Quan at Arizona State University for introducing me to the Sweet Honey in the Rock version of "Deportees." Lyrics can be located at: http://www.woodyguthrie.org/Lyrics/Deportee.htm.

2. Similarly, over the past twenty-five years, with the increased militarization of the U.S.-Mexico border, the thousands of deaths along the border are harsh reminders of the callous treatment of immigrant labor as disposable and unwanted.

3. Citizenship was equated with whiteness due to the very first act of Congress, the 1790 Naturalization Act that conformed to citizenship narrowly circumscribed to only White, male, property owners. As López (2006, 42) cites, naturalization was limited to "any alien, being a free white person who has have resided within the limits and under the jurisdiction of the United States for a term of two years." When the Treaty was signed fifty-eight years later, it gave Mexicans residing in the northern half of the nation, ceded to the United States, the option to move south below the newly defined border, claim U.S. citizenship, or do nothing and after one year become de facto U.S. citizens. A vigorous debate ensued in Congress about the "mongrel nature" of the Mexican race, and when the United States claimed remaining Spanish colonial territories after the Spanish American War of 1898, it was clear Congress learned its lesson from making Mexicans *de facto* whites as citizens by denying citizenship to Puerto Ricans, Filipinos, and all other colonial citizens. As John C. Calhoun decried in 1848,

> I know further, sir, that we have never dreamt of incorporating into our Union any but the Caucasian race—the free white race. To incorporate Mexico, would be the very first instance of the kind of incorporating an Indian race; for more than half of the Mexicans are Indians, and the other is composed chiefly of mixed tribes. I protest against such a union as that! Ours, sir, is the Government of a white race. The greatest misfortunes of Spanish America are to be traced to the fatal error of

placing these colored races on an equality with the white race. That error destroyed the social arrangement which formed the basis of society ("Conquest of Mexico," Available at http://teachingamericanhistory.org/library/document/conquest-of-mexico/).

4. "The State asserted that the equal protection clause prohibits discrimination only where two distinct classes exist and that Mexican-American people are not a distinct class. Declaring that 'persons of Mexican descent' are a cognizable minority group for equal protection purposes in areas where they are subject to local discrimination, the Court found systematic exclusion of the members of the class from jury service" (Delgado and Palacios 1975, 395). The important caveat in the decision deemed Mexicans as subject to "local" discrimination, not national that the authors note as the "other white" strategy.

5. The racialized social system approach to racism "refers to societies in which economic, political, social, and ideological levels are partially structured by the placement of actors in racial categories or races" (Bonilla-Silva 2001: 37). My approach does not discount or downplay interpersonal frames (stereotypes, epithets, discriminatory beliefs and actions) but emphasizes the complex interplay between institutional and interpersonal forms of racism. The insidiousness of race is its naturalization at so many levels, from ideological to material, institutional to interpersonal, lived experience to symbolic representation.

6. In David Montejano's (1987) *Anglos and Mexicans in the Making of Texas, 1836–1986*, the author characterizes the time frame of 1920 to 1940 as one of "segregation" and analyzes Anglo-Chicano relations in Texas in terms of "Jim Crow"-style practices. The post-segregation period (from 1940 to 1986) is characterized as a time of "integration." During the integration period, the massive mobilization for the war effort brought a large number of Mexican Americans out of the fields and into the armed forces and the war-production factories. In addition, "[t]he war had also exposed Texas Mexican soldiers to a world of greater freedoms and equalities, an experience that became especially important on the return home" (Montejano 1987, 270). Montejano is well warranted in viewing World War II as the watershed event in the beginning of Chicano integration but the period of 1940 to 1945 did not witness a significant decline in levels of segregation, racist practices, or significant changes in economic opportunities for *all* Mexicans. Formally segregated schools, referred to as "Mexican schools," were still in place as late as 1954 even though Mexicanos fought segregation through legal channels as early as 1931 (see Paul Espinosa's docudrama *The Lemon Grove Incident* for a fine portrayal of events leading up to the 1931 court case to stop the segregation of Mexican children in Southern California schools). Segregation in housing still predominated as Sanchez (1993, 77) notes in his study of Los Angeles. Even though *Mendez v. Westminster* struck down Mexican-Anglo segregated schools in 1947, Mexicans were defined constitutionally as "white" and therefore not subject to segregation (the case maintained segregation for non-White racialized African-Americans, Asians, and Native Americans). European ethnics started leaving the area during World War II and the areas integrated with Mexicans, Southern and Eastern Europeans became Mexican-dominated: "[b]y 1960, residential segregation was significantly higher than it had been in 1880." Racist attitudes and practices did not subside once Mexicans served in the U.S. armed forces. The Zoot Suit Riots that occurred in Los Angeles on June 3–13, 1943, where Anglo servicemen randomly berated and summarily beat young Chicano males attired in zoot suits, attests to the racial animosity, at the same time that Chicanos were enlisting in the service at the disproportionately high rates that continue to this day (Gutiérrez 1995, 124–25; Sanchez 1993, 253, 267). The expanded economic opportunities of Mexican Americans that Montejano associates with the war-time industrialization programs did not translate as gains for the Mexican immigrant population who remained limited to the most undesirable, underpaid, dirty, and dangerous jobs. The events Montejano notes as characteristic of Mexican integration (political incorporation via more political representation, desegregation of schools, and economic mobility) occurred to the greatest extent well after the end of the Bracero Program. They are more indicative of social conditions that can be deemed more truly integrative than events that occurred prior to the Chicano Civil Rights era.

7. Camps were also located in Washington (3), Oregon (2), Idaho (3), Arizona (3), Colorado (2), Texas (8), Arkansas (1), and Florida (9). Workers in Florida were most often Caribbean contract workers. Source: Galarza Papers "Correspondence 1947-6/1952," Box 7, Folder 6.

8. Craig's book was extensively reviewed by fellow his colleagues. Of all the criticisms lodged against the book (e.g., Carey McWilliams criticizes the lack of direct interviews, Manuel Servin bemoans Mexican-American marginalization by the presence of Braceros and Craig's historical spatial amnesia of borderlands, Charles Ornelas criticizes his historical amnesia more in terms of labor organizing suppression, Abraham Hoffman cites lack of personal interviews but doesn't even conceive Braceros as key sources, instead he suggests interviewing domestic farm workers and the Mexican government), David Leary is the only to note "Braceros were real people" in his call for oral histories or direct interviews. In the eleven book reviews of the pluralist analysis by rural sociologists, Chicano and agricultural historians, and political scientists, none explicitly take him to task for his racist characterizations of Braceros. On the contrary, scholarly consensus seems, as Hawley (1972, 559) states, "it should remain the standard work on the rise and fall of the bracero program."

9. Garcia (1980, 227–28) notes that this number was greatly exaggerated by the U.S. Immigration and Naturalization Service. The campaign in Texas and California resulted in the repatriation of 80,127 and 84,278 undocumented immigrants, respectively. The INS claimed that the remainder of the 1.3 million left voluntarily before they were forcibly deported. Garcia finds little evidence of that magnitude voluntarily returning to Mexico.

10. An interesting study needs to be conducted which examines the relationship between Anglo working-class unrest and the Mexican repatriation campaigns of the 1930s and 1950s. Historical periods when union demands, strikes, and protests against unemployment peaked tend to coincide with the removal of Mexicans from their jobs and forcing them south of the border.

Chapter Three

The Bracero Working Day and the Contested Terrain of Class Relations

In *el* "Corrido del Bracero," the popular form of Mexican musical composition tells the story of *un Bracero* who takes the journey *al norte* to secure gainful employment in spite of the suffering he must endure. As performed by *Los Mascarones y Los Alacranes Mojados*[1] (Fernando Leyva, Ramón "Chunky" Sánchez, Ricardo Sánchez, and Marco Antonio Rodríguez), the ballad of the Bracero is one of suffering, hard work, little pay, the good luck of finding a wife, and the bad luck of hard work passed on to their children.

I came from Mexico, in search of money,	De México vine, buscando dinero,
I came as a bracero around the month of April.	Llegué de bracero por el mes de abril.
I left my little ranch, sad and lonely,	Dejé mi ranchito, triste y abandonado
Out there in the hills where I was born.	Allá por los cerros donde yo nací.
I crossed the border there in Matamoros,	Allá en Matamoros crucé la frontera
For lack of any other means, I crossed illegally.	Por falta de modo, crucé ilegal.
Gentlemen, I am telling you about how I am suffering,	Señores les cuento, como ando sufriendo
How they are making me want to go on back.	Que me han dado ganas de volver pa' 'trás.

They tell me that here you can clean up, making money,	Me dicen que aquí se barre el dinero,
But that is not happened with this poor bracero.	Pero no le toca este pobre bracero.
(How sad is the life of the man Who leaves his country. Woe be the braceros, yes sir!)	(Pobre la vida del hombre Que sale afuera de su patria. Pobre de los braceros, ¡sí señor!)
Picking cotton there around Laredo, Washing dishes there in San Antonio.	Piscando algodón allá por Laredo, Lavando platillos allá en San Antonio.
I was in las milpas, there in California.	Anduve en las milpas allá en California.
Picking onion, I started to cry.	Piscando cebolla, me puse a llorar.
Out of good fortune, a little dark woman,	Por mi buena suerte una morenita
Very Mexican, kind of like me,	Muy mexicanita, tal vez como yo.
She appreciated my love and my life,	La aquella apreciaba mi amor y mi vida,
She was the love of my life, with whom I got married.	Fue mi consentida con quien me casé.
Ten years later, my kids grew up,	Crecieron mis hijos despúes de diez años
Because of my misfortune in working.	Por mi mala suerte allá en la labor.
Gentlemen, I am telling you about how I am suffering,	Señores les cuento, como ando sufriendo
How they are making me want to go on back.	Que me han dado ganas de volver pa' 'trás.[i]

i. Lyrics and translation from Smithsonian Folkways Project. Available online at: http://media.smithsonianfolkways.org/liner_notes/smithsonian_folkways/SFW40516.pdf.

The political economy of labor migration imbricates citizenship, gender relations, work, leisure, health, and the social uses of income and wealth along transnational nodes of existence. Cohen (2011) masterfully dissects the relationships between citizenship, class, and masculinity in the transnational making of the Bracero Program, whereas Mitchell (2012) employs a fine-grained analysis of California's extensive use of Braceros to explain changing relations in the state, agribusiness, and landscapes. In the case of U.S.

capitalist agriculture, many scholars familiar with Anglo-Mexican class relations note the despotic nature of the labor process (see Gonzalez 2006, Mitchell 2012, Mize 2006b, Peña 1997, and Weber 1994). For example, Montejano (1987, 197) refers to the "labor controls and discipline imposed by Anglo farmers on Mexican farm workers" as a set of coercive labor relations best described as a logic of labor repression. "Labor repression refers basically to the use of compulsion for organizing the recruitment, work activity, and compensation of wage labor" (*ibid*). Everyday lives of Braceros were often so out of their control that there was almost no ability to actively resist and still expect to remain employed.

The U.S. receiving states (see Table 3.1) and the Mexican sending states (see Appendix V) that incorporated the migrant labor stream into their regional economies were officially sanctioned by the federal governments of the United States and Mexico. The Bracero Program was instrumental in codifying existent streams and solidifying new streams to U.S. locations that had previously relied upon African-American or Caribbean laborers. Mexican states were impacted by the remittances sent back by the Braceros to relatives and the U.S. states were affected by the influx of a labor force whose length of stay was determined by growers and state officials.

The class relations in the fields during the Bracero Program were defined by the proletarianization of the Mexican countryside that created the impetus for migration, the working day, work hazards and occupational injuries, wages and remittances, and class reproduction. The history of class relations in Mexico very much shaped the context for how Braceros are inserted into U.S. capitalist agricultural production. Repression was key to creating a working day that maximized the exploitation of cheap, temporary labor. The arduous nature of the agricultural work, the constant exposure to pesticides, farm machinery and implement hazards, and difficult working conditions are all major contributors to work-related accidents and injuries. The wages paid to Braceros and the structure of remittances allowed for family subsistence, yet the ability to move up the agricultural ladder or find occupational mobility beyond agriculture was elusive for the majority. The last section will empirically examine the "Corrido del Bracero" quip that because of the bad luck of working, the children of Braceros grew up too quickly to provide for the family wage.

PROLETARIANIZATION OF THE MEXICAN COUNTRYSIDE

In order to understand the Bracero Program's impact on local sending and receiving communities, a larger historical frame must be considered as it regards the formation of the Mexican working class in both Mexico and the United States. Worker displacement, from feudal-type agricultural relations,

Table 3.1. U.S. States Employing Braceros, 1952

	Workers Contracted[1]	Workers Recontracted	Workers Employed on 12/31/52
Arkansas	25,658	2,705	500
Georgia	387	209	0
Louisiana	739	83	17
Mississippi	60	0	0
Tennessee	264	142	0
South Region	27,108	3,139	517
Illinois	0	302	0
Indiana	0	483	0
Iowa	110	39	0
Kansas	0	25	0
Michigan	1,463	2,209	3
Minnesota	0	19	0
Missouri	1,790	1,047	88
Nebraska	1,090	49	20
Ohio	0	19	0
South Dakota	147	–	0
Wisconsin	175	142	0
Midwest Region	4,775	4,334	111
Idaho	249	77	1
Montana	1,730	111	0
Oregon	696	127	91
Washington	1,947	14	1
Northwest Region	4,622	329	93
Arizona	19,350	268	12,491
California	57,407	5,790	18,031
Colorado	4,201	758	0
New Mexico	22,539	768	9,211
Nevada	45	0	0
Texas	54,279	6,153	26,710
Utah	124	231	24

Wyoming	1,392	62	0
Southwest Region	159,337	14,030	66,467
Total, 28 States	195,842	21,832	67,188

1. "'Workers contracted' refers to those newly hired and given a contract, no prior contract being involved. 'Workers recontracted' refers to those whose valid but expiring contracts were renewed" (Lyon 1954, 225).

to industrial and service sectors in the U.S. and Mexico's urban centers, is not the straightforward process of rural to urban migration and subsequent proletarianization that Marx (1976) theorized. The proletarianization of Mexican subsistence agricultural laborers is a process that initially arose in Mexico. The wage-labor system of the capitalist U.S. agricultural labor process can be read as the end result in the process of proletarianization as long as we do not narrowly conceive of the proletariat as solely *factory* workers. The key identifying characteristic of the proletarian class is working for wages in order to earn enough to subsist on a day-to-day basis, while creating surplus value that is the source of capitalists' profits.

Capitalist agriculture can be viewed as a facilitating a mediated rural-urban migration where Mexican *campesinos* moved to the rural areas of the United States to perform agricultural labor in exchange for wages. This rural to rural migration, in its binational context, allows us to better comprehend how a shift from feudal to capitalist social relations is more dependent upon the wage-labor system of remuneration than the industrial, urban component of the proletarianization process. The technological developments of agricultural production eventually displaced agricultural workers and pushed them out into the urban sectors of the economy. But the reason why Mexicans left Mexico in the first place was the increasing inability of *campesinos* to reproduce the means of subsistence within a nation-state that viewed its peasants as a surplus population wholly detrimental to the programs of modernization.

Cardoso (1980) traces the destruction of the pre-Revolution *ejido* system of peasant landholdings during the Porfirio Diaz administration's modernization campaign. The campaign expropriated communal land and transferred tenure to *hacendados* (large-farm owners who held power through a system of patronage) for increased export-agricultural production. This state-sanctioned program was a key factor in displacing Mexican *campesinos* from their means of subsistence. The process was akin to the enclosure acts that Marx, and later E.P. Thompson (1968), documented. In both cases of nineteenth century England and twentieth century rural Mexico, subsistence forms of agriculture were destroyed by capitalist production for exchange on the global export market. Massey et al. (1987) document the intrusion of the capitalist market geared toward export-oriented economies in Mexico as precipitating migration and destroying community bonds. The shift from subsistence farmers to wage-laborers makes the Mexican Bracero predicament a well-suited case for understanding the processes of proletarianization.

Ernesto Galarza (1956, 2) was one of the earliest to document the specific patterns of proletarianization in Mexico. He noted that Braceros originated from ". . . thousands of small villages lying in Mexico's countryside where living is dear and life is cheap; by hundreds of *ejidos* or collective farms still struggling for survival; and by the overflow of service and industrial workers from the city slums." Most often, these urban dwellers were displaced from the rural Mexican villages during the Porfiriato, or the dictatorship of Porfirio Diaz (1876–1911). In the name of modernizing the Mexican economy, Diaz concentrated land holdings in the hands of the few *hacendados* and forced hundreds of thousands from their communal lands and into the cities for work. The reason why rural and urban migrants moved was the same: the promise of wages for subsistence. Workers could earn in a day in the United States what they earned in a week in Mexico.

The Braceros interviewed by Dr. Chavez in 2005 spoke to their experiences living in Mexico prior to the Bracero Program. Whether landholders in the *ejido* system or workers on *haciendas*, the respondents talked about the life difficulties associated with extreme poverty and starvation.

> Don Lupe: Well, then we all used to suffer and on top of all of that we heard that the agrarian department was coming to divide our bosses' hacienda right. Then they asked us if we would enlist so that they would give us land, a parcel. Well, then we said yes and we signed-up. So the boss of the hacienda found out and he fired us from the land.
>
> Int: So they would have you on a list?
>
> Don Lupe: Umh there you go. Because all of the *hacendados* would have a meeting and there they would talk about everything. . . . The *hacendados* each one of them had their own list. The list would say all of us who were outside of the list. Those of us who were excluded for causing revolt . . . I worked like fiftten years, eh, and my father he worked all of his life. The people who knew more would tell us the people who would go there to give instructions to explain to us would tell us, "you have the right, it's not that you are being in revolt, it's not that what you want what is not yours. You have the right to be given a parcel and the law says, the Constitution says that. The Article 30 of the Constitution. You have the right to a small piece of land at least to live and it should not cost you one penny." Like that it is. Then, like I tell you, all of that came and they redistributed the land but to us, me and my father, he signed up in a list of *aparcerarios* [those who showed up, as in a waitlist]. It was special [the list] and it was called new center of population. There they told us that the government was going to give us [land] to make a neighborhood. They were going to construct us homes and all of that. And the land was going to be the best land because the haciendas had 65,000 hectares of arable land . . . And we were dying of hunger.

> Int: So the land was concentrated in the hands of very few?
>
> Don Lupe: Exactly. When they were going to distribute the lands, they said they are going to begin to measure the land to redistribute it. . . . The *hacendado* sent the *federales* so that they would destroy the homes because they were the workers and it got done. They went and destroyed their houses and the families began to cry. The families were crying and they had to leave their homes their rooms . . . Back then there was a lot of fear of the federales. They did not leave one home standing. There were about fify homes, and they destroyed all of them. All because they were going to redistribute the hacienda . . . You know where the politicians then came out of? They were the same hacendados. When they did the topography they gave all of the lands to the ejidatarios. Then they began to cultivate their lands [the ejidatarios] (Life Story of Don Lupe 2005).

Don Lupe's extensive recollection about the land redistribution process was corroborated by all of the respondents who talked at length about conditions in Mexico. Don Andres talked about earning three pesos per day for agricultural work in Mexico. Don Ramon was working on his own by the age of ten even though, by his account, Sinaloa was well-off in comparison to other states in Mexico.

> Int: So at ten years of age you left Mazatlan?
>
> Don Ramon: No, at ten years of age I left Mazatlan and came to a pueblo called El Dorado. I thought I was going all the way until it [the train] left me. In that time, there was Don Joaquin who was the owner of all of the lands. That is why I know that when people get a lot of money. That man had one hundred haciendas. He used to treat people like animals. Now the new generation of youth do not know the stories that I know that were real (Life Story of Don Ramon 2005).

The animal-like treatment they received would later be replicated in the process of securing a Bracero contract. Don Ramon earned his first paycheck of 3.50 pesos in El Dorado. The combination of difficult work, poor pay, coercive bosses, and the ensuing starvation was often how the Mexican countryside was depicted by former Braceros.

COERCION AND CONSENT IN THE FACTORIES IN THE FIELD

The despotic factory regime, which characterized nineteenth-century capitalism in England, is not simply a "pre-modern" relic of interest to Marxist historians. Rather, the parallels between bourgeois-proletarian relations of the Lancashire wool mills and grower-migrant laborer relations in post-war U.S. agriculture make Marx's original analysis particularly pertinent to the Bracero Program.[2] Work is accomplished by coercion and force. Relations are in the form of domination, not the engineering of consent with workers. Capitalist production is organized with two purposes in mind: (1) the creation of a commodity to be exchanged on the market, and (2) the exploitation of labor, to the maximum extent, in order to maximize profits and minimize labor costs. The drive for maximizing profits impacts workers since they are solely responsible for making products. In the despotic regime, capitalists push workers to the margins of existence by simultaneously increasing the duration and intensity of work while decreasing wages to the lowest feasible rate. It is a labor process ruled by force and intimidation: all in the name of maximizing profits.

But this is not to say that resistance did not happen when some workers felt that they were being overworked, underpaid, malnourished, or treated poorly in general. As Gamboa (1990, 75) notes of his study of Braceros in the Pacific Northwest, "This prevailing stereotype of Braceros as docile, undemanding and incapable of organizing themselves to press for better working conditions does not hold true in the Northwest, where Braceros were constantly on strikes and this made the region unique from other parts of the country." Those I interviewed collectively worked in every other region of the country (Southwest, South, East Coast, and Midwest) that employed Bracero labor. The sole story that emerged was of a food strike in North Carolina that was met with fierce grower repression.

Gamboa (1990: 75) identifies that in 1944, Ernesto Galarza noted found that workers in Illinois, Colorado, New Mexico, Michigan and California would rarely speak critically in the presence of camp managers or labor officials. Galarza conducted studies in each of these states and stated that basically if workers wanted to voice complaints, they were told to "shut up or go back." Ten years later in the Salinas area of California, Galarza found that the situation had not changed. Of the 181 Braceros he interviewed, none of them reported "instances of intimidation, any form" (Galarza Papers 19:2). Regardless of conditions—where twenty-six of the workers earned as little as $20 or less in some weeks, thirty-seven workers described the quality of food as "fair or poor," fifty workers lived in housing they deemed "fair or poor," and 105 of the 181 respondents were charged three to seven dollars for the "complimentary" blankets they slept under—there were no reported threats or intimidation.

During the Bracero Program, the threat of returning a contractee to Mexico if he did not meet the demands of the job without complaint was usually enough for workers to conform to grower expectations. If a worker did not comply—deportation. If they caused a ruckus or started making demands for better working conditions—deportation. Living under the threat and fear of control, violence did not have to be inflicted by the grower because workers were made well aware of the history of state agents (local law enforcement) who were recruited to do the dirty work of punishment. Collective action was not an option afforded to the Mexican worker pushed to the margins of existence. The power imbalance was often too great to begin seriously talking about leverage for the worker in negotiations.

Asked about working conditions, another bracero said:

> Three days ago our crew stopped work right in the field. There were fifty men in the group. It was explained by one of the men who could express himself that it was not our desire to make a strike but we wanted to have eight hours work or to have our board without charge if we worked only one or two hours. The foreman said that assuredly there would be plenty of work and we went back to cutting. The next day the bracero who had spoken for us was not in the camp. The foremen said he had been taken to the Association but he did not know the motive. In the field, the boss said there are plenty more where we came from if we were disgusted. I have read my contract, but it is not worth the pain to insist on the clauses. Here, the contract has no value (Galarza 1956, 18).

For the entirety of the program's existence, if Braceros wanted to continue working, they had to accept a pay schedule that changed from day to day. They had to cope with rancid food that was deducted from wages and the illegal deductions for blankets and work supplies. They also had to accept the housing they had to live in, even if it meant living in a tent, "converted" barn, or chicken coop. They risked personal safety riding in overcrowded flat-bed trucks. And they had to be willing to endure the extreme loneliness of living in a country whose language they did not speak. They also endured isolation in a labor camp where surveillance was the order of the day and outside contact was infrequent or completely non-existent. The central means for ensuring that the Braceros would suffer through these deplorable conditions was the threat, implied or actual, that malcontents would be replaced if they publicly voiced their grievances.

One only needs to enter the fields and listen to the farm labor contractor shout out commands or watch the way he berates workers for their stupidity, laziness, and carelessness to understand that Gramscian notions of consent (in the form of grower concessions) and moral leadership are not prerequisites of the capitalist agricultural labor process (see Mize 2006b). Consent is dictated by growers and their representatives through the means of enforcement, control, and domination of workers. In 1997, I worked in the fields to experience agricultural work firsthand, being the first generation in my family not forced to work in the fields. My participant observation working in the agricultural fields of Fresno County allowed me to understand firsthand the constitutive elements of the capitalist agricultural labor process. Direct grower-worker relations were irrelevant in the fields I worked in because I never saw the owner of the land. Every aspect of production was dictated by the farm labor contractor. Whether one found work, what rows one would work in, when breaks would be taken (in actuality, if one received a half-hour break for lunch, one would be considered fortunate), how much one would be paid, and whether one would be paid by piece or hourly rates were all decisions made by the FLC.

One of the key agents of social control was given significantly more power during the Bracero Program. As many growers formed agencies to pool labor resources, they relied upon third-party contractors to manage the labor force. It was the recruitment of men to work in U.S. agriculture by farm labor contractors (FLCs) that was codified and legitimated by the state-sanctioned Bracero Program. Recruitment was strictly male-based and was clearly a grower/FLC-initiated practice since growers believed that productivity would be maximized with an able-bodied, young, male workforce. The capitalist agricultural labor process during the Bracero Program facilitated social control by a strict physical separation of men from their homeland and families. Labor camps were designed often to separate Braceros from the rest of the population. This social isolation was only compounded by the physical distance of Mexican nationals from their homes and families. The Bracero Program extended the employment of Mexican nationals to every region of the United States. In the contemporary situation, an almost total reliance on Mexican nationals (legal, undocumented, and contracted) in large-scale agribusiness production can be traced back to its origins in the Bracero Program.

THE BRACERO WORKING DAY

What Braceros experienced in a typical working day was anything but typical from the perspective of the U.S. workforce.[3] The immense scale of production led to the intensification of the working day to harvest perishable crops in the shortest period of time. Class relations operated to exert control over a workforce and maximize productivity. Growers and their intermediaries (associations, farm labor contractors, and crew bosses) orchestrated a web of labor controls that defined the job tasks of the labor process with profit as primary pursuit and as a result, work hazards and occupational injuries became a necessary byproduct of a wanton disregard for safety.

The general system of corporate farming, what I refer to as large-scale agribusiness, was the main user of Braceros. At the disposal of agribusiness was a labor supply that was suited to growers' needs and delivered to their doorsteps by the U.S. government. Arrangements, on the behalf of growers, were often made through food processing companies or the grower associations. Depending on the crops, the standard work contract lasted forty-five days and coincided with the harvest season. The key feature of the Bracero Program, in regard to the labor supply, was the batch-handling of Mexican workers at every step of the contracting process as it relates to recruitment, processing, transportation, work, housing, and boarding. In addition, the labor supply was designed to be pliable in terms of the duration of contracts and the temporary nature of migration.

The Bracero Program was established and maintained with large-scale agribusiness or its grower associations in mind, not for the benefit of small growers. Some small growers did use the Bracero Program but it did require them to provide housing and food for the Braceros. Growers were required to recontract Braceros, if they wanted to keep them for extended periods of time. The other option for growers was to violate the terms of the contract as it related to the amount of time a Bracero could spend in the United States during a single duration. In addition, small growers needed workers who could do a variety of tasks, such as operating farm machinery, which was also expressly prohibited under the terms of the contract. Quite simply, the Bracero Program was not designed for small farmers who needed year-round labor that could perform general farm tasks. It was a program designed to meet the needs of large growers and their short-term labor requests. If the Bracero wanted to remain working in the United States, they learned to accept the agribusiness-set terms of work and living or else they could expect to be deported or denied further contracts. The sharecropper system partially employed a Bracero labor force in the key states of Arkansas, Louisiana, and Mississippi, but other cotton belt states still held the African-American sharecropping labor force in place. Thus, Bracero labor was superfluous to the exploitable labor force of the plantation economy.

The contracting system of the Bracero Program consisted of short, temporary individual work contracts that were tailored to the labor needs of growers. Highly perishable crops such as fruits and vegetables were contracted out for the standard forty-five-day contract. On the other hand, sugar beets were contracted for a minimum of three months because each task of the labor process (planting, tilling, irrigating, weeding, thinning, and harvesting) was labor intensive. Growers who needed workers for longer periods of time were allowed to recontract workers at their discretion. But on the whole, the contracts were not designed to fulfill a full-time, year-round labor need. Agribusiness needs large numbers of workers for short periods of time and all with the guarantee that workers would return to Mexico. One way the Mexican federal government "guaranteed" the return of laborers was the institution of a 10 percent savings plan. U.S. growers withheld 10 percent of each laborer's wages and the federal government of Mexico arranged with the state-controlled rural *bancos* to hold the savings until Braceros returned in person to claim the earned wages.

The large-batch handling of Braceros was much more cost effective for growers' associations that were comprised of a number of large-acreage growers who pooled their resources to reduce the costs of recruiting and maintaining the labor force. Every day, growers could request the number of workers from their association and those workers would be transported to the worksite. From their perspective, it was an efficient use of labor since they did not have to keep men on the payroll if they did not need them for work. Workers were paid for the days they were needed and the number of workers on a payroll could fluctuate at the whims of the growers. Transportation, housing, and boarding costs were cheaper in batches since individual growers contributed less to maintain one centralized camp and one fleet of transportation.

Scale is what distinguishes the industrial model of agricultural production from other forms of agriculture. Agribusiness, by its very definition, coordinates production on a large scale. In terms of those scales of production that employed Braceros, they can be categorized into three groups: associations, food processors, and individual farmers. Associations consisted of growers who coordinated their labor needs and prevailing wage rates. Food processors are the vertically integrated capitalist organizations that control the production process from seed to store. Great Western Sugar Company was the example I previously mentioned, but a number of large corporations (e.g., Dole, Del Monte, and other non-agricultural firms with substantial agricultural holdings) also fit this definition. Finally, the small farmer also utilized Bracero labor but they only employed 11 percent of Braceros in 1959 (see table 3.2).

During the Bracero Program grower associations were the driving force behind the distribution of workers to the various work sites. Every aspect of cooperation in the fields during the working day was dictated by the crew boss. Determining who picks where, what rows will be picked, and how much will be harvested are decisions made by either the crew boss or the farm labor contractor (FLC), but certainly not the workers. In the U.S. capitalist agricultural labor process, it is the pecking order of the FLC and then the direct supervisor in the fields, the crew boss, which coordinates the

Table 3.2. Employers of Bracero Labor, 1959

Associations		Food Processors		Individual Farmers	Total
Number	Members[i]	Number	Farms[ii]		
305	38,715	86	4,942	5,131	44,788

i. "Members" refers solely to those association members who employed Bracero labor in 1959.

ii. "Farms" refers to those growers who had exclusive contracts with large-scale, corporate agribusiness to produce pre-specified crops for the food processor. Most often, these farmers received contracted labor arranged by the corporation or its intermediaries. For example, in the case of the Great Western Sugar Company of Northern Colorado: "Usually the Great Western paid all the recruitment and transportation costs in obtaining Braceros for grower who held contracts with them" (Crisler 1968, 88).

working day. The history of the FLC precedes the Bracero Program but is intricately tied to the companies that depended so heavily on the program to meet its labor needs.

The Great Western Sugar Company, headquartered in northern Colorado, as Garcia y Griego (1983) notes, was the most important innovator in the use of the FLC to coordinate recruitment, hiring, and the oversight of picking, packing, and canning crews.

> Among the efforts of employers to recruit Mexican labor, perhaps those of the Great Western Sugar Company of Colorado were most noteworthy. This company relied upon thousands of Mexican laborers to cultivate and harvest its northern Colorado sugarbeet crop every season. In 1920, the company sent advance agents throughout the states of New Mexico, Texas, Colorado, Kansas, Nebraska, and Missouri, who worked from house to house in Mexican communities, held public meetings, ran newspaper ads, and offered free transportation to the fields. That same year the company opened an office in El Paso to recruit laborers throughout the season, whereas in Fort Worth and San Antonio it used established labor agents (Garcia y Griego 1983, 51).

Though the control over securing the labor force was rooted squarely in the hands of Great Western, the job tasks and everyday activities of laborers were controlled by those farmers who grew the sugar beets for Great Western or the company-appointed FLCs. But this is not to minimize the power that the sugar processor wielded. As Deutcsh (1987, 130) notes, "Great Western Sugar remained the recruiter and not the direct employer of beet labor, but it taught its agricultural fieldmen Spanish, retained files on each of the laborers it recruited, and mediated in grower-labor disputes." In effect, Great Western was able to construct "company towns" in the regional communities where their operations dominated. They controlled the flow of labor, the production schedule, the local economy, and many of the regional political decisions by virtue of the vast scope of operations.

Since the work crews employed by Great Western were historically Spanish speaking, the FLC was most often bilingual and usually Mexican American. The Great Western practice of using Spanish-speaking FLCs spread throughout the agricultural industry. During the Bracero Program, this arrangement was prevalent in the majority of agribusiness. In places like California that did not have the hegemony of one firm controlling an area, large-acreage growers formed associations to meet their labor needs and they hired FLCs whose duties were to oversee the labor process.

Crew bosses are one step lower than the FLC on the chain of command but in exchange for a slightly higher wage than the workers, they assume responsibility for the specific aspects of workplace productivity and quelling discontent. Since the FLC makes decisions in terms of the labor process, transportation, housing, and boarding, the crew boss serves as an important direct supervisor in ensuring that the pace of work is at the level expected by growers and FLCs.

During the time of the Bracero Program, the FLC had a major role in recruiting and selecting workers from Mexico and worked with grower associations to provide transportation. Growers were responsible for transporting Braceros to and from the U.S. reception centers located on the border. They also had to transport workers between labor camps and work sites. Some FLCs coordinated the feeding and housing of Braceros in addition to paying them wages directly. In those cases, compliance with state regulations still fell upon the shoulders of the FLC. This hierarchy of management is very much an integral part of agricultural operations to this day. Don Lupe's (2005) characterization of the foremen in charge of the cotton labor camps in Arizona corroborates my field research about the role that FLCs and crew bosses played in managing workers.

> Int: And those who were in charge of the barracks were they Mexicans or Americans?
>
> Don Lupe: They were Mexicans only, they were pochos. They were the so-called pochos. They were the ones who frankly treated us bad. Right? The pochos.

Farm labor contractors and crew bosses dictated the tasks of the working day, played a major surveillance function, and kept workers in line often by threats and intimidation. Growers reaped all the benefits of a controlled labor force without having to enact the social control themselves. Don Roberto (1997) verified the class relations in the fields: "Yes. In that time, we hardly [had contact with] the owners. Just the labor bosses [*mayordomos*]. What are they called in English? With the boss."

All of these factors enable capitalist growers to call for a large, highly mobile workforce to be employed for short periods of time but at an extremely fast pace and for as long a working day as sunlight will permit. Of course, agricultural technology—not to be outdone by nature—enabled several types of lighting systems to work during the night. California cotton growers were notorious for employing local youth to shine flashlights and car headlights on growers to enable Braceros to work through the night (the practice referred to earlier as "swamping"). If pickers work a "light-day" of six to eight hours, they often seek night work in the canneries. In response to a question about the working conditions in the fields, the tortilla provider in Colorado stated, "Yes, in the morning, you see I know that for a fact, they would get up at 6:00, they'd have breakfast around 6:00 and by 7:00 they bussed up in the fields. These guys were . . . depending on what the demand was on the market, but they would work from 7:00 'til basically 5:00, and depending on how much time they got in the fields for lunch."

"That was basically twelve hours. When the demand was down, they got out by 3:00 or 2:30. Sometimes the thinning time was straight through. It was pretty much for 12 hours" (Interview with Señor Palmas 1997). Since steady work is available only sporadically for a maximum of nine months during any given year (if a migrant is willing to move at the very least three to four times throughout the year) workers try to earn as much money as possible and work as many hours as possible when the work is available.[4]

In a normal crop cycle the major tasks include planting, irrigating, thinning and weeding, and harvesting. Per the Bracero work contract, growers found a myriad of ways to describe these five major job tasks. Galarza (1964, 88) compiled a list of assigned job duties including: bailing, digging, knocking, pruning, spraying, training, boxing, dusting, lidding, pulling, stacking, transplanting, bucking, emasculating, loading, rolling, stemming, trimming, bunching, feeding, packing, sacking, stringing, turning, capping, filling, picking, seeding, stripping, vining, carrying, girdling, picking up, shaking, swamping, weeding, casing, grading, pitching, shoveling, thinning, wiring, cleaning, hoeing, planting, sorting, tying, wrapping, cultivating, hulling, propping, spawning, topping, windrowing, cutting, and irrigating.

If these descriptions did not suffice, "general orchard work" and "miscellaneous crop activities" covered other job duties to be performed (Galarza 1964, 92). From 1942–1949, no mechanical operations were to be performed by Braceros and in many contracts, the practice of using Braceros to operate farm machinery and drive tractors was expressly prohibited (see Appendix III). In the late 1950s, Don Jorge was employed in Santa Clara, California, as a tractor driver. His job was primarily planting crops. The job was to plant, and drive a tractor to plant broccoli.

> Don Jorge: In a shed I had a tractor, and making loops you'd go planting the little plants. I did other jobs too: plant celery and cut the celery, cut beans, tomato. Cleaning and weeding.
>
> Int: The first contract was for planting. The first time you came, how long was the contract?
>
> Don Jorge: The contract was for six months.

If Braceros were used in this manner, they were to be compensated at a higher pay rate. Those interviewed (see Table 3.3, Column 4) for this study mostly harvested crops (the most labor intensive component of the growing cycle) but they also planted, irrigated, thinned, topped sugar beets, and performed job tasks expressly forbidden by the terms of the contract—that is, driving tractors and the construction task of laying irrigation pipe. One of the standard lines in the contract Don Jorge had, along with all of the other Braceros under contract, was they were expressively forbidden from operating machinery. Though Don Jorge later found a tractor job in California, his first experience on tractors was in Texas at a time when Braceros were not allowed to operate machinery.

> The picking was over, then the boss told me "Do you know how to drive?" Well drive, yes. Then he asked me if I knew how to drive a tractor. Well yes, but I never worked with them. But if you show me how, yes. "Good," he told me, "I'm going to put you on a tractor." Then he placed some wood blocks on the tractor so that I could reach the brakes. It went well. The first time I drove the tractor there was a wire, for a fence, it was the first time and I took off with the fence. "No Shorty, no, you'll wreck," they yelled at me. The second time he got on with me and taught me how to use the brakes (Life Story of Don Jorge 1997).

This fairly detailed recollection of the work done as a tractor driver was extremely relevant to the interviewee because he was doing a high-status job task that most Braceros did not have the opportunity to perform. The jobs of operating farm machinery were the best paying in the fields and were to be reserved for domestic workers (per the contract agreed upon by both federal governments), but Don Jorge was asked to operate tractors in California and Texas.

The nature of the job tasks varied according to the types of crops. The most difficult tasks, in most of the respondents' evaluations, were the harvesting of cotton and sugar beets. Tomato production is also discussed due to its large proportion of employment of Braceros in California. As a grower from Arkansas stated to the President's Commission, "cotton is a slave crop, nobody is going to pick it that doesn't have to . . . and the [Mexican] national is about the only reservoir of labor that we know of that really wants to pick cotton, because he gets more money than he ever saw in his life before, or ever expected to see, and people that can get anything else to do, don't want to pick cotton" (U.S. President's Commission 1951, 20).

> Well, we would arrive and we would work all day and they would pay us about three dollars. It was by contract for how much work we did. I don't remember what it was per pound, [again], we would get our lunch half way through the day, we wouldn't take too much time because we were doing contract work. Sometimes they put us into some pretty bad places. Like cotton for example. Places where the cotton was very small [arm gesture to knee] and those that were from here, they would put them in the better places. So there were still locals working here and they got the better jobs. We don't know how much they paid them. They had restrooms. Water wasn't very good it was kinda salty. They didn't have fresh water but where could we get better water from. We would take soda but we would bring our own (Life Story of Don Antoñio 1997).

Table 3.3. Summary of Braceros' Testimony

Respondent[1] (Years Contracted)	States Worked	Crops	Job Tasks	Pay Rate Blank= "No recuerdo"
1. Antoñio Guanajuato (1958)	Texas	Cotton Beans	Pick Pick	
2. Liberio Michoacan (1947-49, 1952, 1964)	Utah North Carolina Michigan California	Sugar Beets Green Beans Potatoes Cucumbers Lemon Peaches/Tree Fruits Tomato	Topping/Pick Thin Pick Pick Pick Pick Pick Pick	$180-200/wk $.40/bushel $8/week $1.50/100 lbs. $2.40/wk
3. Jorge Colima (1956-59)	Michigan Ohio Texas California	Sugar Beets Cucumber Cotton Broccoli Green Beans Tomatoes Wheat	Hoeing Plant, Irrigate Thin, Pick, Tractor Driver Tractor Driver Pick Pick Hoe	Sharecropping $2.40/hr[2] $2.40/hr $2.40/hr $2.40/hr
4. Francisco Zacatecas (1960-64)	California	Asparagus Chiles Tomatoes Fruit Trees Strawberries Tomatoes Tomatoes Grapefruit Grapes Beans	Pick Pick Pick Weeding Pick Pick Plant Pick Pick Install Irrigation Pipes	$45/15 days $.13/box $.13/box $.90/hr $45/15 days $5/bin @ 2 bins/day
5. Roberto Sonora (1960-64)	Arkansas Michigan California	Cotton Cucumber Cantaloupe Tomatoes	Pick Pick Pick Pick	Paid per box
6. Daniel Oaxaca (1958, 1960, 1962)	California	Tomatoes Lemons Avocados Grapes-Raisins Melons	Plant Pick Pick Pick Pick	$.50/hr $.50/hr $.50/hr

7. Pablo Chihuahua (1956)	Arkansas	Cotton	Pick	
8. Jose de Michoacan	California	Grapes	Pick	Piece work
9. Emilio Sonora	California Michigan	Lettuce Oranges	Pick Pick Pick	
10. Hector Coahuila	Texas	Cotton	Pick	
11. Nicolas Michoacan	California	Grapes	Pick	
12. Crecencio Colima (1958-1963)	California	Tomato Lemon Melon	Pick Pick Pick	$.20/box, 60/day
13. Lupe Guanajuato (1959-1960)	Colorado Arizona	Cotton Cotton	Pick Pick	$80-200/45 days
14. Ramon Sinaloa (1956-1962)	California Arizona New Mexico	Tomato Chile Melon Cotton Squash Carrots Lettuce Cotton Cotton	Pick Pick Pick Pick Pick Pick Pick Pick Pick	
15. Andres Guanajuato (1959, 1960, 1963)	California	Strawberry Lettuce Celery Chile Asparagus	Pick Pick Pick Pick Pick	$1/box $50/day
16. Baldomero Durango (1945)	Pennsyl-vania	Railroad	Spike Ties	$5.20/day
17. San Luis Valley[3] Respondents	Colorado	Lettuce/Spinach/Potatoes	Irrigate/Thin/Pick	$.75/hr

1. To preserve the anonymity of respondents, all names are fictitious. But to convey a sense of where workers were coming from in Mexico, all last names connote the state they were born.

2. In a later interview with Don Jorge, he stated that his memory may not have served him well and this was an overestimation. Maybe, he said, "it was because he was such a good worker they were just throwing money at him." Don Liberio's high estimates of sugar beet topping were never confirmed as I lost contact with him after the interview.

3. The summary of crops, job tasks, and pay are based on recollections of those interviewed in the valley who had associations with the program. It was estimated by one source that $3 a day was deducted for room and board but deductions not included are mandatory, non-occupa-

tional health insurance premiums and other non-sanctioned deductions. That would be a net of $20.25 per week if workers could work a full week of five and a half days from 7:00 to 5:00 ($41.25 gross salary minus $21 in minimal amount of deductions).

The idea of the Bracero as a privileged worker in terms of how they were treated as compared to domestics was often countered by Braceros' testimony as to how they were treated in the fields and the camps. The quality of water, lack of facilities, and work in low-yield crops all combined to place Braceros squarely at the bottom of the labor process in terms of receiving the lowest pay under the harshest of conditions.

Similar to the cotton working day, the thinning and harvesting of sugar beets was also a labor-intensive activity. Mechanization was introduced in stages during the program but full-scale mechanization did not occur until after its completion (Grove 1996).

> After the sugar beet ground was ploughed and seeded, the plants sprouted thickly, each ordinary seed sending up four or more shoots. The worker had to go along the rows and *block* out the plants into clusters several inches apart. Also, each cluster was *thinned* so that only the strongest plant remained. This activity was performed with a short-handled hoe, generally eighteen inches long. The worker, therefore, had to work in a "bent over" or squatting position. The work was usually done under pressure, since the plants had to be thinned quickly before they became too large and crowded. The worker often worked from twelve to fifteen hours a day (Crisler 1968, 80).

The aim of blocking and thinning is uniformity of spacing between seedlings and control over the number of developing seedlings in each row. After this process, which continues up until the crops have fully matured, the harvest begins. Harvesting was either done via mechanical aids or the sugar beets were topped by hand.

> In Utah, we were thinning the rows with *cortitos* [short-handled hoes that required one to stoop over]. During those times, they did not have the big ones for us. We would also top the beets. With a knife, we would take the top off. . . . The way we did the sugar beets was a machine would pull up the plants from the ground and way up to here [signals up to his chest] and we were topping the beets and throwing them in a ditch where another machine picked them up and put them in a truck (Life Story of Don Liberio 1997).

Don Liberio was fortunate in that certain aspects of his difficult work were mechanized. The topping of sugar beets, without the type of machinery described, would be done by the workers stooping over. The beets would be pulled from the ground, the tops would be cut off, then stored in a sack. This sack was attached to his shoulder and would be carried until it was filled to capacity (about forty to fifty pounds). Then, the worker would carry the sack to the end of the row and dump the beets in a box that would eventually be transported to the processing plant. At that time, hoeing was most often done with *cortitos* so workers would not damage seedlings. This was based on the assumption that it was easier to view their work if they were forced to bend over and reach almost to the ground to clear away weeds and other debris (e.g., rocks, clay, and litter).

From 1943 to 1946, Braceros were employed on Oregon farms to harvest sugar beets, peas, cucumbers, hops, beans, prunes, onions, beets, hay, grain, walnuts, mint, sweet corn, potatoes, lettuce, asparagus, flax, and tomatoes (Oregon State College Extension 1947, 11). As is evident in Table 3.4, the employment of Braceros, in California (1956), in the harvesting of tomatoes far surpassed the peak employment of Braceros working in every other area. One particular tomato operation in California used this system as detailed by Galarza (3:1): "All [of the] boxes [were] punched for on [a] card held by worker and checked by him on the spot. Box piles [were piled] six high. Boxes [were] dumped on the field when considered below grade and charged to worker. Re-sorting of rejects made at workers expense." The seven Braceros I interviewed, who picked tomatoes, had very little in common since some were paid an hourly rate while others were paid per box or on a piece rate. For example, Don Liberio was paid at a piece rate, Don Jorge recalls receiving an hourly wage of $2.40 per hour, and Don Francisco was paid an hourly rate on one contract and 13 cents a box on another. Piece rates force workers to operate as quickly as possible to fill as many boxes as possible. Thus, the source of pride by many of the men in terms of the number of boxes they could fill, as that translated into dollars. The hourly wage ensured steady work but I found out working in the fields in 1997 that if the pace was too slow, workers could easily be threatened by piece rates if they did not pick up the pace of work. My experience also introduced me to the shifting pay scale, which operated to minimize growers' or FLCs' payout while maximizing exploitation. At the beginning of each work day, I rarely knew if I would be paid hourly or piece so work operated at an amazingly quick pace regardless. But when the pickings were good and the harvest required little cleaning, people were often paid hourly. Conversely, after a big rain when mold sent in or after the first few passes through the rows, we were paid on a piece rate or how much we picked. This practice would have been strictly forbidden during the Bracero Program but it was also forbidden by law in 1997 so it is likely the practice I experienced is more widespread and long term than my personal experience.

WORK HAZARDS AND OCCUPATIONAL INJURIES

The incredible pace of work often led to injuries and the repetitive stresses associated with stoop labor creates chronic conditions that marked ex-Brace-

Table 3.4. Peak Employment of Braceros in California by Crop, 1956

Asparagus	6,037	Grapes	6,270	Pears	3,848
Almonds	1,749	Lemons	6,050	Prunes	2,548
Brussel Sprouts	1,225	Lettuce	5,975	Strawberries	4,098
Carrots	1,714	Melons	2,255	Snap Beans	2,351
Celery	2,245	Olives	1,771	Sugar Beets	4,209
Cherries	1,068	Oranges	5,299	Tomatoes	44,837
Cotton	9,000	Peaches	4,957		

ros' bodies for life. Most of the men interviewed complained of back pain and several had severe issues with the ability to stand up straight or walk unimpaired. The short-handled hoe, *los cortitos*, placed major strains on backs and legs. With the introduction of machinery, the lessening of stoop labor was often replaced by increased work hazards. For example, I noted in 1997 how tractor drivers negotiated the narrow gaps between grapevine rows to pick up full trays of picked grapes and drop off empties. The crew consisted of a tractor driver and one or two loaders working on a trailer attached to it. Before the cheap availability of large-scale farm machinery, pickers had to run their boxes to the end of the row or back to packing sheds. To preserve space and maximize land usage, the space between rows is enough to fit a tractor in such a way that they won't damage vines. Of course, people are in the gaps too and the space left to avoid the tractor when it comes through for trays is about six inches if a person places the majority of his or her body under the vines (grape vines are grown on elevated stands made of two by fours and grapes usually grow at eye level). On days after a rain and the soil is muddy, it is easy to see how feet might slip under a tractor tire or how easily it is for people to lose their balance and fall under the tires. This scenario is all the more likely considering the fact that workers have been doing the same job task under the hot searing sun of the central California summer.

Workplace injuries were the norm and the Bracero selection process most often disqualified those with "pre-existing conditions."

Don Emilio: I tried to receive a contract three to four times. In the medical examination, I would get disqualified because I had a back operation.

Don Jose: [Interrupting] It was the luck of the draw if you found work.

Don Emilio: [Continues] I eventually found work picking tomatoes in Michigan. I picked lettuce and orange in California. But in oranges, I was injured and did not recontract.

Not only did Don Emilio suffer through the humiliation of the processing centers only to be turned away four times, he also ended up injured in a subsequent contract that ended his career as a Bracero. No matter how much the FLC Don Jose attempted to minimize his experience to "the luck of the draw," it was clearly by design that Don Emilio was turned away from a program that sought to maximize the efficiency of workers. Don Jorge started off similarly situated in that he was injured on an earlier sojourn as an undocumented worker.

> Int: Before you were contracted, had you come to the US?
>
> Don Antoñio: Yes, I came. No. No, I don't remember. It seems like it was before. It seems. Maybe I've got it wrong. But it seems like I came before. That's why I started getting used to dollars. (Laughs). It seems so.
>
> Int: For work or for vacation?
>
> Don Antoñio: Yes, I came to work. I was far from Corpus, but I don't remember the ranch. What happened is I came back [to Mexico] because I fell. And I felt really bad here in my back. I couldn't work anymore. With the boss. He couldn't take me to get cured [to the doctor] because I was illegal.

Don Antoñio was one of the men who suffered from chronic back pain and to add insult to injury his undocumented status led to not only a lack of medical treatment but also a swift return to Mexico.

The testimony of Don Crecencio attests to the sheer dangers associated with the lemon harvest. When asked about job task segregation, his response invoked memories of lost co-workers.

> Int: Did you used to only work with Mexicans?
>
> Don Crecencio: Yes pure Mexicans. Only the contracted. In that time there was no one without papers. At least the ones who worked there were the ones with mostly papers. . . . They would take lists there and some got killed. Like two fell from the trees and they would get stabbed by the trees. "And so and so is missing" [then someone would say,] "oh, I think he was working by my row." So they would say, "get off because there is someone missing" [they would tell the braceros at the end of the day when they were taking row to get off the bus and look for the missing person]. Check to see if he is dead by there. "There was one right next to me" I said. "I don't remember what his name is" [said Don Crecencio] "Well then look for him" [said the foreman]. I then looked through my row and passed through it and then jumped to the next row to see if . . . I then saw him with his head hanging down. There was a stick stuck on him his face full of blood. I went to go tell, "he is here."
>
> Int: When you saw the dead man did you get scared?
>
> Don Crecencio: I never found out if they sent him back to his land. I am not sure where he was from. You know that from distinct places people came there

[as braceros to work in the U.S.]. They would tell us "you go over there to pick lemons." They would never ask us where we were from. The foreman would never ask us. We did not know where they were from. Because there are too many and I did not know where they were from. I did not like to ask where they were from.

The anonymity of batch-handling on a mass scale in many ways made these deaths even more tragic. Fellow workers had no idea who was dying in the rows next to them. The level of control dispatched by the foreman for Braceros to go "look for him" and the fact that the ultimate fate of the worker's dead body was never released to his co-workers are both less than subtle reminders of how Mexican immigrant labor was viewed as disposable and workers were rarely treated as people, much more as the category of abstracted labor inputs.

Another respondent mentioned a fellow worker who disappeared and though the circumstances were sketchy and difficult for him to recount, Don Antoñio (1997) shared how the death of a worker disinclined him and his fellow countrymen from returning to the United States.

Int: Whether you arrived or not. Did you meet men who came and didn't ever go home?

Don Antoñio: Yes, yes, I always met some who didn't go back home. There were some of them. I think one was killed. And the rest, yes, they went back.

Int: They killed him here?

Don Antoñio: In the rivers, I think it was . . . How was it? Now we . . . Now we don't want to go back there anymore.

Int: Why?

Don Antoñio: It's so much bother . . . it is, one's death.

The same threats are still used against the undocumented worker. Death threats are obviously the extreme but the constant threat of being deported, replaced, or fired often secures compliance.

The character of work for the Mexican Braceros is probably unimaginable for those who have never worked in the fields. Those affiliated with the program indirectly all stated that their work was "hard," not something most people would want to do. And quite simply, stoop labor is not the type of work people do because they want to, they do it because they feel they do not have any better employment options. As a life-long worker in the fields described his work:

Don Francisco: The work is hard. You get all sweaty and dirty and wet.

Int: What does it do to your body?

> Don Francisco: The cuts on your hand from the knives. You have to be careful or you'll cut your fingers off. You get tired. It hurts your lower back, your shoulders from the weight. You are never going to come up. You are always bent over.

From my supplementary interviews in the San Luis Valley of Colorado, one respondent who at the time of the interview worked for a migrant services agency detailed the effects of agricultural work on one's body. The respondent worked in the valley's potato harvest as an adolescent. "You get a terrible sunburn on your neck and back if your shirt exposes skin. You couldn't wear the gloves to pull the potatoes since you were sweating too much. . . . You had to carry the bags of potatoes to the end of the row when you filled them up and I would get blisters on my leg where the bag rubbed up against me."

Respondents noted that they were required to use a short-handled hoe when thinning and harvesting asparagus, strawberries, sugar beets, and other vegetables. This farm implement required one to bend over and stoop down for the vast majority of the work day. Respondents complained that they felt like they would never be able to stand up straight after a day with *el cortito*. As Murray (1982) notes, the tool was eventually banned from agricultural work due to its negative effects on workers' backs, shoulders, and arms. At the time of the program, agriculture was one of the most dangerous occupations. Anderson (1961) notes that in California, only mining and construction jobs were more dangerous than agricultural employment. In California (one of the few states to collect data at that time), disabling injuries occurred at a rate of almost 50 per 1,000 workers from 1953 to 1957 and though all other industries saw a steady decline in rates, agricultural rates remained stable.

> Int: That time when you came back because your feet were swollen . . .
>
> Don Francisco: That was when I was kneeling in Santa María.
>
> Int: Yes, for the strawberries. Why did they swell?
>
> Don Francisco: Because I was kneeling and all wet . . . that we are going to pick tomorrow, they water it in the afternoon. There are times in the morning when there are still puddles of water and all the strawberries are rotten and they make a muddy mess. They give you rubber knee pads and . . . It made me sick. No, I did it like that, without anything.

Rarely did any of these injuries, caused by the horrible working conditions, simply go away and the chronic nature of workplace injuries cannot be minimized. Ex-Braceros invariably looked physically exhausted from a lifetime of toil. Band-aid solutions like knee pads rarely resulted in minimizing the injuries and deaths associated with agricultural labor. A conversation between Don Jorge and Don Francisco (1997) captured the difficult nature of stoop labor, the particularly difficult strawberry harvesting methods, and how their worth as a worker was often subjectively assessed by the number of boxes they could fill in a day.

> Don Jorge: The asparagus is hard work because you have to go around bent over all day.
>
> Don Francisco: Everywhere it's like that! I got used to it. You know what was hardest for me was when I started with strawberries. I picked strawberries here in . . . There I lasted . . . there . . .
>
> Don Jorge: Oooh, I picked strawberries too. In Watsonville. I was forgetting about that. In Watsonville, it was strawberries with the Japanese there.
>
> Don Francisco: Me too, I was also with those Japanese. And there when we started to pick.
>
> Don Jorge: You forget things sometimes.
>
> Don Francisco: In a little while I . . . no, man, in the afternoon, I went to the afternoon and I went slowly. They gave you rubber kneepads. You have to go kneeling on one leg, to rest a little as you go. It's really tough. . .
>
> Don Jorge: In '95 one of my sons was there in Arizona and I went to pick chile. I had picked chiles to eat to take home, but I had never picked to fill demand [to sell]. I got sent to pick chile there in Casa Grande, Arizona. And, oof, another guy who was there said you didn't earn much. I said, why doesn't he earn, he's young, he's eighteen. And I went with him. It took like three hours and I said to myself, don't cry. My back was tired. And at first this boy called, I did fifty, he did forty.

WORTHY WORKERS: ON WAGES, DEDUCTIONS, AND REMITTANCES

Even though the work was difficult, dirty, and dangerous, one rarely heard complaints from the ex-Braceros about hard work or their occupational injuries. Rather, hard work was often a measure of pride and their worth was often measured as how good they were as workers. Don Crecencio was most insistent in identifying that he often filled sixty boxes of lemons per day and often brought the conversation back to this measure of dignity. When he was asked, "how much did you get for each box of lemons that you picked," Don Crecencio (2005) noted, "twenty cents in that time," and reiterated that he regularly filled sixty boxes per day even though it translated to about 12 dollars per day. When asked where he worked, Don Crecencio replied, "Saticoy, California. It is close to Santa Paula. . . . The most that I picked was sixty boxes daily." The conversation was brought back to the measure of hard work and his pride in the good job he performed. Similarly, Don Francisco (1997) stated, "I was good at the boxes. They never returned a single box to us. The numbers flew."

When remuneration practices were so paltry, the men identified other aspects of work that would validate their worth as hard workers.

> Don Andres: The boxes that we would fill up, they would pay us $1.00 per box.
>
> Int: How many boxes did you do per day?
>
> Don Andres: I would make as many as 80, sometimes, even 100 depending on the strawberries. You could not put any rotten ones or anything like that.

The wage labor system is an integral, if not *the* defining, component of capitalism. Classes can be delineated between those who pay others' wages and those who earn wages. Those who purchase the labor power of others and own the means of production may ultimately decide the type of wage scale that is used, how much workers are paid, and what will be deducted from paychecks. The two means of remuneration at the disposal of both U.S. growers are the piece schedule and time schedule. Piece rates are based on how much a worker produces and they are usually paid a flat fee per item produced. Time schedules, or hourly rates, are based on the amount of time spent working so a worker earns a fixed amount per hour of work. I discuss how these two wage schedules were specified in the individual work contract of Braceros. In addition, I utilize both the life stories and other sources on wage data to show how much workers were actually paid despite the contract specifications. The amount and type of deductions becomes central for calculating the actual wages earned by Braceros. As for the money that was earned, I also discuss the remittances that were sent back to Mexico and how the Braceros used their earnings to support their families. Finally, I discuss different survival strategies in forming a family wage of subsistence and how the Bracero Program subverted the family as wage-earners in favor of employing solely men.

During the Bracero Program, the use of piece rates was officially sanctioned in the individual work contract, which would specify whether pay would be based on a piece or hourly rate. The Bracero arrangements guaranteed that the wages paid would be equal to those paid to American workers for similar jobs in the respective regions of the United States (*Secretaria del Trabajo y Prevision Social* 1946, 85). Some of the recent research on the program (see Grove 1996 and Calavita 1992) assume that the wage guarantees were in fact a lived reality for Braceros since growers complained about this stipulation and the U.S. government agreed to the guarantees in writing. On the standard work contract, it did state how much the worker would be earning in each crop he was contracted to harvest. But the direct testimony by

Braceros attests to the cunning of authority in the remuneration practices of Braceros (see Table 3.4, Column 5).

> Don Antoñio: We got up at five and we made our lunch and we went to work. There it was by weight for what you made or what you got. And . . .
>
> Int: How many hours was it?
>
> Don Antoñio: No, well, sometimes . . . it took us . . . what can I say? If we hurried all day in those times we'd earned three pesos (dollars).
>
> Int: A day?
>
> Don Antoñio: A day.
>
> Int: It was by contract or by piece?
>
> Don Antoñio: By contract or what it weighed. But I don't know how much it was per pound. I mean I don't know how much we got per pound.

Certain factors varied to ensure workers that they would never really know how much they were making from week to week. The availability of work, the number of hours worked per day, the shifting wage schedule (piece or hourly), the amount of deductions, and the changing pay rate all served as means at the growers' disposal to pay whatever wage they deemed appropriate.

The wages that Braceros received varied a great deal but a consistent pattern did occur. The few workers who could earn what was guaranteed to them only did so by working extremely long hours. In 1946, Washington pea farmers boasted that their workers averaged ninety dollars per week, but in order to do so, Braceros had to work fifteen hour days, seven days a week at 85 cents per hour (Gamboa 1990, 88). Since the minimum wage for non-agricultural jobs in the United States was 75 cents per hour and agricultural work was exempt from minimum wage laws, the 85 cent hourly wage was rarely paid to Braceros. After deductions for non-occupational medical insurance, board, and transportation, the wages they were paid were rarely enough to live on in either the United States or Mexico. Considering that most Braceros were sending upwards of 80–90 percent of their paychecks back to Mexico, this really puts into perspective the meager livings they were barely subsisting on in the United States.

An explanation for why Braceros were willing to work in such harsh conditions for poor pay only makes sense when comparing their earning options in Mexico. One respondent stated, "One worked in the fields over there in Guanajuato, you earned three pesos all day from six in the morning to five or six in the afternoon. Three pesos [ponders while he repeats the amount the second time]. Well of course everything was a little cheaper but no no no. It was very little" (Life Story of Don Andres 2005).

The wages paid to Braceros varied a great deal from crop to crop and region to region, but both hourly and piece rates were employed by growers. In terms of an hourly rate, the respondents reported a range of fifty cents per hour to ninety cents per hour. Piece rates were specific to the crop but a sample of the different rates were forty cents per bushel for picking green beans, thirteen cents per box in tomatoes, five dollars a bin for grapefruits (the respondent averaged two bins per day), and $1.50 per 100 pounds for picking cucumbers. One respondent I spoke with, Don Liberio, recalled earning between $180–200 per week (before deductions for which he could not remember that amount) using a short-handled hoe to thin sugar beets in Utah. This was the highest amount any respondent reported and he later told me he overestimated the amount. His next assignment sent him to North Carolina to pick green beans. He earned $.40 per bushel and was able to collect about fifty bushels in a week for which he earned a net wage of $8. He also worked in potatoes during this contract but stated that the grower had hired too many workers so the job didn't last for the duration of the contract. He was sent back to Utah where he topped and harvested sugar beets. All of this work was on a single 45 day contract. In the following years, he earned in Michigan $1.50 per 100 pounds for cucumbers, $2.40 per week harvesting lemons in Oxnard and later harvested citrus fruits and tomatoes in other parts of California for varied amounts.[5]

Working the California chile harvest, Don Andres (2005) recalled: "It was also by day and it was also about 50 dollars per day." His recollection about earning an hourly or day wage was similar to Don Lupe's (2005) extensive recollection of a week's wage.

> The rancher was an American. He would say, "you are going to pick cotton." Well then go get your sacks. Well then we would enter and they would give each of us 2 sacks. More or less 80 pounds would fit in each sack. And from there, they would take us to the field. The fields were huge. It was the type of cotton that they called, *chapo*. Then they would take us and tell each of us to select two rows [of cotton fields]. In only one attempt [collectively], we would complete a whole field like of 50 acres. What would we do we would do nothing. Why? Because we would only earn more or less in a week we would earn like $150–200 dollars, per week. So in the whole season, that we were there the weeks would not always be the same. Sometimes we would come out with $100 dollars sometimes $80 dollars. It was a small amount that we would earn. It was 45 days. We suffered because frankly it was very little to send right? Then we expected to complete the contract of 45 days and then return back. Then when the contract was complete we would be taken back to Mexico again. We would return to our homes again. Can you imagine that money was very little.

One of the more interesting aspects of the self-reports on wages was that there were a number of silences, the "*no recuerdo*," "I don't remember" type of responses. One explanation for the lack of recollections on wages is that it might serve as a source of embarrassment. The Braceros tended to take pride in their work and the conclusion reached by them might be that they are measured by their worth in wages. The more likely reason why respondents stated they did not know was because the wage rate varied so often, unexplained deductions, and shifting work schedules combined to make it completely impossible to verify actual wages. Even though the contract clearly specified the wage and piece rates for each contract, after speaking with Braceros and personally working in the fields, I found that the wage schedule changed on a daily basis. On the most labor-intensive days when the crops were not producing or needed to be cleaned to remove mold or insects, the pay was the worst and on a piece rate. Vice versa, when pickings were good and the work was comparatively easy, the pay was usually done by the hour so it did not make a difference how much one picked. The pay was the same for everyone, based on the number of hours worked on those days when workers could pick the largest amount.

Another source on wages, other than self-reports and contract stipulations, is the pay stubs Braceros received with their paychecks. Ernesto Galarza collected hundreds of pay stubs from Braceros and they document a consistent pattern. After deductions and off-time due to inclement weather, Braceros were consistently making just enough for themselves and their families in Mexico to subsist. Of the 181 workers that Galarza interviewed in the Salinas area, 160 reported earning less than forty dollars (net) in a one-week period. The highest weekly net earnings never exceeded seventy-five dollars for 171 of the 181 interviewed (Galarza Papers 18:6). The factor that tended to account for the differences in earnings, whether the pay was based on a piece or hourly rate, was the amount of hours worked. The more hours in a week that the Bracero worked and the less he spent in the United States, the more he could send back to Mexico.

But certain aspects of the wage structure were simply out of his control. The amount deducted from paychecks also varied in the reports by Braceros but most often the question posed about deductions was met with a "*no recuerdo*" response. The standard work contract stated the amount that would be deducted for food. As Galarza (3:1) notes, the $1.75 per week maximum deduction for food that was set by the government was translated into the minimum amount deducted by growers. This amount was intended to guarantee that Braceros would be charged at cost for the food prepared. Other deductions that were officially sanctioned by the binational agreement was a mandatory non-occupational health insurance policy that cost Braceros $3 per month ($3.50 at one camp that Galarza surveyed). "In conforming with the established international rules and contracts, of the amount paid to the Mexican braceros of their salary ten percent was deposited into a savings fund [in Mexican National Banks] for each worker" (*Secretaria* 1946, 88).[6]

This money would not be returned to the Bracero until he fulfilled the conditions of his contract and had returned to Mexico. Galarza (18:6) also exposed the illegal deductions made by growers in the Salinas, California area. Braceros were charged for blankets and a smaller number were charged for the twist ties used in banding carrots together.

For most Braceros, remittances were the main reason for migrating in the first place. "The majority of the braceros sent money to their family in Mexico. . . . [Almost 97 percent] of those sent money and only 3 percent did not send any" (*Secretaria* 1946, 91). In California, the Postmaster General reported the money sent during 1951 to Mexico based on where money orders were purchased: Brawley—$22,817.80, Calexico—$3,101.37, and El Centro—$19,845.54 (Galarza Papers 17:3). Regardless of the marital status of the Bracero, the wages they received were earned so that money could be sent back to Mexico for family members' well-being. "The money was good because we did not have a house [in Mexico]. We sent all our checks and they bought a permit and built a house. I was not married, and my brothers were young, they were studying. So, my money served a purpose, to support them" (Life Story of Don Jorge 1997).

All of the Braceros acknowledged that their money was sent back to Mexico to support their wives and children or larger, extended families. In the San Luis Valley, remittances were handled by the post office in Alamosa. "And it was all sent back in the form of money orders. I understand that they had some problems when they sent cash through the mail. It disappeared and what not. In the form of a money order and they did register the letter also. That way someone had to sign for the letter" (Interview with Señor Freemont 1997). A former crew boss/bus driver detailed what Braceros brought home with them after working in the San Luis Valley of Colorado—used appliances, dry cell battery radios, used and new clothes for kids, and trundle sewing machines (Interview with Señor Paulo 1997). These purchases were in line with those reported to the Mexican government upon arrival at the recruitment centers. The goods purchased with wages was dispersed in the following manner: "food (29.14 percent), clothing (10.95 percent), cleaning of clothes (2.11 percent), entertainment (5.49 percent), savings fund (10 percent), voluntary savings (8.88 percent), and money orders to Mexico (33.43 percent)" (*Secretaria* 1946, 87).

The reliance on remittances for subsistence is a unique characteristic, to the extent that it occurred, of the Bracero Program. Primarily, the labor demands of growers for young, unattached males substantially limited the options for families in Mexico. For years prior and even subsequent to the program, Mexican agricultural laborers have been comprised of families that work as a team for subsistence wages.

Int: And what advice do we to give a man whose thirty-two years old and has a family?

Don Antoñio: It's better that he stays in his family. What does he earn with forty-five days?

Int: About your feelings about leaving your wife and your kids alone while you were here. Was it hard?

Don Antoñio: Yes, it was hard. Because there wasn't anyone who could help them out. More than you who were tightening your bills to be able to maintain them. What else could you do?

Int: Did you send money back, or did you have to wait until the end of the season?

Don Antoñio: When they pay you, then you send it.

Int: Did they pay you weekly?

Don Antoñio: Weekly, or every fifteen days. But you could hardly send money, see? You sent what you could while it lasted. If it got lost, well, it was better to take it yourself. If it got lost, it was better to transport it yourself. It was just forty-five days. How much is that? You left them *[money]* until you came back. "Have this. I leave this for you." Or "Here there's so and so much." . . . You can.

With the pay as poor as it was and has traditionally been, translating wage-labor into forms of subsistence required a family-earned wage. If Mexican families wanted better lives (i.e., living above a subsistence level), men went to places where they could maximize income opportunities in trades they were prepared for. Agricultural work paid much better in the United States than Mexico. If they had their own crops (most likely corn for subsistence), it was not grown for exchange on the market. The Bracero Program codified the guidelines workers had to follow if they wanted to work.

It was the recruitment of men to work in U.S. agriculture by FLC's that was codified and legitimated by the state-sanctioned Bracero Program. Recruitment was strictly male-based and was clearly a grower-initiated practice since growers believed that productivity would be maximized with an able-bodied, young, male workforce. The capitalist agricultural labor process during the Bracero Program was characterized by a physical separation of men from their families. Even men who sought contracts with siblings were intentionally separated. Don Andres recalled the way he was separated from his older brother. "'It's because I come with my brother' [he tells the inspector]. [The inspector then replies], 'you over here' [Don Andres raises his voice mimicking how the inspector responded] 'and your brother over there'. [The inspector replies] 'there is no such thing as I came with my brother here'. And then he says, 'how do we do it'? He got chosen for Salinas and I got chosen for Watsonville. We got separated" (Life Story of Don Andres 2005).

Viewing the Bracero Program as a total institution is discussed in greater detail later (also, see Mize 2006a) but Goffman's views on the incompatibility of the family and total institutions are worthy of note here. "Total institutions are also incompatible with another crucial element of our society, the family. Family life is sometimes contrasted with solitary living, but in fact the more pertinent contrast is with batch living, for those who eat and sleep at work, with a group of fellow workers, can hardly sustain a meaningful domestic existence" (Goffman 1961, 11). The immense physical distance of Mexican nationals from their homes only amplifies the problem.

So the question may remain in some minds: if they endured hardships, mistreatment in their "host" country, and threatened family stability; why did men *van al Norte*? Quite simply, many felt that they had no other choice, given their economic chances in Mexico. Given the choice, many Mexican male workers stated that they would prefer to be with their families and a few even stated that they prefer to work with wives and children to maximize their earning ability. The Bracero Program attempted to establish the exact opposite of the Braceros' intentions by keeping women and children in Mexico while fully exploiting Mexican detached, unencumbered men in U.S. fields. It was a combination of direct surveillance by FLCs and crew bosses, social isolation, and low wages that placed Braceros in the vulnerable positions they found themselves in.

CLASS REPRODUCTION

In a seminal article by Burawoy (1976), he notes that what makes labor migration so palatable for receiving nations is the costs of reproduction are separated from the costs of production. What the United States gained from migrant labor is the costs of reproducing families on a daily basis or from generation to generation remained in Mexico while the costs of agricultural production (mostly wages but also room, board, and transportation) were isolated as the sole costs bore by U.S. agricultural employers. This system of labor controls make it very difficult to escape and the working conditions remain remarkably unchanged since the time of the Bracero Program. Similarly, for the workers I interviewed, very little had changed and the overwhelming majority did not occupy positions outside the agricultural sector. The lack of occupational mobility, as evidenced by Don Antoñio's family situation, was fairly typical.

Int: When you came, after the bracero, when you came the other way, did you continue in the fields?

Don Antoñio: Yes, I continued in the fields.

Int: You never left the fields?

Don Antoñio: No, always the same field.

Int: Your three children, did they continue in the fields?

Don Antoñio: Yes, they're all in the fields. There are five.

Int: There are five. Sons? No daughters?

Don Antoñio: Two daughters. And they're also in the fields.

Once the *hijo/hija* confusion was resolved, it was clear that all seven of Don Antoñio's children ended up working the fields. His lifetime toiling in the fields was very typical of the Braceros interviewed in Fresno. Nine of eleven were still working in fields or did until they retired, at the time of the interviews. One was a painter with the Catholic Church and he was the only one who did not work in agriculture growing up in Mexico. His dad was a leathersmith who made saddles and *huaraches* (sandals). Of the daughters I interviewed, two of their fathers remained in the fields while one found a unionized butcher's job in Los Angeles. She was able to earn a college degree (the only second generation who witnessed significant upward mobility in this study). Based on other contacts, I was able to trace the occupational histories of other Braceros who also found union jobs in Los Angeles working as butchers for large-scale, corporate slaughterhouses. One Bracero who settled out in the San Luis Valley brought his skills as a mason to the valley where he works on sub-contracted construction jobs and still winters in Mexico.

The respondents on the border had much more varied work histories and their offspring have also found work beyond the agricultural sector, but because they are taking service and manufacturing positions in Mexico, their wages are still minimal. Don Lupe, at the time of the interview, was working as a security guard with his son. Don Crecencio never married. Don Andres unfortunately no longer has any living children and Don Ramon has lost contact with his former wife and three children over the years. Tracking the work histories of Don Baldomero's nine children proved difficult but of his offspring, three daughters are employed as a housewife, in the hotel industry, and a factory worker.

The children of former Braceros tended to reproduce the class positions of their parents as nearly all of the respondents' children were to be found in working-class occupations. The children of former Braceros were overwhelmingly in two industries: manufacturing and agriculture. If children resided in Mexico, they owned small parcels of land and were almost exclusively female. This land is rarely enough to provide subsistence for the family so other jobs must be done to provide for the bare essentials. One respondent had two sons living in Mexico and working in the construction industry. The other occupational titles held by the sons and daughters of former Braceros were butcher, construction worker, laundromat attendant, and hair stylist. These children all currently resided in the United States and occupational status depended on the communities they were living in. If a son or daughter lived in Los Angeles, Fresno, or Denver, they were working in factories or the service sector. If they were living in a rural community, they were doing agricultural work. If they were in Mexico, it was equally possible that they would be employed in either agriculture, manufacturing, or services.

Most of the Fresno respondents were at one point married but most were currently widowed or their wives were not living in the United States. Three of the respondents were never married and had no children. Another respondent had a common-law wife but she still remained in Mexico with their daughters. Each of the daughters were married to men who owned land. According to Don Francisco, "the United States is no place for women and . . . they [his daughters and common-law wife] would never come North." He had not returned to Mexico since 1987. The State Housing Inspector discussed the blocked opportunity structure of the Braceros' offspring compared to Mexican-American parents working in the fields.

> And that was one of their [Braceros'] disadvantages, they didn't have the opportunity for education that the local people had, the local Hispanic people. Like I said, their kids are getting out of this and that's daddy and mommy telling you that. "My kid is not going to be doing this. They're going to get an education. They're going to teach school. They're going to be lawyers and doctors. They're not going to be out there." Well the Bracero, where was he going to go? Those programs were not available in Mexico. Still aren't, I guess (Interview with Mr. Allen).

CONCLUSION

One of the defining features the labor process was the ever-increasing scale of production. U.S. agribusiness typifies this trend. During the Bracero Program, grower associations and processing companies took full advantage of the contracted labor that was delivered to their labor camps and fields. For instance, in 1959 the 305 grower associations represented 44 percent of all growers who utilized Braceros. Growers were rarely in charge of controlling the labor force. That task was left to the intermediaries—crew bosses and farm labor contractors—who oversaw production on a daily basis. The working day for the Braceros was characterized by those interviewed as hard, dangerous work. The introduction of machinery did not have the effect of lessening the workload or making it less dangerous. On the contrary, the introduction of "labor-saving" mechanical implements increased the dangers associated with agricultural production.[7]

The wages that Braceros received rarely followed the guidelines that were agreed upon by the Mexican and U.S. governments. Even though workers were guaranteed wage rates and schedules, they most often changed to coincide with the interests of growers. Piece and time wages were employed interchangeably to benefit growers. If the harvest cycle was relatively easy and workers could pick a large amount in a short time, they were normally paid hourly rates. If the work was more difficult and the pickings were slim, workers received the piece rate. Rarely did the pay schedule work in the interests of Braceros. Deductions also served as a source of profit for growers. Rather than adhering to the program guidelines, workers reported that they were charged for items (blankets, housing, and farm tools) that were supposed to be provided free of charge. Excessive deductions, for legitimate items, also were found in the pay stubs that Galarza collected. It is all the more unfortunate when one considers that most Braceros were not even guaranteed minimum wage, per the contract, due to agriculture's exemption from federal minimum wage standards. In addition, wages were often sent back to Mexico, in the form of remittances, in order to allow the Braceros' families to subsist. The family wage, which many Mexican immigrants relied upon as a survival strategy, was hampered by the Bracero Program's insistence that workers be males. Perhaps the most unfortunate aspect of the treatment the Braceros received is in the issue of class reproduction. Of the Braceros interviewed, the vast majority of their children shared similar class locations. All of the factors, racially and class-based, have had the overall effect of severely limiting the life chances of Braceros and their sons and daughters.

NOTES

1. Roughly translated as the Figureheads and the "Wetback" Scorpions.

2. In the literature on the capitalist labor process, the workplace is characterized as the arena where consent is engineered. Workers are, in a way, complicit in their own exploitation by willingly conceding to the expectations of capital and management. Burawoy (1979, 1985), and those who use his framework to examine the capitalist agricultural labor process (e.g., Thomas 1985 and Wells 1996), see the owners of capital as making certain concessions to ensure their positions of leadership in capital-labor relations. For Burawoy, the concessions consist of state-enforced rules and regulations that guarantee workers' wages, safety, and benefits. In addition, collective bargaining and other elements of union representation result in "the hegemonic organization of work [that] is based on consent predominating over coercion" (1979, 194). Both agricultural workers and immigrants are not protected by the National Labor Relations Act so it's difficult to locate where in the Bracero Program concessions were ceded by capital or the state.

3. The similarities of the post-war U.S. agricultural labor process are more in line with Marx's "despotic regime" of the country and time frame that gave birth to the capitalist industrial process—nineteenth-century Britain—than the late capitalist production processes of the contemporary U.S. economy. An elucidation of the labor process in Marx's *Capital, Volume I* is most applicable to the U.S. capitalist agricultural labor process. A more extensive comparison can be located in Mize (2000) and Mize (2006b) but this first half of this section

focuses on the key features of the working day (increased scale, wage labor, surplus value extraction, class relations, and workplace injuries) as Marx (1976) detailed in comparison with working day conditions during the Bracero Program.

4. For point of comparison, the National Agricultural Workers Survey has been collecting data continuously since 1989 and finds that farm workers' earned on average hourly wages of $9.42 in 2009–2010. The average wage in 1999 was $6.68 an hour. See https://naws.jbsinternational.com/5/table4.pdf.

5. Based on these amounts, it appears that the first report was in pesos, not U.S. dollars, but I was unable to recontact the respondent after our initial interview.

6. The savings fund is a source of controversy because it appears that few of the Braceros were able to claim their money from the Mexican National Banks. This controversy will be discussed in the concluding chapter.

7. U.S. agriculture currently has one of the highest rates of work-related deaths and agricultural workers can expect to die sooner, on average almost twenty years sooner, than the general U.S. population. The average life expectancy of a male farm laborer is fifty-four years (Broyles-Gonzalez 1994, xi). In comparison, the life expectancy for all men and women in the United States is 71.4 and 78.3 years respectively (U.S. Census 1990). In 1988, agriculture had the highest rate of work-related deaths (48 per 100,000 workers) than any other industry (U.S. Census 1990). The second highest death rate was construction (34 per 100,000) and the rate among all industries was 9 per 100,000 workers.

Chapter Four

The Making of the Bracero Total Institution

When I interviewed one of the two state housing inspectors who investigated housing conditions of Colorado's migrant labor camps, Mr. Allen (1997) stated, "the Braceros were actually stoop laborers. In fact, we always said the first Braceros were led out of Egypt by Moses." By linking to a longstanding story of enduring suffering and humiliation, the person responsible for the enforcement of the Bracero Program's housing provisions noted the peregrinations that Braceros were forced to endure necessitated suffering of biblical proportions. From the moment they entered a recruitment center in Mexico to the time they were returned to that center, the Braceros' lives were in the hands of others. Officials in Mexico determined whether they were worthy to work in U.S. agricultural fields. Representatives of growers' associations chose whom they wanted to employ as workers and decided what work they would do. Decisions were already made as to where the Braceros would live (whether it be in labor camps or on growers' ranches), whom they would come into contact with, what they would eat, and what tasks they would be doing. Due to the remoteness of the camps and ranches, it was predetermined for most Braceros that they would have little or no contact with the local community.

The recent literature on the Bracero Program identifies specific examples of relationships between Braceros and the local Mexican American population in specific communities. Whereas Martinez (2010, 165) confirms that in West Texas towns such as Pecos many Mexican Americans avoided Braceros on their weekend shopping trips or mistreated them as *mayordomos* in the fields or socially in dancehalls, López (2010) identifies that in Santa Barbara, California, his Mexican American father created close, longstanding relationships with Braceros. "My father's involvement with the Bracero Program is characteristic of other Mexican Americans who were associated with the program. There is a history of Mexican Americans who married former braceros, who served as cooks and who even worked alongside them at the canneries" (López 2010, 187). Gamboa (2000, 107) notes a 1944 Cinco de Mayo celebration in Medford, Oregon, that brought Braceros into contact with the local population that culminated in a "dance, complete with orchestra, where the growers' wives and daughters danced with the Mexican workers." But it was these rare celebrations that were exceptions that proved the rule. The holiday interactions were brief interludes of community interaction that were marked as stark contrasts to the daily isolation Braceros mostly endured. By design, the Bracero Program isolated men as "local officials virtually quarantined contract laborers in their migrant camps, limiting the mobility that might provoke desires to establish new families in a new country" (Rosas 2014, 147).

Living conditions came very close to military specifications: Braceros were most often housed in army barracks complete with a mess hall that served institutionally prepared meals. Lest we forget, these men were not soldiers. They were laborers who were hired to do a job. For almost everybody else in the U.S. workforce, this meant their time devoted to earning a wage was all that they owed their employer. Every other aspect of their lives was within their own control and there was a distinction between the private and public. However, the Braceros' private was public and very few options existed for deviating from the imposed regimen. I mean this quite literally as a precondition for receiving a contract was a very public display of their private parts. If they lodged a complaint about negative treatment, the fear of reprisal was very real and would result in deportation. They were not allowed to shift to another job because the contract stated that those who did not meet the requirements of the contract and sought employment elsewhere in the United States would be subject to deportation. Workers were all too often powerless in their bargaining positions.

The Bracero Program was instituted with the interests of agribusiness in mind. First, the needs of large-scale agriculture are highlighted. The batch-handling of large numbers of Mexican immigrants, to be employed for short periods of time on an "as-needed basis," was best suited to fulfill the labor demands of agribusiness. The second issue of concern is the high degree of social isolation manifested in the lived experiences of former Braceros. Since I discussed how social isolation is related to racial segregation in chapter 2, I explore two other aspects of social isolation: linguistic isolation and isolation in terms of "leisure" time. Leisure time consists of not only what the Braceros did if and when they had days off from work but also how the dictates of the labor process impacted "break time" during the working day. Finally, I discuss the situations where Braceros actively resisted the conditions they experienced and how growers dealt with this opposition to their authority.

The theory underlying the making of the Bracero total institution will be discussed in depth in Appendix I, with the goal that the lived experiences and memories of former Braceros reside squarely at the forefront in this chapter.

CONDITIONS OF DEPARTURE: AGRARIAN CHANGE AND RURAL MEXICO

The main impetus for migrating *al Norte* often stemmed in the deplorable living conditions in rural Mexico. The men interviewed discussed how they often started working in the field at an extremely early age, why their families required all family members contributed to a family wage, and how they were subjected to abject poverty. Don Ramon discussed why he started working on a hacienda at the age of ten. "When I left it was because they would hit me really hard, my grandma. I would hear the boats nearby and knew that that was going to help me [to escape]. When I leave, I will leave and never return back home. And I did it. I took the train and got on top of the cargo trains until I got to my destination" (Life Story of Don Ramon 2005). Don Ramon left the relatively comfortable confines of Sinaloa (where food was plentiful), due to the domestic violence he faced, but he found his life in the haciendas would not improve markedly. He recalled the conditions in Mexico because he felt the new generation did not understand how tough conditions were in post-revolutionary rural Mexico.

Don Baldomero (2005) described life as very precarious: "Well my life was, what word would you say, well it was like an adventure because we did not have work. There was no work there. There was only one hacienda. I began to work like at 12-13 years of age in that hacienda. And they would pay me two pesos for all day from the time that the sun rose to when it fell. There was no one who could give you work." In further detailing of his life working on the hacienda, Don Baldomero explained how official work began when he harvested maize, beans, and oats. Informal grass cutting began when he was five years old.

> Don Baldomero: I began to work, well not work, but doing . . . where was I? I am going to tell you that my brother and I, so you can see for yourself, since we were young. I must have been about five years old. And my brother must have had seven years. And my brother the one he prepared the land for agriculture. Between both of us, we had farm animals but no one could come and help because the Ox would not let them. . . . In that time, I had nothing. The rattlesnakes would try to bite me but I was too fast. So that is our life since I was really young I began to work so that we could earn something. It was a lot of suffering because my father . . . lasted seventeen years ill. All of our lives since we were small my father was sick.
>
> Int: And your mom?

> Don Baldomero: Well she was the one that was there in the house. But there was work for no one. There was nowhere where she could go to earn something to eat. Then our life was . . . our life since really small [was about] suffering [since] we did not have anything to eat. Our father was sick and he lasted seventeen years.
>
> Int: How many of you were in the family?
>
> Don Baldomero: Ten in the family, there was ten of us . . . but when I got to be twelve years of age, I began to work and I would make enough for everyone to eat.

Life complications such as ill parents were all too prevalent in overall conditions of poverty and starvation. Don Baldomero recalled that his paid labor at twelve years old was enough to feed his mother and siblings.

When Don Lupe was asked "what was life like in Mexico before you became a bracero," he detailed the difficulties his family endured.

> Don Lupe: Well it was difficult. They would pay us very little in the hacienda. There were many of us in the family. Right. In that time there were seven, eight of us in the family because there were fourteen total. . . . When we were there working in that hacienda, I tell you it was really heavy [a burden] because we worked lots and got paid very little.
>
> Int: Who would you work for? You were not owners of that hacienda right?
>
> Don Lupe: No. No we were simply workers.
>
> Int: And in that hacienda what would you do.
>
> Don Lupe: In that hacienda they cultivated chile, maize, beans. Only those three things. . . .
>
> Int: How old were you when you began to work?
>
> Don Lupe: In that time when I began to work I was like nine years old.

Working by age nine, helping a family of fourteen subsist with eight active wage earners, and often in conditions described as overworked and underpaid, Don Lupe's experience resonated with all of the men who grew up on haciendas. He provided very detailed examples of the starvation his family had to endure and how he was reduced to begging for survival.

> I thought it would go well over there right. So that I could keep going frequently. But unfortunately the contracts were too short and the wage was too low. Well then I thought that if it went well I am going to remove some of the hunger because unfortunately we were hungry. We were really broke and because we were such a big family. When I did the military service. So we would go in the morning to do the service. And my mom, it was Sundays. She would say, "there is nothing more than cinnamon with some old tortillas and then god bless you. Go do your service." And then to get to the point, there in

> the small town I found some people in San Diego de la Union [stresses the name of the town] in the state of Guanajuato that would help me who would give me food that was leftover so that I could take to my younger brothers. So the lady would give me food she would give me the left over tortillas that were really hard so that I could take them to my mom for by little brothers. So I would arrive and my mom would say, "how did it go son?" "Look I brought you some tortillas even though they are hard" [said Don Lupe to his mom and his mom responded] "no that is good." Well then she would say come on then and come to eat . . . And that is what we used to eat and also chile done on a pestle and mortar. And that was our dinner. And in the morning when we used to go and eat, she would make us some taquitos with beans and a little bit of lard . . . You would eat the taco and it was only animals in it. That is what we would eat. So on Sundays when we rested [pauses] my mom would make us a pot of about 10 liters of white *atole* and red chile and with some warm tortillas. Two or three [tortillas] each one and some chile. And my father he also used to work, so frankly we did not have enough (Life Story of Don Lupe 2005).

The deplorable conditions in Mexico were defined in terms of abject, absolute poverty and starvation. It was Don Andres that detailed how these conditions directly related to the decision making process to become a Bracero. "Well there was a lot of poverty, much poverty, and one had to leave out of necessity, not because of pleasure for necessity, so that one could progress a little, right. And because with family one had to help my mother and brothers, there was nine siblings in my family, right, now there are eight of us, one has died, so that one could be well that is why we would go over there as Braceros" (Life Story of Don Andres 2005).

MIGRATION AND CONTRACTING PROCESSES

The decision to migrate from Mexico to the United States constitutes the first step in the process that led to the contracting of Braceros. The life stories of former Braceros shed light into how the decision-making process was determined. The major factors shaping the decision were influenced by both the living conditions in Mexico and the interrelated pulls of economic opportunities in the United States. The formation of recruitment centers in Mexico by the Mexican government represents another obstacle that potential Braceros had to surmount in order to secure passage to the agricultural fields of the United States. But before would-be migrants went to recruitment centers, they had to obtain letters of support from local government officials, find a way to have their names placed on lists of potential contractees, and secure the financial means to afford transportation to the recruitment center. The processing centers established in the United States facilitated the next stage of the batch-handling of Braceros. Medical and prior work-experience examinations were administered to determine the fitness of laborers. It is from a discussion of the contract and recontracting process that further insight is gained into the power relations between growers and Braceros.

The Decision-Making Process to Migrate

The decision to migrate is one aspect of the subjective nature of the life stories that provides a fairly uncomplicated correspondence between past and present subjectivities. The decision to uproot or transplant one's social existence to a new locale is certainly susceptible to *ex post facto* interpretation but most often, particular circumstances directly result in the decision to move. Manuel Gamio, in *The Life Story of the Mexican Immigrant* (1931), found that the form of the "reasons for migrating" stories were based on three recurrent themes: the Mexican Revolution, the good money to be made, and the friends and community members (those who were former migrants) who coaxed others to migrate. The Revolution still holds a particular salience in shaping the stories of later Mexican-American generations whose parents, grandparents, and great-grandparents migrated around that time (1910–1917). But from that time forward, it was the money to be made and friends' encouragement that structured the story of why one migrated. Coupled with the difficult living conditions in many parts of Mexico, migrating *al Norte* was a clear decision for many to make.

> Int: Were you working in Mexico prior to entering the military?
>
> Don Jorge: Yes, I started working when I was eleven years old, in the fields. Over in our country there's work for the children, cutting lemons, oranges . . . there's a lot of work that children and women do. There they would plant cucumbers, cantaloupe and watermelon. There was plenty of work there. But sometimes one would have to venture out to see if there was more, or better, work elsewhere. The money one earns is usually spent day to day. There's not an opportunity to save money, to buy a house, it is also just to survive.

The living conditions in Mexico, particularly in its rural areas, were barely at a subsistence level. In 1958, the incomes of the richest 5 percent of all Mexicans were twenty-two times those of the poorest 10 percent.[1] The wages to be earned in the United States, even though they were paltry by U.S. standards, were important boosts for local Mexican economies.[2] The wages one Bracero sent home were enough to put three brothers through school. All but one of the Fresno Braceros interviewed were working in agriculture prior to their contracts. The Braceros interviewed in Mexico had extremely varied work histories prior to and after working in the Bracero Program. A few (four) were working their own parcels in cooperatively owned farms (*ejidos*). In this arrangement, corn was grown strictly for subsistence. The majority of those interviewed were working on haciendas that exported cotton, fruits, and vegetables to the United States, Europe, and Japan. In Mexico, they often picked the same crops that they would eventually pick in the United States. Two respondents who picked lemons in Mexico were contracted to do the same work in California. Initial contracts were based heavily on the crops the workers had experience with. It was not until later contracts that the work diversified to other crops.

The migration process started by friends and family that had previously migrated eventually led the Braceros I interviewed to begin the process of securing work contracts. "I came to the United States because I had a lot of friends, who were older than me, and they were already coming to the United States. And they would tell me that it is pretty, and there's a lot of work and all. But I could not come because I was doing my military service" (Life Story of Don Jorge 1997). Don Andres joined his older brother for his first trip as a Bracero but they were quickly separated at the recruitment center. Stories of the wealth one could accrue in the United States were major factors in the decision-making process. As Hector Coahuila stated earlier in the group interview: "It's the money, once you get used to having the money, it keeps you coming."

Galarza (1964) also notes the use of newspaper advertisements to recruit workers, but of those I initially interviewed, each of the respondents heard about the Bracero Program from fellow community members and not from mass media sources. Don Ramon was the only Bracero interviewed who recalled newspaper ads in his home state of Sinaloa. The state was not in as dire straits as more populous interior states, so advertising was more of a necessity to fill the local government lists of would-be Braceros. Don Ramon (2005) noted:

> Because there was of everything there was no necessity. There were many farms of diverse crops. There was much food then. Then life it was not difficult as it was in other states because it was believed that the Bracero Program opened up because there were states with lots of necessity. That is why they gave preference to those states. But us no. The reason why we were called was because there was a list [the list was created by a female politician]. They then began to announce it in the newspapers and we began to go and we began to sign up with her. Then there was a person called El Negro Durazo who was the person who gave the good list. If you were not on the list of El Negro Durazo then it was no good. They would return you. But there was not as much necessity in Sinaloa as I said because there was much to eat and work. There was fishing. On the boats you made lots of good money because there was shrimp.

His experience was rather exceptional, due to the family circumstances that forced him onto haciendas, as it was the large haciendas that were cultivating the export crops that gave the men requisite experience to secure contracts.

Advertising to populate the lists of willing applicants was often not necessary in the major sending states where the hacienda system predominated.

Most often, informal networks planted the seed to seek a contract. As Don Baldomero (2005) recalled:

> But then came my twentieth birthday but I did not have the age to enter [the bracero program] because it was twenty-one and over. Nonetheless, I signed-up for the bracero program because a man told me, "Baldomero you know what? Let's go north. That is how you would say it in that time. Let's go north." Then I say, "No, how am I going to go. I say I don't have [any money]." He said, "let's go, let's go if you want I will loan you 25 pesos. It was a lot of money 25 pesos." Then we left from there."

As Don Baldomero identified how he found out about the program, it was "through Rosendo, he was a neighbor of ours." Yet, the informal networks only brought one in contact with the government officials who maintained lists of eligible applicants. It was *mordidas*, or bribes, that defined the main protocol associated with getting one's name on the list.

In some cases, men made decisions for the family whereas other cases involved other family members making decisions for them. Most decisions were made in a more cooperative arrangement of decision-making. The remittances were the key to a better life in the form of small appliances (sewing machines, dry-cell battery radios, and small electronics), a savings (no matter how meager it might have been), and a glimpse at U.S. standards of living that encouraged a large numbers of Braceros to settle permanently in the United States with their families.

The Recruitment Centers in Mexico

The entire recruitment process was touted by the Mexican government as being "free." None of the Braceros I spoke with were able to find these "free" contracts since there were fees associated with every step of the process in order to become eligible for work in the United States. Before one could qualify, a potential Bracero had to obtain a letter from the local government official stating that there was not a labor shortage in the community and this person could be spared (see Appendix III). This "complimentary" letter, in actuality, cost potential Braceros on average 200 pesos. The 200 pesos worked like a bribe for local government officials in exchange for this letter of recommendation. "Well, they were taking letters to every country [municipality]. They gave you the list and asked for people from your municipality, and there they called you. And then the letter that they gave us to come here cost 35 pesos" (Life Story of Don Francisco 1997). For the elite who had access to Mexican government channels, the process of registering for a contract became a significant source of unjust enrichment. Like the current day *coyotes* that transport undocumented workers across the border for an exorbitant fee, men with inside connections to local governments were in the business of selling contracts.

Another informal arrangement developed that circumvented this process. Men who were able to pay at least 500 pesos could be put directly on the list. "There were the lists that came from *Gobernación* (the government), they said. And there you were signed up, and there they began to . . . what's it called? We were already signed up on the list. *Fulano, Sutano, Vengano,* right? They started to . . . to be able to cross. And there they brought us in a cargo train" (Life Story of Don Antoñio 1997). The majority of those interviewed took the latter route and did not recall having to obtain letters from local officials.

> Don Liberio: I had to pay. I always had to pay to get on a list. I had to pay money.
>
> Int: How much?
>
> Don Liberio: Around 500 pesos.
>
> Int: Who received the money you paid?
>
> Don Liberio: A man. Like *coyotes*. I would pay the man in Empalme about 500 pesos to get on the list and he would get me to Monterrey . . . I would pay the recruiter in Michoacan to be put on the list. It was a very long list, four-five-six hundred men. And then they would write you to show up in Monterrey and then they [the associations] would come and get you.

The final means of securing paperwork consisted of buying papers from men who decided that they could no longer wait outside the recruiting centers. As Don Ramon (2005) recalls,

> Oh after Empalme, they would call the list and one would run to get in line. There was an inspector there who would call you by your name. There were some that would buy the letters from others. They would go and buy the letters [those that left would say] "no I am leaving to my *tierra*." This is no good. [They would further say], "I will be able to live better off my land." They would return and whoever bought the letter they had to memorize [all of the information that was in the letter]. But not everyone would do it. They would forget one of the last names when they were called because it was not theirs. He couldn't remember the last name because well it was not his. There was this small guy from Oaxaca who they called his name and he turned around and said, "what is my name?" "What do I know, I don't even know you."

The purchase of other people's identities to secure temporary contracts would become the *modus operandi* in the ensuing years of undocumented migration, but the humor associated with forgetting one's name was also squared with a significant cost to the would-be Bracero from Oaxaca.

The transportation costs associated with travel from one's home to the recruitment center were also covered by Braceros. In Mexico, the recruitment centers were moved three times during the program. The Mexican state wanted the centers close to the major sending areas of central Mexico. The U.S. state, for the purpose of easing transportation costs for growers, pushed to have the centers along the U.S.-Mexican border. A publication by the Mexican government (*Secretaria del Trabajo y Prevision Social* 1946) stated that the Mexican government wanted to use the program to alleviate unemployment in populous central Mexico, possibly even urban areas with high unemployment. U.S. growers wanted seasoned veterans (i.e., *campesinos*) in a way that minimized their expenses. This played out in the determination of where the recruitment centers in Mexico would be located. In 1942, the sole center was in Mexico City. This remained unchanged until 1944 when the Mexico City location closed and operations were relocated to Irapuato and Guadalajara. In 1947, centers were moved to Zacatecas, Chihuahua, Tampico, and Aguascalientes. In 1955, centers were again moved to Monterrey and Hermosillo (see Illustration 4.1) with the Chihuahua location remaining open (all located in northern border states). These three centers continued operations until the end of the program in 1964 (Durand 1994, 130).

These changing locations shifted the economic burdens of travel expenses from the U.S. government and growers to the Mexican Braceros. The northern border states of Mexico—Baja California, Sonora, Chihuahua, Coahuila, Nuevo Leon, and Tamaulipas—sent only 21.92 percent of all Braceros contracted to work in the United States from 1951–1964 (Garcia 1980). For the remaining 78 percent of the Braceros who migrated during that time, the increased burden associated with a bus ride or train ticket to Sonora, Chihuahua, or Nuevo Leon fell directly on their shoulders. Often, workers had to request loans from the local elite in their places of origin to cover the costs. One Bracero spoke about how the shifting locations of the recruitment center raised the costs associated with securing a contract. Don Jorge lived in Colima and when he first came to the United States under contract, he traveled less than 200 miles to the recruitment center in Irapuato, Guanajuato. His transportation costs were minimal and consisted of a bus ticket as compared to the hardships he endured almost 700 miles away from his hometown.

> Then I returned again, April or May 1958. This time I went to Monterrey, Mexico, we were there three months in the streets. There were so many people there, we just had to wait and see who was chosen, and finally they contracted us. At that time there was money sent to me from home to get back because I could no longer afford to stay there. But when the money got there I was contracted (Life Story of Don Jorge).

The cities hosting recruitment centers became the way stations for those waiting for their numbers to be called. The streets became temporary homes for those who hoped to be contracted (see illustrations 4.2 and 4.3). In every step of the way for the potential Bracero, they were simply numbers (see illustration 4.4) and usually handled en masse for everything from work experience inspections and health examinations to paperwork processing. The recruitment centers represented their indoctrination to the high degrees of social control they would experience as Braceros. Potential contractees, from all regions of rural and urban Mexico, were brought together for the common purpose of tending to the fields of U.S. growers. The waiting period tended to be the most difficult aspect for would-be Braceros because it was often at great personal expense that they would have to wait in an unfamiliar city, often without housing or jobs, until their numbers were called. As Don Jorge Colima recalled about the three months waiting outside the recruitment center in Monterrey, in order to survive he had to have money sent from home.

If an individual was lucky enough to be contracted, his own situation suddenly was grouped together as a general condition that every Bracero faced. The treatment they received in the recruitment center served as preparation for a life beyond any individual worker's control. The images of how the Braceros were treated at the recruitment center are evidence of their mass-handling. If they did not feel enough like a number, the placards they wore around their neck would remind them. The practices, associated with the total institution, were passed on to the U.S. counterparts of the Mexican recruitment centers.

U.S.-Border Processing Centers

A small number of processing centers were opened on the U.S. side of the border to connect Braceros with growers. Eagle Pass, Texas, was the main center for associations that recruited workers to the East and Midwest. El Paso was the way station for the Rocky Mountain states and the Midwest. For Braceros to the San Luis Valley of Colorado, the majority of contractees were from Chihuahua and the northern states of Mexico since the processing center was in El Paso. Calexico and El Centro, located in the Imperial Valley, processed workers headed for California and the Pacific Northwest. It was here that medical tests were administered, delousing occurred, and the workers started their long bus rides to their eventual work sites. "Upon arrival at the United States labor reception center, the worker and his luggage are thoroughly dusted with DDT powder as a sanitary measure and to prevent insects from being brought into the United States. His [the Bracero's] next stop is for a chest X-ray, then for a photograph for passport purposes" (Colorado Agricultural Experiment Station 1958, 63).[3]

Illustration 4.1. Braceros at the Hermosillo Recruitment Center. Recruitment and Processing Procedures, circa 1950s. Courtesy of Department of Special Collections, Stanford University Libraries: Galarza Papers Box 65, Folder 3.

The Braceros more recently interviewed on the Mexico border were very forthright about the humiliating experiences they endured at the processing centers. "They would take off our clothes and would throw powder on us and it had a small smell like DDT. They would take off our clothes and would take out our penis and they would stick their fingers [in the anus] to see if we had a hernia" (Life Story of Don Ramon 2005). From the Fresno interviews, where the Braceros did not want to recall their experiences in the processing centers, the changing social conditions (particularly the weekly get togethers) allowed the border-based ex-Braceros to recall their humiliating past in ways that placed the blame squarely on those responsible for inflicting the mistreatment rather than internalizing the humiliation. The shift in recollections

Illustration 4.2. Braceros, Waiting to be Contracted. Town of Hermosillo (ca. 1957) where Ernesto Galazara photographed would-be Braceros living on the streets while awaiting their contract. Courtesy of Department of Special Collections, Stanford University Libraries.

is best noted by Don Andres' response to what he best remembered about the program.

> Int: What would you say that is most that you remember as your days as a bracero?
> Don Andres: Well that when we got there to the check-in where they would pass us they would disrobe us, disrobe us. And they would pull the penis like that [demonstrates using finger how foreskin was pulled back] to check to see if they had gonorrhea or some infection. En Empalme? [he asks the wife sitting across the room]. And then they would open your anus to see if you had hemorrhoids. And the doctor would stick a finger to those who had a hernia. If you had these, you would not go all of that. All of that. They would disrobe you completely then they would fumigate you. All of us were healthy, the majority of us we were young. Only the older people but they would not go it was mostly the young people. I was 23-24 years old. But that was their requirements.

A similar recollection by Don Lupe was elaborated upon in quite full detail.

Illustration 4.3. Braceros, Contracts in Hand. Galarza photographed the "lucky ones" who solemnly display their contracts. Courtesy of Department of Special Collections, Stanford University Libraries.

Don Lupe: And then with one of these how would you call them, compressors, they put powder on us for [lice]. They told us, "unbutton your shirts." We unbuttoned our shirts. Then he said, "now unbutton your pants" then they put a tube on us and powdered us again. Then once we were inside they told us, "now take off all of your clothes." "Now all of you take off all of your clothes. All of you take off all your clothes. Do not leave any clothes on. Put the clothes there [points to corner of the room]." And then they put us in a circle where they had us inside. All of us naked [says it really slowly so that I capture it on the recorder]. We saw each other one with the other. Right. Then he says, "now turn around." Well then we then all turn around. And they [inspectors] were in the middle of the warehouse where they had us. And then after they did all of that to us, they then gave us vaccinations. Can you believe it. Yes they also vaccinated us. But with an injection. [They would tell us] "Go on through this door there are the medic . . . Walk fast." Like that, like animals.

Int: Was this the Mexican or the American government who was doing this?

Don Lupe: The American! You would pass and they would dig the needle in you. Like an injection. And then they passed us all. Once we all passed they told us, "alright now go ahead and dress yourself. Alright now dress yourself and you are going to walk to the offices where the señoritas are located so that you can give them your information, so that they give you your passport." Good, then we passed one at a time. And the Americans really [pauses to

Illustration 4.4. Braceros, Waiting for their Numbers to be Called. The contracting process was handled en masse with a very dehumanizing effect. Courtesy of Department of Special Collections, Stanford University Libraries.

> search for word] they treated us bad. They treated us like animals. . . . Well each one of us gave our information. [Then they said] "Well then go ahead and leave like that in a line go outside as the buses are out there that are going to take you to the other side." Then we got in line and we took off on the buses and, then yes, they were giving us a ration of food for the road. When we left there we lasted more or less [ponders thinking] we arrived the next day. . . . Until the next day until almost like at 5:00 p.m.

I found this detailed recollection interesting in comparison to Don Lupe's other major recollection (to be discussed in the housing section below) that he was working in Colorado as a cotton picker and the location of the Granada internment camp that he was initially transported to. It is highly unlikely that Don Lupe ever picked cotton in Colorado as it is not a crop grown in the state as the climate prohibits it. The Granada camp was used to ship Braceros into the sugar beet fields of Eastern Colorado and possibly in the nearby Arkansas Valley minor crops (cantaloupe, onions, tomatoes, and cucumbers). The Granada camp was according to Don Lupe "in the main part of Colorado" yet, its extremely remote location in the southeast corner of the state would seemingly stick in one's head. Upon follow-up with Don Lupe, he apologized for his "bad memory" and stressed that his first contract took him to work cotton in Arkansas, and he didn't remember the former Japanese internment camp turned Bracero labor camp was in the town of Jerome, but most likely this is where he was housed. Regardless, the recollections of the processing center at the forefront of Don Lupe's memory mark an important shift in how the program is publicly recollected. How the ordeal felt was best capture by Don Crecencio's comment that the experience made him feel ugly, and though he mentioned that after it, he changed (presumably referring to his clothes) his word choice is crucial for understanding that what was changed was also the man.

> Int: To become a bracero what was it that they asked you?
>
> Don Crecencio: They would ask for your birth certificate. Where you lived and everything else. Where are you from they would ask us. They would ask us, "do you have your birth certificate?" They would take our fingerprints. They would take off our clothes there. They would take off our clothes and fumigate us. . . . Then they would [demonstrates how they would pull back the foreskin of penis to inspect him using his finger, then points to anus and says that they would also stick their finger there].
>
> Int: How would you feel when they did that to you?
>
> Don Crecencio: I am not sure what I would feel. I felt ugly in those terms because what the Americans would do to us [laughs]. They would fumigate us then one had to go take a shower. One then changed.
>
> Int: Why have you never forgotten what they did to you?
>
> Don Crecencio: No because we were all naked. We were all naked. They would fumigate us and all. It was really hard in that time.

The U.S. processing centers represented the epitome in batch-handling. The delousing, medical exams, interviews, and paperwork processing were all done *en masse*. Having to stand naked in a large group of other like-situated men to be fumigated, poked, and prodded is certainly not what most prospective employees go through in the application process. "The first time I came I was placed in Sonora. They were contracting there. I got my contract and came to Calexico where the bosses, and the Department of Immigration, was there and all. They would check the hands, how they looked, and if some had calluses on their hands 'oh come over here.' But if your hands were clean they would say 'no, you're a secretary.' And I, ever since I was young I worked in the fields, I had huge balls of calluses" (Life Story of Jorge Colima). The idea driving the selection process was to find the most experienced men who would not require training upon entering the fields. The processing centers, in a way, were responsible for delivering a homogenous product. When he received a contract to pick lemons, Don Crecencio recalled, "They would choose mostly short people. I am not sure why this was. I am not sure maybe it was so they could work faster. The short ones they would set to one side and the tall ones they would set to another side [in the contracting centers]."

> Don Andres: They would inspect your hands and if you did not have them like if you worked in the fields [in Mexico] they would tell you that you do not work in the fields. So I got a shovel and made some calluses [he explains that he would get the handle of a shovel and run his hands up and down the wood handle until calluses would form in his hands through constant friction]. Then I would get to Empalme which is where they would contract them, they saw my hands and said, "ok."

Regardless of individual differences, the Braceros sent to the U.S. fields were touted as disease-free, unattached, hard-working, experienced and, above all, subservient young men.

Vocal critic of the Bracero Program, Henry Pope Anderson, visited the Calexico processing or "reception" center in 1958 and was told by his guide the characteristics of the "ideal bracero" and those rejected.

> Those deemed expendable were described one at a time: this one is too tall, he is too "cocky," that one a "loafer," another "lazy and irresponsible," he's a "smart aleck," this one a "ladykiller" and not "peon" enough. On the other hand the "right man," according to the guide, was "built right. He's a farm worker, you can tell that . . . he hasn't any big ideas. He's got the right attitude. He's humble, not fresh and cocky. He's an Indian type, probably from Jalisco or Guanajuato" (Gonzalez 2006, 119–20).

Anderson concludes that what he witnessed was in many ways a re-enactment of the slave markets in the U.S. South from a century ago and his subsequent work was entitled "Fields of Bondage" (1963) to make the connections unequivocal.

The Standard Work Contract and Recontracting

The Bracero contract was signed by the grower or grower association, a Mexican government official, a U.S. Department of Labor representative, and the Bracero (see appendix III). It specified both the agreed-upon work tasks, duration of contract, and pay rate. Unfortunately, all three provisions were systematically ignored by growers and their intermediaries. The discussion of class relations in the fields (chapter 3) provides the supporting information regarding how the job tasks and pay rate provisions were systematically violated. The individual work contract specifically barred Braceros from engaging in non-agricultural work and operating farm machinery. But respondents stated that they operated tractors and installed irrigation pipe while under contract. A World War II-era Bracero, who was interviewed for a 1999 newspaper article, claims that he was contracted as a "janitor—someone to clean streetcars and trains transporting wounded soldiers from ports in Los Angeles" (*San Diego Union Tribune* 9/26/99, A1).[4]

Even though the pay rate was specified on every individual work contract, there was no guarantee that the amount represented on the piece of paper would equate to the amount they would be paid. In the previous chapter, the section on wages detailed how the pay schedule varied (hourly or piece rate) to minimize grower expenses. In addition, the amount deducted from paychecks for legitimate expenses such as boarding and non-occupational insurance was at times supplemented with illegal deductions for room, board, transportation, and farm tools/supplies. Galarza found that some growers in Salinas, California, were charging Braceros for the ties that they used to bundle carrots. Even if all of the rules were followed and deductions were legitimate, growers still held a comparative advantage over non-agricultural U.S. employers because agriculture was specifically exempt from minimum wage, overtime, collective bargaining, child labor, and worker protection laws.

> Under the terms of the August 1, 1949, International Agreement, contracts for work in sugar beets may be for not less than 6 weeks; employment in cotton may be for not less than 3 months; for all other employment, the contract period is not less than 4 months. No contract may be for more than 6 months. However, with the consent of the Mexican consulate, the worker, the United States Employment Service, and the United States Immigration and Naturalization Service, workers may be contracted for additional periods provided that the worker shall remain in the United States no longer than 1 year (U.S. President's Commission 1951, 46).

As discussed in chapter 3, growers stated that the contract was one-sided and discriminatory because it guaranteed conditions and wages rarely, if ever, enjoyed by domestic farm labor. But it was most often only the Mexican Bracero who was expected to fulfill his portion of the agreement. "If you violated the 45 day contract and didn't come home on time, they wouldn't renew your contract. They wouldn't let you go back" (Life Story of Don Liberio 1997). If growers wished to extend the stay, it was solely at their discretion regardless of whether they were violating the contract that stated workers could not stay more than six months in any single stay. One Bracero I interviewed stated that, while under contract, he worked for the same association in Santa Clara, California, for over four months on a single fort-five-day contract.

> Don Francisco: The contracts were for forty-five days.
>
> Don Jorge: Yes, that was the minimum.

> Don Francisco: But I was lucky, I recontracted and recontracted. . . . In Santa Maria, the grower said we had to stay. They gave us three contracts so I was there from March to July. But my feet got swollen as I injured myself when working. After that, I returned to Mexico. I had to get back to do the planting in my fields.

Don Francisco recontracted because he was *told* that he had to stay. As a result of the limited bargaining power and the amazing amount of effort and money required to gain the "free" contracts from the Mexican government, many Braceros decided it would be easier to stay in Mexico or come over illegally than subject themselves to harsh conditions that they could not alter. Don Antoñio (1997) discussed the difficulties associated with renewing his contract and the border-crossing options available to him.

> Int: Why not renew?
>
> Don Antoñio: Because it was kinda bad, bad bad. Times got bad. . . . Things were getting bad and bad for them and us and it was time to leave.
>
> Int: Why didn't you apply the following year?
>
> Don Antoñio: Because one suffered much. Trying to get the same contract. It took a lot of effort and money to come over here again. It took a lot of effort to buy the contract to come. It's like today, we had coyotes. The government wouldn't give us a card. They would pocket the money.
>
> Int: How much [did you] paid for the contract?
>
> Don Antoñio: No I am not really sure. I don't want to lie. I can't remember. I don't remember how much I paid. They were coyotes who got the cards (cartas). They would get them from over there. One would struggle to get these cards and I just didn't make the effort. And there were some that weren't able to get it. And sometimes we would find other ways to get there. Undocumented through the river. . . . The last time they gave me this card [he removes his Bracero identification card from his wallet]. Yeah, but the problem here is they put the wrong date.
>
> Int: Can we make a copy?
>
> Don Antoñio: Will this affect me in any way?

In the interview process, the amount of effort expended to elicit information on the negative aspects of the program required a great deal of persistence. Even with repeated follow-up questions, Don Antoñio was never willing to elaborate upon which specific aspects were "bad." Though housing was incredibly cramped and poorly ventilated, pay was barely enough to subsist, working conditions were substandard, potable water was tainted, the recruitment process was fraught with deceit and graft, that is, overall things were very "bad"; Don Antoñio was one who endured, one who was willing to sacrifice for the chance to work. His concern over sharing his thirty-nine-year-old expired Bracero identification card is indicative of a very real and sustained fear of retribution, of being perceived as recalcitrant, and paying the costs associated with mounting a resistance.

The Bracero Program was a significant source of revenue for local government officials in Mexico. The patronage system of politics, endemic in rural Mexico, allowed local elites to further the disparity between rich and poor by funneling the hard-earned funds of the working poor and depositing the money directly into their own coffers. As Don Antoñio referred to the practice, the government would "pocket the money" that was taken in a process that was intended to be free of charge to Braceros. The U.S. government was charged with enforcing grower compliance. Housing conditions were supposed to be monitored by state housing authorities. To check compliance with wage contracts, the Department of Labor was enlisted for this task. A question posed to a former housing commission officer, in order to better understand the government agencies responsible for enforcement of the contract, gives us substantial insight into what happened to Mexican migrants after the program.

> Int: Who enforced the length of contracts to assure that workers did not remain after their contract ended?
>
> Mr. Allen: Wage and Hour Division, State and Federal Labor Departments . . . Which was an advantage for these people [Braceros] because later on when they were replaced those people had trouble collecting their wages and everything else because there was nobody controlling . . . same people controlled it but to get some of these people to risk their jobs to stay in this country by reporting anybody was a little rough. And finally immigration officers began to try and collect it. I seen Border Patrol would collect wages for people they picked up and found out they were owed wages. They'd pick it up for them and demand they pay them before they took them back. Otherwise, they'd never get the money.
>
> Señor Freemont: So what was happening was they were being exploited actually.
>
> Mr. Allen: Well a lot of places what they would do is tell these people that they would hold the money for them and give it to them when they left. And then call the Border Patrol themselves and then Border Patrol comes and picks them up and if they didn't do something the guy's gone and his money is still here. Some crew bosses did that and some growers did that.

The fact that the agencies, in charge of monitoring compliance, were severely understaffed made it difficult if not impossible to ensure that the stipulations of the contract were met by growers, both during and after the program. Mr. Allen was one of two state agricultural housing inspectors for the entire state of Colorado while the Bracero Program was in operation.

ON THE ROAD AGAIN: BRACEROS AND TRANSPORTATION

In order to get to the recruitment centers in Mexico, Braceros had to save up to pay their own way. Employers "would pay all transportation costs and guarantee the workers' return to their points of origin" (Scruggs 1960, 145). Of course, those "points of origin" were only the recruitment centers in Mexico, not their hometowns. The vast majority of Braceros still had to cover transportation expenses after their work contract expired. Growers were expected to be responsible for transportation from the recruitment centers to processing centers but the U.S. government covered the expenses initially. No similar subsidy was made available to Braceros who had to find transportation to the recruitment centers in Mexico. Transportation from U.S. processing centers to labor camps was the sole responsibility of growers or more often the associations that represented them. According to a bus driver of Braceros in Colorado, "the bus ride was direct with one stop for food. It was the law that the men had to be fed one meal. They stopped at a diner or restaurant where the Braceros purchased their own meals. A ride on the 24 passenger bus lasted for 15 hours from the processing center in El Paso to the labor camps in the San Luis Valley" (Interview with Señor Paulo 1997). This law was intended for the safe steerage of livestock, but was subsequently applied for worker protections.

During World War II, the War Food Administration and land-grant university extension offices handled the transport process. Extension offices in fourteen states also housed temporary workers (see Table 4.1). The allocation of Braceros was often in conjunction with the allocation of prisoners of war, conscientious objectors, Japanese internees, inmates, military personnel, and local women and children as temporary agricultural laborers. After the war, Braceros and domestic migrants were the exclusive employees of agribusiness.

Once the Braceros settled into the labor camps, they had to be transported to and from their various worksites. It was the transportation of Braceros within the United States that resulted in the largest number of accidents and safety violations. Galarza (1977) was commissioned to conduct a study of unsafe transportation practices during the Bracero Program. He found drivers who were overworked, mandatory rest stops that were ignored, and too many workers loaded onto flatbed trucks without any safety rails or harnesses. In addition, many of the buses and trucks, which were involved in accidents, did not meet code. Galarza documented some drivers who were not qualified to drive the modes of transportation they operated or were driving with expired licenses. There was a wanton disregard of safety measures that was poorly, if ever, regulated by the state.

The episode that warranted the initial investigation by Dr. Galarza was a bus accident in Chualar, California, that left thirty-one Braceros dead. The

Table 4.1. War-Time Labor, Braceros and "Foreign" Workers Transported and Housed By Extension and WFA: August 1943

State	"Foreign" Workers	Transported by Extension	Housed by Extension	Transported by War Food Admin
Pennsylvania	311	342	510	0
Delaware	267	230	0	0
Maryland	2,406	98	220	0
Ohio	234	35	139	205
Indiana	172	65	0	106
Illinois	546	0	600	0
Michigan	743	2,400	219	734
Wisconsin	325	121	0	0
South Dakota	12	0	0	200
Virginia	998	75	75	0
Florida	66	0	0	23
Tennessee	416	230	230	0
Texas	15	35	0	0
Montana	495	87	160	173
Idaho	1,698	0	1,877	0
Colorado	200	0	0	388
Wyoming	139	124	204	333
Nevada	112	111	0	0
Oregon	2,950	42	215	0
Washington	2,595	0	0	634
All Other States	6,320	1,093	445	5,851
Total (48 States)	21,020[i]	5,088	4,894	8,647

i. This compares to the 23,607 Japanese internees, prisoners of war, armed service members, conscientious objectors, and penal inmates enumerated in the October 1943 report. The totals transported and housed include all enumerated, including Braceros. Numbers adapted from Oregon State College, Extension Service (RG111). SG2, Folder 10.

accident occurred when a converted flat-bed truck that was formerly used to haul vegetables (but at the time was equipped with a canopy that made it a "labor transporter") collided with a moving train. Another accident in Visalia, California, was also investigated by Galarza. At the time of the accident, it was the second trip of the night for the driver. He was transporting re-contracted Braceros from El Centro to the San Joaquin Valley. On the trip before the accident, the driver transported Braceros to the San Joaquin Valley from the Coachella Valley. In the accident, two Braceros died and fifteen were injured (Galarza Papers 17:2). The driver's total mileage behind the wheel would have exceeded 800 miles in the one-day period. Galarza (1977, 86) notes other accidents occurring in the same month (September, 1963) near Woodland, California, and in the Imperial Valley. Though accidents were not part of the collective memory of the former Braceros, one interviewee recalled that similar types of transportation were utilized. "They would bring us to the field in a van or truck. They were flatbeds and we would be standing sometimes 10–15 per truck" (Life Story of Don Antoñio).

Transportation served another purpose related to social control. Since Braceros were required to get to the job sites or the local community with grower-provided transportation, the schedules of the buses and trucks determined their schedules. As one Bracero noted, if you were not on the bus on time, you had to find you own way back to the labor camp. In many instances, this was not a viable option so workers simply had no other choice but to submit to the schedule of the transportation that serviced them. "Large concentrations of aliens in camp barracks call for mass transportation, quite different from the sort of transportation that domestic laborers, in family groups of neighborhood car pools, used in years past" (Galarza 1977, 87). This batch-handling in terms of transportation, coupled with lax safety enforcement on the part of the state, put a number of Braceros directly in harm's way. The deaths attributed to the transporting of Braceros represents one of the most unfortunate, and ultimately preventable, aspects of the Bracero Program.[5]

"SU CASA ES LA CASA DE NADIE": BRACEROS AND HOUSING

The structure of the labor camps and other housing types were in line with the aim of social control and isolation, as the compounds were designed to physically separate the Braceros from the rest of society. In addition, the conditions within the camp were designed to treat the workers homogeneously. That is to say, workers were treated as interchangeable and replaceable. The three main state agencies that provided or oversaw housing included federal work camps under the U.S. War Food Administration, state-level housing agencies, and county extension agents. Housing was also handled directly by grower associations or the growers themselves. As a result of different agency oversight and beliefs about the housing Braceros were deemed worthy of receiving, three main types of housing structured the living conditions of the Bracero Program.

First, former Japanese internment camps, in operation during World War II, and government work camps from the New Deal programs for employing the Depression-era working poor were used by some associations, growers, and farm labor contractors who leased the grounds.

> Int: What part of Colorado was this concentration camp located?
>
> Don Lupe: Well in the main part of Colorado [author clarification: the internment camp was in Granada, which is in the desolate southeast portion of the state, and later interviews confirmed Don Lupe picked cotton in Arkansas]. Umh. And then there, the ranchers began to arrive. But they would not select one or two [braceros]. They would take them by the 100s. By the 100s because we were not the only ones that arrived. All of the rest of the people were there already. Around more or less 3000 in that concentration camp. From there they designated us to the ranchers. But because the ranches were companies like factories that they would take 200-300-1000 and of 2000. Then, when we arrived there, there were some huge barracks. More or less like 25 meters. There wasn't only one barrack there were many of them. There were more or less like 6 barracks. There were two files of beds, doubles right? That is one on the top and one on the bottom. More or less about 50 beds fit on each side of the barracks. Like 200 people [per barrack].

Second, a much less frequent but very important type of housing consisted of houses, barns, tents, and converted chicken coops that could be found most often on small-acreage operations. Galarza (1956) found in California that Braceros were housed in tents, converted chicken coops and barns, and other makeshift housing. None of the respondents I interviewed stated that they personally lived in housing of this sort. Gamboa (1990) noted that in the Pacific Northwest, Braceros were housed in a former Japanese internment or "prisoner-of-war" camp near Toppenish, Washington. In addition, Braceros also lived in tents in Idaho, Oregon, and Washington. Placing workers in former internment camps and tents was justified according to government officials and growers because "braceros deserved nothing better than their own homes in Mexico" (Gamboa 1990, 93). Don Jorge (1997) had the very atypical contract in Texas where he worked on a farm with one other contractee and they both had living quarters on the farmer's land. When the Mexican government interviewed returning Braceros, they found the following housing types by percentages:

Railroad Box Car	47.5
House Constructed of Wood	17.7
Room Constructed of Wood	15.8
Shed Constructed of Wood	12.2
Partitioned Room	2.3
Partitioned House	1.7
Canvas Tent	1.5

Hotel 1.3

The majority of those interviewed likely worked in the railroad Bracero Programs due to the nearly one-half residing in box cars, but housing also included houses, sheds, tents, and hotels (*Secreteria del Trabajo y Prevision Social* 1946, 75–76). "The absolute majority of the workers . . . lived in groups and only a small minority, 3.34 percent, lived alone" (*Secreteria del Trabajo y Prevision Social* 1946, 76).

Finally, the majority of housing was provided by grower associations that consisted of temporary barracks or alternate-use structures such as an abandoned school in Blanca, Colorado, and a converted gym in Ft. Garland, Colorado. The camps housed from 35 to 2,000 Braceros according to those interviewed.

> Int: Where did you live?
>
> Don Roberto: In barracks. Lots of beds, one next to the other.
>
> Int: How many men lived in the barracks?
>
> Don Roberto: In a big barrack, some 200 fit. There there were some 2000. They had lots of barracks.

In California, Galarza noted that the quality of housing was directly related to its visibility to the general population. Labor camps located on highways, major streets, or at least within visual sight from the road tended to be the housing in the best condition. Housing that did not meet state regulations or was in decrepit condition was usually located on growers' properties where it would not be easily visible (Galarza Papers 3:1). Private housing was the norm after the war but state housing agencies in California assumed the housing role during the war.

The California Farm Production Council (FPC) was a key captured agency that provided various state subsidies to growers. Mitchell (2012, 60–62) catalogs that by September 1943 the FPC housed 20,000 workers and subsidized private operators of labor camps for another 10,000, adding yet another 38,000 in the following year. Though financial figures are not disclosed, the FPC massive housing subsidy clearly denotes its impact as the "largest, most comprehensive, and most rapid program of state-sponsored and subsidized housing in the history of the state—and its transformative effects on the landscape . . . were profound" (Mitchell, 53).

In Oregon, the Oregon State College Cooperative Extension oversaw the allocation of housing and distribution of workers across the state. During the war years, twelve Bracero camps were located in Jackson, Klamath, Malheur, Umatilla (2), Hood River, Multnomah, Columbia, Washington, Marion, Yamhill, and Lane counties and administered by the War Food Administration (see illustration 4.5). The close working relationship between the WFA and Extension agents ensured workers were moved from hop yards in the central Willamette Valley to peach orchards in Jackson County, from strawberry farms in Hood River to potatoes and sugar beets in Eastern Oregon. Internal documents in the Cooperative Extension files at Oregon State University identify that labor surpluses were dealt with by reassigning Braceros to other regions of the state or, at least in 1943, shifted to non-agricultural employment. By 1945, this flagrant disregard for the terms of the contract meant reassignments did not stretch what qualified as farm work. "During the present low employment period in seasonal crop harvest around 200 or more Mexican farm workers have been temporarily assigned to seed cleaning plants, food processing plants and similar labor closely related to strictly agricultural work" (Oregon State College 1945).

For example, the Extension Service of fourteen states provided housing for 4,894 Braceros in 1943. The totals to date ended in October 1943, primarily the 1943 harvest, but numbers may also include the 1942 fall harvest. Though the majority of Braceros were housed in Idaho (1,877), sizeable numbers were housed in Illinois (600), Pennsylvania (510), Michigan (219), Maryland (200), Oregon (215), Tennessee (230), Utah (280), Wyoming (204), and lesser numbers in Ohio, Virginia, Oklahoma, Montana and New Mexico (Oregon State College Extension Service 1943).

In 1946, the Mexican government surveyed returning Braceros and emigrants on the issues of housing and boarding. Of those Braceros and Mexican emigrants they interviewed, the vast majority had lived in railroad boxcars. This certainly reflects that the sample contained a large proportion of railroad workers, as this was an oft-used housing option in the industry. Unfortunately, the survey did not provide information as to the exact dates of data collection, where respondents were surveyed, what industries they worked in, and what U.S. states the respondents worked in. The findings contradict both the established research and my regionally focused analyses that found the majority of Braceros were housed in barracks. If we had more information about the source of the sample drawn, we might have a better basis for speculating on the divergent findings. Don Baldomero was the only railroad Bracero located for this study and his recollection of housing was minimal though he remembered living in a labor camp, having water to shower with, and generally comfortable conditions.

The living conditions were generally viewed as favorable when respondents were asked but again, the specific details of their experiences contradicted their own subjective general assessments. Most of the men recalled living in army barracks with about forty to forty-five other Braceros. They slept on army regulation cots, according to their descriptions. Some who worked on smaller farms lived with two to six other men.

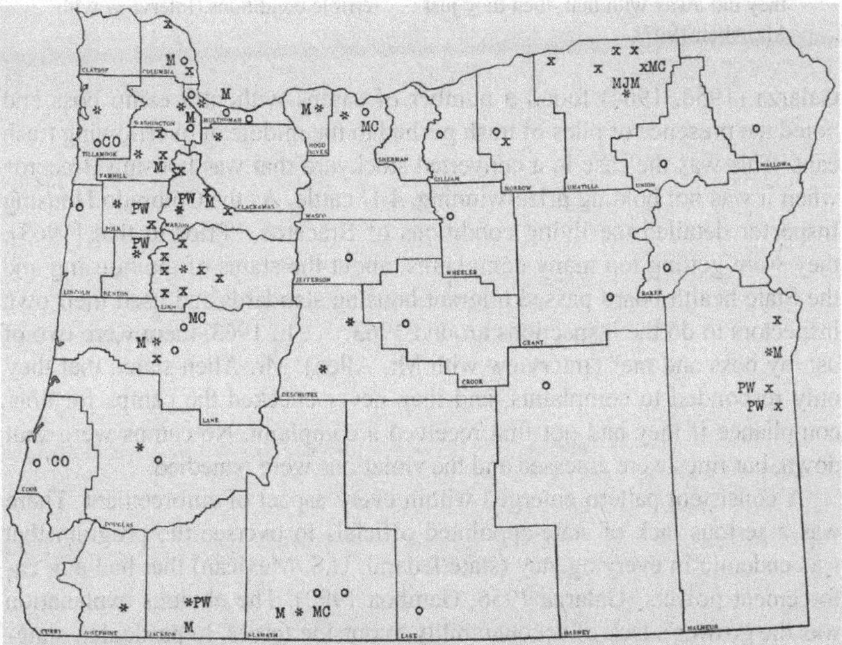

Figure 21. Placement offices and farm labor supply centers, 1945.

* Year-round offices
o Seasonal county offices
x Seasonal sub-offices

M 12 Mexican camps (WFA)
J Jamaicans
MC 4 Migrant camps

PW 6 Prisoners of War Camps
CO 2 Conscientious objectors on individual farms

Illustration 4.5. Extension Offices and Farm Labor Camps in Oregon: 1945. Adapted from Oregon State College Cooperative Extension 1947, 17. Used by permission of Oregon State University Libraries, Special Collections and Archives Research Center.

> Int: How were the conditions?
>
> Don Antoñio: Well the houses were pretty much like they were here. It was summertime, not wintertime, if it got too hot we would open the windows. Many of us endured, we stayed.

Since this Bracero was working in the hot, humid summers of central Texas without any type of ventilation, it was certainly a lot to endure. The Colorado state housing inspector noted that the mass handling of Braceros led to difficulties in keeping barracks clean.

> The Bracero housing, a lot of it wasn't too bad. The problem was its single dormitory style and you get a guy working in the fields for twelve hours a day and then have him come back and want him to clean up the housing and so forth. It's like any places, if you don't have a sergeant around, the military wouldn't do it. So they used to put a camp boss in, a guy that had nothing to do

> but take care of the camp. Generally, those guys did pretty good. But when they did away with that, then they just . . . terrible conditions (Interview with Mr. Allen 1997).

Galarza (1956, 1964) found a number of camps without a camp boss and noted the presence of piles of trash pushed to the middle of overflowing trash cans. This was the case in a converted stockyard that was housing Braceros when it was not holding prize-winning, 4-H cattle. As the Colorado Housing Inspector detailed the living conditions of Braceros, "Prior to that [1963], they were getting too many complaints, about the status of the housing and the State health board passed migrant housing standards and used their own inspectors to do the inspections around 1963. . . . In 1963, there were two of us: my boss and me" (Interview with Mr. Allen). Mr. Allen stated that they only responded to complaints, and they never checked the camps for non-compliance if they had not first received a complaint. No camps were shut down, but fines were assessed and the violations were remedied.

A consistent pattern emerged within every aspect of enforcement. There was a serious lack of state-appointed officials to oversee the program that was endemic in every agency (state/federal, U.S./Mexican) that had any enforcement powers (Galarza 1956, Gamboa 1990). The obvious explanation was the grower's lack of accountability to outside forces. In particular, state-appointed overseers were consistently hampered in their efforts due to a serious lack of staffing, resources, and at times commitment.

In regards to the housing situation, the conditions that Braceros faced were rarely seen or questioned by government officials. The state of Colorado only investigated labor camps when a claim was filed by a resident or concerned citizen. As a result, the labor camp conditions rarely came under the government scrutiny that was dictated by the contract. Housing served the purpose of placing Mexican Braceros into similar conditions, cutting them off from U.S. society, and dictating their schedules to center around work. The military-style housing enabled the mass handling of workers by keeping them in a centralized location. By housing workers together, it also allowed for the efficient distribution of labor to meet the short-term needs of growers. The deplorable housing conditions that some Braceros faced (whether that consisted of living in internment camps, tents, converted barns, or high school gymnasiums) attests to the lack of regulatory control by the U.S. government. Quite likely, this control was intentionally lax because the notion of developing a program to meet the needs of large-scale agribusiness did not coincide with instituting a strong system to ensure compliance on workers' rights.

"Y LA COMIDA?": BRACEROS AND BOARDING

The institutional preparation of food was a central component to the Braceros' mass handling. Food represented not only the major source of deductions from Braceros' paychecks but also one of the major areas where discontent was expressed. According to the standard work contract, Braceros were to be given a choice whether to prepare their own food or have food prepared for them at cost. What actually happened for the Braceros I interviewed was that the choice was made for them.

According to the Mexican government's (1946, 78) survey, almost 80 percent of the Braceros were fed in a commissary or labor camp cafeteria. Approximately 15 percent were fed in their own house, 4 percent in a restaurant, and 2.2 percent in someone else's private house. In addition, the types of food prepared for Braceros were limited to those foods that could be bought in bulk and institutionally prepared. The list of foods documented by returning Braceros included by percentage eggs (16.8), milk (12.4), potatoes (11.6), bread (8.9), vegetables (8.7), fruits (8.4), meat (7.5), oats/cereals (6.3), rice (4.1), beans (3.5), soup (1.4) and a little of everything/*poco de todo* (10.4) (*Secreteria del Trabajo y Prevision Social* 1946, 79-80). Don Roberto's (1997) experience corroborates both the institutional room and board arrangement as well as the types of food consumed: "During the program, everyone had barracks. Fresh water to drink, the big dining room. They gave you good food. Meat in the morning, eggs, oatmeal, milk, and at noon, to the dining halls for even more." Growers were allowed to deduct at most three dollars a day for food and were expected to give lower rates to those who prepared their own food.

Since growers had to provide the necessary items to prepare food, they were allowed to deduct those expenses from Braceros' wages. As Galarza notes, that maximum became the *de facto* minimum in assessing deductions from paychecks. None of the respondents I spoke with were able to recall the exact amount deducted from their pay for boarding.

> Int: And the food.
>
> Don Antoñio: The food, we had to buy it ourselves.
>
> Int: Who cooked it?
>
> Don Antoñio: We would cook it ourselves. To some they would give, to others, no.

A similar answer was given by Don Pablo who also paid for food and cooked it himself but could not recall the amount of deductions for food per paycheck. According to the contract, Braceros were supposed to be given the choice whether they would have food prepared or fix it themselves. That choice, in every case, was determined for them. In the large camps, food was institutionally prepared, usually by a professional commissary, but several Braceros do recall they had to buy and prepare their own food. Companies, or commissaries that specialized in catering to institutional groups, often submitted bids to grower associations in order to exclusively provide food for the laborers. In the San Luis Valley, the food preparation and distribution were handled by commissaries. The only food item subcontracted to a local business was corn tortillas. An extended conversation with the tortilla supplier gave substantial insight into how the food was institutionally prepared and what were the best of conditions with fresh corn tortillas supplied daily.

> Señor Palmas: They did, because I remember there were meat suppliers, milk suppliers, dairy product suppliers, etc. etc., and of course the basics, beans, rice, and usually it was some kind of stew with real meat in it. They did fairly well. You know, our kinds of stew . . . general stews. . . . And every once in a while they'd have an actual piece of meat. Meat and beans and rice. That was a standard . . . Of course we'd supply the tortillas. So they got tortillas at least one meal a day and usually everybody got that at the evening meal, some demanded it in the morning. If they demanded it, they got it. Some demanded it at noon, not very many because that was done in the field, and . . . I got to see what they were cooking, and being Mexican, I could survive on that diet really well. Beans, rice, some form of meat too, Kool-Aid or that type of thing, tea, so . . . I don't think I heard a lot of complaints, except that one over there at Tilden's. . . . Now they were complaining that they never, ever, ever ate any fresh fruit. But most of them got some kind of fresh vegetable and fruit daily.
>
> Int: All these different suppliers, were they mostly local farmers, then? The dairy that came in, was it coming from farmers around here?
>
> Señor Palmas: Well, not necessarily. The standard supply houses . . . They usually came through big supply house chains . . . butter, cheese, a lot of produce probably, but they usually came through regular supply house chains.
>
> Int: So the supply houses did not have corn tortillas available?
>
> Señor Palmas: They were available but not as fresh products. . . . So they were piping hot when we served them. And that was very important, see because that's an item that most people I know out there in agricultural regions . . . and that was something we could provide for these guys so they'd be happy.

Noting that food choices only changed when workers "demanded," Señor Palmas identified how food was a central source of contention and the exceptional case of providing fresh corn tortillas made the San Luis Valley boarding experience unique. Yet, the major shared recollection in the life stories was that complaints about bad food abounded. The objections were not necessarily about taste, but incidents of food poisoning due to spoiled food. One respondent noted the salty drinking water in a Texas camp where he picked cotton. Gamboa (1990) noted that wage strikes rarely resulted in change, but food strikes were more successful in the short term.

> Reports of food illness continuous. Mostly individual reportd [sic]. Planada camp group reported that some fifteen men were ill for several days. Some stayed in the hospital for three days until recovered. Cook changed from camp to another after too many men complained of stomach trouble. Men ask what['s] the best laxative is when they discuss stomach troubles with interviewers. Observe kitchen practices closely and criticisms of these practices often leads to "trouble" in the camp when men protest to cook. Practices most common seem to be: use of food left over from previous meals; sour beans; smelly meat. Men report that they have seen no food inspectors in any of the camps (Galarza Papers 3:1).

In North Carolina, Don Liberio reported that the food served in the camp occasionally would be rancid. If the workers would unite and complain, the quality of food would temporarily improve. But this was transitory since a couple of days later, workers again would be served rancid food. It was a continuous cycle for the month and a half he spent there. A sister of a former Bracero who worked for one of the railroad companies during the program was fed chicken. Initially that sounded great but he got chicken parts for dinner, other chicken parts for lunch, and other chicken parts even for breakfast. Chicken was the only meal he and his coworkers received. It was most often prepared the same way, unless the cooks were running low on whole chicken parts and had to make stew. The sister was told that the Braceros were not served side dishes to supplement the main dish of chicken. All of the parts were eventually fed to them (gizzards, hearts, and the more traditional servings such as thighs and drumsticks). This lasted for one contract, three months, and he vowed he would never return to the United States again. His sister summed up his experiences as "hard work for little pay, not worth the price of coming up" (Interview with Dolores Chihuahua 1997).

As for the other respondents, talk about the food, the housing, and the transportation was sparse. Most were not willing to talk about the details of their living conditions. They only would say that it was fine or adequate. Silence characterized many of the responses in terms of the exact details of how much was deducted, how often they were served food that they did not like, how they were transported, and what their housing situations entailed. For one Bracero who voiced what most knew but were not saying, how the workers were treated was of little concern. After all, as Don Daniel (1997) told me, "we were here to work."

LINGUISTIC ISOLATION AND THE SOCIAL CONTROL OF "LEISURE" TIME

Erving Goffman (1961) described the "total institution" as denoted by its spatial separation from the rest of society (see Appendix I). In addition to this spatial component (see Illustration 4.6), one of the unique characteristics of the Bracero total institution is the high degree of linguistic isolation that was fostered in its design. Of the Braceros contacted for this study, only one interviewee considered himself bilingual. The remaining interviewees all listed Spanish as the only language they spoke. The one respondent who had a good command of English was, not coincidentally, the only Bracero who integrated into the local town, via upward mobility, where he was originally contracted. The high degree of social isolation was partially diminished by the one-day-a-week trip to town where many Braceros were allowed to shop, send remittances back to Mexico, and co-mingle. I explore how even this leisure time was managed due to the strict rules (both highly formalized and informal) that they had to adhere to, in the local towns, in order to retain their contracts.

The physical isolation of labor camps from local communities was one way that Braceros were kept separate from the rest of society (see chapter 2).

Illustration 4.6. The Bracero Total Institution. Near Yuba City, CA, circa 1957. Photo by Dr. Ernesto Galarza. Courtesy of Department of Special Collections, Stanford University Libraries.

In many of the communities outside the Southwest, Braceros were also cut off linguistically from the community. The only Spanish speakers that Braceros found in places like Michigan, Ohio, and North Carolina were their immediate supervisors and possibly a few local Mexican-American merchants who specialized in supplying goods to Braceros. Thus, the language barrier served as another effective source of separation from the community.

Even in the San Luis Valley of Colorado, where a sizable Mexican-American population resides, the Braceros were cut off linguistically from the local citizens. The specific dialect of Spanish spoken in the valley is much closer to sixteenth-century Spanish spoken by the Spaniard colonists than the dialect of Spanish spoken by Mexican nationals. The unique history of the San Luis Valley—in terms of the its isolation from the rest of the Spanish empire and the Anglo intrusions—allowed its inhabitants to develop and preserve a linguistic artifact that has remained intact, with particular Anglicized modifications, for nearly four hundred years. This linguistic conflict served as another source of separation between Mexican nationals and their Mexican-American counterparts (Lopez Tushar 1992, Trujillo 1983, Interviews with Mr. Allen and Señor Freemont 1997).

The rare occasion that Braceros were allowed to interact in local communities was on their day off. If they worked a half-day on Saturday, the remainder of the day was spent in the communities. If workers had six full-day schedules and the nearby town was large enough to accommodate stores opening for business on Sunday, workers were allowed to enter towns. Because of the large distances between towns and labor camps (often a direct result of locals not wanting "foreign" workers near their towns), Braceros had to be transported to the nearest town. Growers and crew bosses sometimes offered this service for free, but a few Braceros stated that bus rides were deducted from their wages if they wanted to enter town. In contrast to the short shrift that respondents gave to detailing their job tasks in the fields and the daily experiences in the labor camp, the day-on-the-town story was expounded at great lengths by most Braceros.

> Our days off were only on Sundays. Or if the cotton picking wasn't very good, we wouldn't work. On those days we would stay in the barracks. Some people would go out—they'd leave. The barracks were in the camps. The ranchers had their own homes. We would be at the camps and if the ranchers needed eight or ten, they would come and get them. The association is where all the buses come, where all the people are (Life Story of Don Antoñio 1997).

By describing the general issues of transportation and housing, Don Antoñio offers substantial insights into the degree of social isolation from non-Braceros. He lived in a labor camp, housing only Braceros, which kept the workers separate from the growers who belonged to the association, the fields where they toiled, and the local community. The only day Don Antoñio and his compatriots could leave the labor camp was on Sunday. He was not able to recall if transportation was deducted from his paycheck but he did state that he elected to stay in the barracks on his "leisure" time. The Sunday trip was one of the few topics that Don Antoñio spoke of at any length.

Don Jorge also devoted a great deal of time to discussing the Sunday trip-on-the-town.

> Don Jorge: On Sundays, they would ask us if we wanted to go to Church. Many would say "yes" and many would say "no." They would even take us downtown. They would pick us up at a certain time and whoever was not there would have to find their own way back. They would take us downtown to allow us to walk so that we didn't get bored, because we worked all week. I, in reality, have nothing to complain about because they treated us well. Sometime during the contract there was a period of fifteen days with no work because it was raining really bad. The company would send someone to bring us money, usually about ten dollars to buy sodas, or things like that. We were not working, we had our checks, but they would give us money anyway.
>
> Int: Did they deduct that amount from later paychecks?
>
> Don Jorge: I don't remember if they deducted that from our paychecks, but they did give us money. They also told us that if someone had an urge to go home, that they would lend us money. They did give some loans but they [would] be deducted from their checks. I did not ask but it [the loan] was available.

Even though Don Jorge states that he had nothing to complain about because he was treated well, the last line casts a doubt on the benevolent grower and his intermediaries. Loans were provided by *ellos* (this unspecified "them" in the account refers to growers, FLC's or crew bosses), not necessarily out of good faith, but because the lending scheme proved to be very profitable. The loans offered to Braceros were similar to the company store where workers surrendered to a form of debt peonage in the perennial, yet futile, effort to restore a zero credit balance. When interest was assessed and loan repayments were automatically deducted from workers' paychecks, the fact that Don Jorge never requested a loan makes him very fortunate. For the sake of comparison, note how Don Jorge and Don Antoñio's fairly detailed responses differ from the brief testimony of one Bracero who claimed he was not given days off. Even when pressed, this was all he had to say about his experiences during his time spent in the fields and the labor camps.

> Int: What did you do when you weren't working?
>
> Don Francisco: There was no time when we weren't working. We worked all the time. From morning until night. No holidays, *dias de las santas* (holy days recognizing patron saints), nothing.

Int: Every day?

Don Francisco: All of the day. Yes, even if it was raining. We would work in the rain and they'd call us *mojados* (wetbacks) but we kept on working.

The experience of not being allowed to take time off is a frequent complaint of former Braceros. Any leisure time or downtime became another source of control by growers and FLCs. In one camp that Dr. Galarza visited in California, Braceros told him they "need a permit to [go] anywhere out of the area on 'off-day.' Usually, they were told that they can't go" (Galarza Papers 3:1). As evidence of the degree of control exercised by some growers and their intermediaries, not allowing workers time off certainly represents a basic infringement on their rights. For those who did receive a day off, these days were spent exclusively in the company of fellow Braceros. Local community members only entered this world when they provided a service or had something to sell.

> The only contact I had with them was strictly on Saturdays. That's when they came in from the fields or their encampments and that's when they transacted their business. . . . I wasn't really involved in their all-day activities but I assume that's the day they came in and did their personal shopping and make personal contacts and I understand that quite frequently they would have a gathering and maybe a celebration of sorts where they roasted a pig or a goat or something. I mean it was their day on the town, it was. From what I was able to observe time and again they had some real good times (Interview with Señor Freemont 1997).

The interviewee went on to explain that socializing was strictly limited to a Braceros-only affair even though he personally wanted to join them as they seemed to know how to have a good time. But this practice of co-mingling was explicitly forbidden for community members to consort with Braceros on an anything-but-business basis. The Braceros were certainly welcome in the valley to pick the crops and purchase items from local shopkeepers but beyond that, they were not welcome. A large Mexican-American resistance was mounted in Alamosa, Colorado, when it was suggested that Bracero housing would be erected on the south side of town. Local community members were effective in opposing this proposal. Labor camps were eventually placed in smaller towns or directly on growers' property.

The remaining six days of the week the Bracero spent in the fields or labor camps were almost completely managed for them. As Don Ramon (2005) responded to the question, "What would you say that you most remember of your days as a bracero," he stated, "[t]he days of rest is that what you mean? When you go to work to the U.S. it is from work to the barracks the food and go to sleep. And the lunch had to be prepared [the night before] so you could take it with you ready to go the next morning." The work day ran according to the food schedule since all workers were fed at the same time. The work schedule was enforced by the crew boss who responded to the wishes of the grower. At harvest time, the hours worked could be pushed up to the limits of the day-time hours in order to pick the fresh produce. As Don Andres noted of his work schedule, "We would get up at 4 a.m. so that we could get breakfast. And then the buses would come for us like at 5:30 a.m. We would then come back at 7:00 p.m., 8:00 p.m." When this was not enough, some growers (particularly in the cotton industry that utilized "swampers," that is, people, often local teenage-boys, who were paid to illuminate the harvesters' paths) used flashlights, car headlights, and flood lamps to enable workers to toil through the night.

The pace of work was most often related to the pay schedule utilized (piece or hourly based). Those working at piece rates would make their lunch as short as possible and work as many hours as possible in order to maximize their earnings. If it was in the growers' interests to switch remuneration to an hourly rate, Braceros accepted this as an inevitable part of the job. Since the pay schedule could change from day to day and even from morning to afternoon, the incentive to work harder was induced by the indeterminacy of how one would be remunerated. In the end, the expectation was that the Bracero work hard, extremely hard without breaks or rests since there was always the threat that workers would be paid by a piece-rate (on the amount they picked) if they were picking too slowly on the hourly rate.

DESERTION, DEPORTATION, AND ENDURING "BAD TIMES"

In order to control the workforce, outright physical intimidation was not often necessary because the role expectations of the dominated worker were hammered into their psyches, even before they arrived in the United States. The Mexican government indeed played a role in establishing the role expectations as to the Braceros' conduct in the United States. Galarza (3:1) noted how Braceros were indoctrinated by Mexican government officials at the contracting centers:

> You are going to be representatives of Mexico in the US. Be an example of honesty and show what good workmen you are. Do not spend your money there but send it home. Don't go on strikes or make trouble for your *patrones*. Remember if you make good you will be wanted again and again in the future.

Even if they were intimidated or threatened, most Braceros did not see it as a viable option to report such practices to a Mexican government official, who made it clear that those who made trouble would not be viewed favorably for future contracts. As a result, many men "deserted" or left their contracted work arrangements.

Int: Did you get to make a lot of friends?

Don Crecencio: Many of them would leave.

Int: Why would they leave?

Don Crecencio: They would get bored and they would leave.

Though Don Crecencio did not dwell on why men left, others who were interviewed identified the harsh working and living conditions as the impetus to exit.

The rate of desertion was significant enough to seek further explanations for why men often skipped out on contracts. Don Jorge, though he never deserted, gave it some more thought and identified the fear of not being able to recontract was sufficient justification to fulfill the terms of the contract.

> I was never in the factories. Since I was from the field, I felt good there. It was my area. . . . And I felt, well . . . I'm going to say that during the time that I came contracted, if I heard that *Fulano* didn't appear, that they left, that they deserted, like what a soldier leaves, he deserts, . . . They deserted because they had family and they went with their families to other states. Since they were already here, taking advantage of the fact that they were already here, they deserted the contract. Because it is deserting because they are contracted and have to complete the contract. Some didn't complete it, and we told them that they should not desert or break the contract, because if they broke the contract, there would not be more contract. When someone deserts, it's reported, and when a person wants to come, they can't any more. So this card they gave it to me after, and when I entered they didn't deviate to me, they gave it to me later. I don't know why they should have a record of people. I don't know if they gave it to everyone (Life Story of Don Jorge 1997).

Knowing he needed future access to the Bracero Program, Don Jorge endured a range of working and living conditions to receive his Bracero identification card and solidify his spot on future eligibility lists.

If Braceros had complaints to register and sought to keep all other parties who signed the contract responsible (growers, grower associations, U.S. and Mexican state representatives) for holding up their ends of the contract, they found a cumbersome compliance process that was often completely out of their reach.

> To expect the Mexican contract worker to locate one of the nine United States Employment Service inspectors or to relay his complaint to them through the State employment service is to expect much more than is within his capability. Consequently, if he can get in touch with the Mexican consulate, that is about the best he can do. This cumbersome and complicated procedure, involving several government agencies in general and none in particular, encourages desertion in the place of making a complaint because every complaint has the

> potentiality of being lost or ignored (U.S. President's Commission on Migratory Workers 1951, 45).

It was very difficult for Braceros to lodge any complaint to the authorities because the channels of communication were rarely established. If Braceros wanted to complain about their housing conditions in Colorado, they had to locate either of the two state housing inspectors who were responsible for investigating complaints in the entire rural Colorado area. Complaints were rarely registered so the concern of "lost or ignored" complaints became increasingly irrelevant. Worse yet, complaints also had the consequence of losing one's job, being deported to Mexico, and placed on a list of "undesirables" that made the acquisition of future contracts impossible.

The main means of resistance was to exercise the exit option (referred to in the government documents and academic literature as "deserters" or "skips").

> In one region in which we have information, desertions from contract were 20.8 percent in 1948 and 20.2 percent in 1949. Of the Mexican nationals under contract in the United States on August 31, 1950, one-third were in illegal status, primarily by deserting their contracts. Desertions from individual contracting employers range from as low as 4 percent to as high as 50 percent. Moreover, it is noted that there is a tendency for those employers having a high desertion rate in one year also to have a high desertion rate the next. We interpret this to mean that desertions from contract vary with individual management and working conditions. Where these are good, the desertions are low (U.S. President's Commission 1951, 46).

In addition to those Braceros who exited before their contracts ended, there was also the more significant (but uncounted) number of Braceros that refused to go back to the United States as contract workers after their contracts expired and they were returned to Mexico. None of the Braceros interviewed for this study stated that they had deserted on a contract. More often they stated that when times were bad, "they endured." For example, Don Antoñio (1997) noted the options: "Yes, on that contract. The people arrived . . . the day when it was over, many deserted. Many left. Others hung on."

Yet, the high rates of desertion during the Bracero Program demonstrate that when work stoppages or strikes were not feasible options to protest abhorrent working and living conditions, individual Braceros exercised the only form of resistance available to them—exit. A partial list of reasons why Braceros would exercise their exit option would be low wages, bad food, excessive deductions, too little work, too much work, poor housing, domineering supervisors, and on-the-job injuries. The reasons abound for why Braceros would skip on their contract but the desertion phenomenon speaks directly to the limited options available to workers who wanted to resist the working conditions or officially register complaints (U.S. President's Commission 1951).

By making a public example out of suppressing individual malcontents, the growers successfully deterred others from expressing their dissatisfaction. For those few Braceros fortunate enough to remain working after making a complaint, Galarza (3:1) notes of their subsequent treatment: "Forms of punishment used by contractors on recalcitrant men who ask for improvements: deprivation of work for one or more days; scheduling the same crew to leave camp last in the morning; keeping men waiting entire day for their pay." Elsewhere in Galarza's field notes, he states what happened to three active resisters. One "[s]poke up for group and got ten days in jail," another died in fall from truck, and the third was deported (18:1).

The main way that most "agitators" were dealt with was deportation. When acts of resistance were made public in the attempt to convince others to strike or participate in work stoppages, they were dealt with by a swift and immediate return trip to the recruitment center in Mexico.

> Señor Palmas: Any infraction by any one of those individuals would constitute immediate deportation in terms of conduct, insubordination, or this type of thing. They weren't mistreated or anything, they simply . . . you're gone. You violated the terms of the contract . . . and you were gone. It was as simple as that. At some point there was guys that were kind of chow-hall lawyers type of people, you know what I mean? and I got to see plenty of this. These guys says "You know these conditions aren't going to work," he says, "this, this and this." And I see him standing on the table . . . if you want to call it inciting these guys to go on strike and call for better conditions. Well this guy would be immediately deported simply because he was upsetting the balance of the whole operation. Now how much there was in fact a reason for him to do that I don't know. Maybe the conditions that they lived under and this, that, and the other would come to bear on this particular guy's mind and he'd start pointing it out to all these individuals who were his comrades. He says you know, "we can demand better conditions than this" and most of those guys would sit there and listen then just walk off. Of course there are always those people that would follow anything that pops up. But anybody like that would immediately be deported and that's the end of that. His contract, in other words, would be ended.
>
> Int: Did this happen a lot?
>
> Señor Palmas: There's only two camps that I saw this actually happen. Now I heard about it in other camps. . . . Normally they were guys with a little bit of educational background, a little bit well maybe a little bit more ambitious than the run of the mill Bracero who was up here, who was up here simply to fulfill a contract to make enough money to maybe carry over the rest of the year in Mexico, and that's the end of that.

Whether the method of deterrence was deportation, worsened working conditions, jail time, or even death, it was almost irrelevant that the one *individual* agitator was punished. What really mattered was the symbolic value of what happened to those who rocked the boat or voiced demands to improve conditions. Quite simply, if Braceros wanted to continue working under contract, they met the expectations of remaining silent, even if they had complaints. Braceros were expected to endure the conditions, not of their own making, to which they were subjected.

In an exchange between Don Francisco and Don Jorge, the focus on strawberry harvesting in the Salinas Valley of California shed considerable light on the exceptionally good treatment by Japanese-American farmers they were accorded as opposed to how so many of their other contracts operated.

> Don Francisco: And they treated us really well. I don't have to talk badly about them. They gave us good food. Good sleep. Good beds and everything. The bosses and the overseers were good. They didn't scold us. As long as we didn't make trouble, nothing. Right? They didn't fire anyone. Your actions were what fired you.
>
> Don Jorge: I arrived to see many who stayed behind. And in everything they said, even if it was in front of you, "Go back." But that was all the time. All the time they were taking us out. The people stayed not for days, but for . . .
>
> Don Francisco: Yes, but it's that they didn't have the spirit. And later the checks came as we were owed. They came and distributed the checks. And those who worked they told us what we were due. The check matched. But that was when they renewed the contract. But they treated us well. I was pleased.

Though the men were quite reticent to talk about anything other than the best of experiences, it is clear that they were comparing the best of times with what could clearly be identified as the worst of times: bad food, uncomfortable beds, scoldings, paychecks that did not match either hours worked or contract-specified wage rates, squashing resistance, and firings were the order of the day. The reason attributed to this good treatment was the absence of troublemakers, not necessarily the Japanese-American farmers, and it is only Don Jorge's questioning of the "troublemakers" justification that identifies the Bracero era as fully replete with the "go back" message.

By squelching resistance, growers were able to control their labor force in the fields, at the labor camps, and in the local communities. The primary means of resisting deplorable living conditions was to exit the situation. The Bracero Program was designed with the interests of large-scale agribusiness in mind and as a result, the batch-handling of contracted labor was well suited to meet the needs of grower associations. Mass recruitment, short-term work contracts, recontracting options, institutional preparation of food, barrack-style housing, and the batch handling of transportation all fit well with how agribusiness conducted its operations.

CONCLUSION

The Bracero Program controlled the lived experiences of the Mexican laborers who toiled in the fields and lived out their daily lives in the labor camps of U.S. growers. From the point of contact with the Bracero Program at the reception centers in Mexico, the men quickly lost their individual identities and assumed the characteristics of the group of would-be Braceros. If they stood out (either in style of dress, mannerisms, or demeanor), their chances of being contracted were negligible. As Galarza (3:1) characterized the selection of candidates in the Hermosillo recruitment center: "Nationals learned to dress strictly ranchero. . . . They will turn you off the line right off if they see you wearing a bit of American clothing." The identities of the contracted were prescribed by a selection process that placed a premium on rural, acquiescent, agriculturally experienced, and unattached men. If one stood out from this crowd, he would most likely not receive the contract.

The other manner in which prior identities were dislodged included the batch-handling of Braceros from the point of contact at the Mexican government's recruitment centers to their return to Mexico following the fulfillment of the work contract. Batch-handling was designed to meet the labor needs of large-scale agribusiness. The costs associated with maintaining the labor force were shared through the grower associations and food processing companies. The needs of small growers were not met by the guidelines set forth by the Bracero Program because it was not designed with their interests in mind.

Accompanying the batch-handling was the resultant social isolation that the workers experienced. Braceros were kept separate from the local U.S. communities, non-Bracero workers in the fields, and even from the Mexican-American population. The linguistic isolation that Braceros suffered from their Mexican-American counterparts was symbolic of their larger isolation from U.S. society as a whole. The only contact that most Braceros had with local communities was the "Sunday-on-the-town" trips that brought the workers in contact with local merchants. But, by and large, the Braceros kept to themselves because they were expected to do so. The Sunday trips represented the only time that was not managed by growers or their intermediaries. Even though this freedom was confined to a prescribed set of acceptable practices, it was nonetheless one of the few activities that went relatively unsupervised. Of course, if the Bracero displayed conduct that challenged the prescribed role of the complacent worker/consumer, the punishment would be swift and harsh—often in the form of deportation. The role expectations that Braceros were subjected to, during both work and leisure time, impaired counterhegemonic responses to domination.

The migration and contracting processes began the process whereby the citizens of Mexico lost control of their individual fates. The "choice" to migrate was structured by the economic necessity that impelled those in poverty to separate families and leave their homeland for the vague promise of better wages. The recruitment centers in Mexico were designed to assemble a qualified labor force of experienced, male workers. But it was the manner in which would-be Braceros were handled *en masse* that eventually defined their lives as Mexican contract workers. The processing centers, ran by the U.S. government, continued this mass handling by conducting dehumanizing medical examinations and delousing in groups. The standard work contract, signed by the Bracero, grower, and U.S. and Mexico government representatives, provided the written codification of the common culture. The like-situated nature of the Braceros' existence was continued in how workers were treated in the United States. The mass transportation, housing, and boarding of Braceros were simply extensions of the batch-handling and social isolation of Mexican contract workers. Any hopes of resisting intolerable housing situations, inadequate safety measures in transportation, or rancid food was quelled by the threat of deportation. Rather than openly challenging mistreatment, the Braceros developed a particular communicative competence in answering those perceived as authority figures in a deferential, strictly positive manner. As the postal worker in San Luis Valley of Colorado explained the way Braceros acted in public:

> The sad commentary there is that the majority of them, they were suspicious, mistrusting, and I think that was an inherent thing that they had always been put upon. They were not really made welcome into these areas. So they were always real cautious. They didn't want to make any waves. They tried to stay out of the way . . . because they were afraid they might be sent home. It would be contrary for why they were here in the first place (Interview with Señor Freemont 1997).

NOTES

1. To this day, living conditions in the rural areas of Mexico are still clinging at subsistence levels. "[B]y 1980 the gap had more than doubled, and the rich enjoyed incomes fifty times greater than those of the poorest sector of the population" (Hellman 1994, 2). A decade later, "[i]n Mexico, the twenty-four wealthiest families have more money than the twenty-four million poorest Mexicans (Lipsitz 2001, 9).

2. Currently, remittances are the second largest source of foreign dollars (after oil revenues and before tourism) to the Mexican economy.

3. The use of DDT, a pesticide banned for use in the United States since the 1970's due to its carcinogenic effect, as documented by the Colorado State Agricultural Bulletin is a credible source of evidence of the "supposed" delousing practice. The article exhibits an explicit Great Western Sugar Company/grower bias so the identification of the delousing chemical comes

from a source that was not promoting a pro-labor agenda. According to the article, the advantages of using Bracero labor are the following: "(1) workers could be moved easily to the beet area at the time they were needed and in number which were needed, (2) workers could be shifted from farm to farm and from area to area as needed, (3) as all people handled were [unattached male] workers, there were no problems of moving and housing women and children, and (4) workers were moved out of the area as soon as the work was done" (Colorado Agricultural Experiment Station 1958, 60–61). During that time, DDT was an extremely popular pesticide and used extensively.

4. There are no U.S. government documents (except an Oregon State College internal report that will be discussed later in this chapter) that document Braceros used in any industry other than railroad construction and agricultural work. It is likely that the person interviewed for the story was contracted to work in railroad construction but used for janitorial purposes.

5. The statistics on deaths and injuries sustained by Braceros in vehicle accidents are difficult to ascertain. Galarza (1977, 86–87) notes: "The number of accidents of this kind [involving farm laborers] have been reduced steadily from 140 in 1952 to 50 in 1962. But the fatal number of injuries was 13 in the former and 13 in the latter of those years. . . . In those eleven years, 1953 claimed the record of men killed—28—and 1958 was second with 18. In the month of September 1963, both records were broken with 34 dead, all braceros."

Chapter Five

Conclusion

The Politics of Reparations and the Contemporary Bracero Redress Movement

In 1997, I sat in on a citizenship class that was preparing for the U.S. naturalization examination, and as the conversation shifted to the Bracero Program, I listened to which aspects of the Bracero Program resonated in the minds of the Mexican nationals in attendance.[1] There are a number of possible sources that inform this historical memory: the mass media, education, and oral traditions to name a few. Sanchez (1993, 27) notes that during the time of the Bracero Program, many of the towns in Mexico that comprised the major sending areas of migrants to the United States were "largely dependent on word-of-mouth communication."

From the class discussion, I was offered a glimpse into the Mexicano historical memory of the Bracero Program.[2] The Bracero Program has a particular salience in the historical memory of the Mexican citizens of the major sending areas of agricultural labor to the United States (Massey et al. 1987, Massey and Liang 1989). In many of these small communities located in rural Mexico, if individuals did not have immediate relatives who came to the United States under Bracero contract, they certainly knew people who did (see Appendix V for statistics on Mexican sending states). One former Bracero was also in this class of ten students who were learning how to pass the U.S. citizenship interview. All of the students were legal immigrants (resident aliens in the INS vernacular) but with the late-1990s changes in U.S. immigration and welfare law, their benefits and some of the group's right to stay in the United States were increasingly in doubt. Even though this group was adopting the label of "U.S. naturalized citizen," their social network ties and hearts were rooted squarely in Mexico. Most traveled back and forth from Fresno to their Mexican hometowns, all had family in Mexico, and all spoke Spanish almost exclusively.

The stories told by the class members about the Bracero Program were ones of horror, degradation, and humiliation. The stories were about the medical examinations at processing centers, consistent short-changing of workers' wages, deplorable housing conditions, inedible food, and the poor treatment of Mexican citizens in the United States. As one of the older gentlemen in the class gestured, in regards to the medical exam, the men were whistled at to spread their legs and the medic would thrust his hand into the men's anuses. When asked if he knew anyone who was treated in this exact manner, the man answered no but the familiar laughs he received from the class told me that stories about the medical examination abounded and that Mexican citizens were well aware of the large-batch exams for tuberculosis, hernias, sexually transmitted diseases, and other infectious diseases. In addition, they were knowledgeable about the practice of spraying chemicals on all contractees to purportedly de-louse them.

The wages paid to Braceros were also a major source of horror stories told by class members. Men not getting paid, outrageous deductions for housing and food when they slept in tents and bought and made their own food, and ever-shifting wage rates that in the end always favored the grower comprised the content of the economic-based stories shared by the naturalization class. Housing for the Braceros was told to have consisted of standard army-style barracks in addition to tents, chicken coops, barns, and stockyards. According to the class, the quality of food ranged from spoiled to varieties completely foreign to Mexican tastes such as bologna or peanut butter and jelly sandwiches for dinner. A sister of a former Bracero was told by her brother that he was fed chicken, every edible part of a chicken, for the entire duration of the contract. Three meals a day of chicken, for a forty-five day contract, would mean 135 consecutive servings of chicken.

The stories of how Braceros were treated by U.S. citizens took on the variety of a "no one could prove it but everybody had heard about it" tale. Braceros were rumored to have been killed off (by whom, it was never specified) to collect on the non-occupational health insurance. Those subject to this practice were said to have been the agitators or those who openly complained about their treatment in the labor camp. A similar story was told by one Bracero I interviewed. "There was a man, he was protesting and complaining about the food. The next day he was gone, nobody told us what happened to him and we didn't ask. Later we heard that they killed him" (Life Story of Don Liberio 1997). No evidence was found during my research that would confirm this popular story, though workplace fatalities were all too common. Don Crecencio's (2005) experience in the lemon fields corroborated the deadly aspects of agricultural work. This myth seemed to be constructed more as a method of deterrence (to keep Braceros in line and provide an example of what would happen to those who openly resisted the existing social conditions) than as necessarily an accurate representation of actual events.

The Mexican historical memory about the Bracero Program, which informs the naturalization class's impromptu conversation, is just one of the numerous components that together form a community identity and common base of reference. Regardless of whether or not the memories are in fact true representations of past events, the fact that these memories are shared throughout the Mexican community is important in and of itself. What makes this particular case so interesting is that the historical memory shared by these Mexican immigrants, who were not Braceros, aligns very closely with the documented, secondary accounts made by scholars such as Herrera-Sobek (1979), Galarza (1964, 1956) and Gamboa (1990) and the recent interviews conducted in the Bracero redress movement era. Barring the discussion that ensued about killing Braceros for financial gain, the issues raised about the U.S. processing centers' medical examinations, poor wages, and harsh living conditions are all prominent themes in the academic literature documenting the Bracero Program. Equally interesting is the dissonance between the Fresno Braceros' retelling of their life stories and the historical memory of the naturalization class. Many of the details are corroborated by Fresno Bracero accounts and Mexican immigrant accounts, but the imposed definitions from above, which influenced the perceptions of the Braceros to talk about the program in favorable terms or personal luck, did not impact those immigrants who were not directly involved in the program. The space opened by the social movement for recouping lost savings has had an important consequence of putting the Braceros in conversation with one another and enabling the men to see the social origins of their previously private concerns.

The savings debacle has served as the touchstone for varied attempts at redress. During the summer of 2002, my research was submitted as expert testimony on behalf of Braceros in a class action lawsuit associated with the Bracero savings program.[3] The 10 percent deducted from workers' paychecks is, from my research, only the tip of the iceberg as it relates to how Braceros were exploited and systematically cheated out of wages and benefits. Illegal deductions for farm implements/supplies such as carrot ties, blankets, room, excessive board, and transportation charges were all commonly documented practices. The affidavit filed from my research was on behalf of a claim of peonage/indentured servitude.

1. As a result of my research I have determined that the braceros were subjected to substantial physical and legal coercion from the time they entered the program in Mexico through the contract periods in the

United States. My findings substantiating this coercion have been published in my dissertation and other writings.

2. Further, as a result of my research, I have determined that braceros were subjected to exploitive work conditions: compelled to work excessive hours for little or no pay; compelled to work under abusive labor conditions; compelled to live isolated from the surrounding communities; subjected to numerous instances of wages withheld without explanation, or withheld for "transportation fees" and "bonuses" with the intention of compelling the bracero to stay through a contract period no matter how abusive the conditions were.
3. In addition, my research shows that the bracero was forced into debt because excessive charges were deducted from wages without explanation or recourse. The bracero did not have access to a grievance process and if the bracero did complain about exploitive conditions, he was threatened, and was sometimes, deported. Furthermore, the bracero was compelled to sign a waiver of liability prior to leaving the United States (Mize Affidavit, Filed 2002).

Critical race theorist and legal scholar Eric Yamamoto not only participated in the legal action that led to reparations for those Japanese Americans interned during World War II, he also provided a scholarly blueprint for how other attempts at redress can learn from the successful example of the internment redress program. He (2000) cites three main nodes where pressure should be applied.

> [1.] There was a congressional commission very similar to that proposed by Rep. Conyers. It gave people an opportunity to tell their stories to the public in a very powerful, concentrated way. It provided for foundational research.
> [2.] There was also extensive legislative lobbying which was multiracial. . . .
> [3.] And third, there were legal efforts. And I was a member of the legal team re-opening the Japanese-American internment cases from World War II based on newly discovered evidence showing there was no evidence of necessity for the internment. I was a member of that team and saw the power of the three-pronged approach.

As crucial as commissions, lobbying, and lawsuits are, Yamamoto inadvertently leaves out an equally important form of pressure in the application of grassroots mobilization on the part of aggrieved communities.[4] Without the pressure from below, it seems highly unlikely that the lobbying, commissions, and lawsuits would survive on their own. When discussing the Bracero litigation claims, I will return to this issue in detail. In this concluding chapter, I will discuss the litigation approach by identifying two cases on the peonage claim (*Jimenez de la Torre v. U.S. Federal Government, Republic of Mexico, Wells Fargo Bank, Banco de Mexico, Banco de Credito Rural*) and the Bracero savings debacle (*Senorino Cruz v. U.S. et al.*), the efforts of Illinois Representative Luis Gutierrez in introducing The Bracero Justice Act, the limited lobbying efforts of Latino serving organizations, and the burgeoning grassroots redress movement in Mexico and partially the United States to hold the Mexican government culpable for past wrongs. Finally, I will discuss the other actors who share culpability for past wrongs and discuss the dangers in calls to repeat history by instituting a new Bracero Program.

A series of class action lawsuits, filed in U.S. courts, were important steps in the recognition of culpability for the past wrongs associated with the Bracero Program.[5] Most of the paltry media coverage centered on the Bracero mandatory savings program.[6] As the rule was explained in a 1946 Mexican government document (*Secretaria* 88): "In conforming with the established international rules and contracts, of the amount paid to the Mexican Braceros of their salary ten percent was deposited into a savings fund [in Mexican National Banks] for each worker." This money would not be returned to the Bracero until he fulfilled the conditions of his contract and had returned to Mexico. What many Braceros found upon returning was that their money was not available at *Banco Nacional de Credito Agricola, Banco de Mexico* (where the Braceros' funds were transferred from Wells Fargo Bank), or the other Mexican federal banks designated as holders of the Braceros' mandatory savings deductions.

The majority of the U.S. movement on behalf of Braceros has been in the courts. The recent consolidation of cases and their dismissal certainly bring us directly back to the insights of critical race theorist Mari Matsuda and the reparations challenges to liberal law standards. One of the pioneering critiques of critical legal studies that helped launch the critical race theory movement, Mari Matsuda's (1995) "Looking to the Bottom: Critical Legal Studies and Reparations" identifies three standard liberal challenges to legal challenges made by oppressed groups. The identification of victims and perpetrators, in reparations claims, is based on horizontal, intragroup and vertical, hierarchical connections rather than simple individual plaintiff–defendant (direct perpetrator) cases. The relationship between the present claim and past acts belies the proximate cause and statute of limitations arguments that are often invoked in the attempt to right past wrongs. Finally, measures of relief for loss of "sovereignty, dignity, personhood, and liberty are incapable of uniform valuation" (72). The savings program suits are interesting and warrant attention, but a neglected set of allegations in *de la Torre v. U.S. et al.* relate to peonage and indentured servitude. The research gathered for this book amply documents that Braceros were required to work beyond their contracted work period, workers were consistently subjected to physical and legal coercion as a precondition for work, the terms of the individual work contract were broken by almost every grower, enforcement of living and working conditions was nonexistent, the grievance procedure was cumbersome if not impossible, and work was marked by complete social isolation. A total of thirty-one counts were filed in the peonage suit, yet the district judge only discussed peonage in terms of those parties not accountable (in particular Wells Fargo Bank). On August 23, 2002, the ruling by U.S. District Judge Charles Breyer stated:

> The Court does not doubt that many braceros never received Savings Fund withholdings to which they were entitled. The Court is sympathetic to the braceros situation. However, just as a court's power to correct injustice is derived from the law, a court's power is circumscribed by the law as well. The plaintiffs are not entitled to any relief from the Mexican Defendants or Wells Fargo in a United States court of law. As currently pled, plaintiffs are not entitled to relief from the United States because their claims are time-barred. The motions to dismiss of the Mexican Defendants and Wells Fargo are hereby GRANTED. The United States' motion to dismiss is hereby GRANTED without leave to amend with respect to the claim for breach of fiduciary; the motion is GRANTED with leave to amend with regard to all other claims.

Matsuda notes that reparations claims do not require all plaintiffs to be similarly situated due to the historical aspect of past wrongs. In his oral explanation of the ruling, Judge Breyer dismissed claim on technicalities claiming before co-counsel and the defendants that it would be difficult, if not impossible to prove that the claimants had similar experiences to constitute a class. The application of statutes of limitations refers to the other major liberal challenge to reparations claims. The defense lawyer for the U.S. government stated upon arrival at the hearing how disappointed he was to be called in on events that happened fifty years ago.[7] As Breyer states in his ruling:

> In fact, the complaint indicates just the opposite. The complaint alleges that plaintiffs did not know "the amount of money deducted from their wages." This language implies that plaintiffs did, in fact, know that some money was being deducted, just not how much. The other complaints also fail to allege that the braceros were ignorant of the fact that a portion of their wages was being withheld. In short, the complaints allege that the braceros knew that a portion of their wages was being withheld. Plaintiffs knew that money was withheld and that it was never refunded. That is, the braceros knew the facts underlying their injury and its cause. See Alvarez-Machain, 107 F.3d at 700. This knowledge is all that is required for the statue of limitations to begin to run. Given this knowledge, it is of no consequence that plaintiffs may not have fully understood their legal rights or the available legal remedies, even if such ignorance was the result of unsophistication or illiteracy. See Barrow v. New Orleans Steamship Ass'n, 932 F.2d 473, 478 (5th Cir. 1991).

Simply stated, if the plaintiffs knew they were being cheated out of wages, then the statute of limitations would bar the plaintiffs from seeking redress. Most of my research, not on the savings program, makes it quite clear that Braceros were unaware of what was being deducted from their paychecks (particularly when paystubs were in English and the Spanish-speaking Bracero may not have even been able to read in their native language). No Bracero could recollect in any detail how much they were charged for mandatory deductions, nor could they specify what those deductions were. Breaches of contract were so numerous (from being required to stay beyond contracted period, underpaying workers, overcharging for items such as food and blankets, charging for non-chargeable items such as housing and transportation) that it seems apparent that the peonage claim should have been duly considered above and beyond the savings deduction debacle. Judge Breyer felt the need to dismiss most claims of peonage against all parties but it is important to remember that no grower, association, or food processor was named in the list of defendants. This might not be the most prudent course of legal action, but on the other hand it might serve to embarrass corporations to the point of providing forms of restitution to meet the needs of Mexican immigrants.

To recoup losses suffered by Braceros during the Program, the struggle for redress in the United States is still in its incipient stages as the statute of limitations may be lifted by an act of Congress. In 2000, one bill was initially introduced by Illinois Representative Luis Gutierrez. Yet recognition of the bill, let alone broad based support, has been elusive to this point. The Bracero Justice Act of 2002 (H.R. 4918), introduced by Rep. Luis Gutierrez (D-IL), is to date the only Congressional acknowledgment of the role that the United States played in the savings program debacle. The bill, which withered in committee, sought to extend the statutes of limitations and waive U.S. sovereign immunity claims. Representative Gutierrez is particularly interesting as he is a driving force in the Congressional Hispanic Caucus (CHC) and is of Puerto Rican ancestry, yet represents the heavily Mexican immigrant and Puerto Rican 4th District of the Chicago metro area.

Given the political climate on immigration issues, the Congressional Latino representatives who were pushing the Bracero cause have backtracked, and the most recent legislation by Jim Costa (D-CA), House Resolution 696, is entitled "Expressing gratitude for the foreign guest laborers, known as Braceros, who worked in the United States during the period from 1942 to 1964." Supported by Representative Gutierrez and other CHC members, the Act would simply say "thanks" for a job well done without recognizing the humiliating treatment accorded to our "guests."

1. Expresses gratitude for the foreign guest laborers, known as Braceros, who worked in the United States during the period from 1942 to 1964; and

2. Recognized the Braceros for their contributions to the war effort during World War II, and for their hard work, which helped to keep the United States strong and prosperous during this challenging period.

If this issue is going to be thrust onto the public stage, there is no question that it needs broader multiracial support and further reach in terms of not only "giving thanks" and recognizing the savings claim but also clearing the obstacles for allowing peonage, unjust enrichment, and breach of contract suits to move forward. The words of the former Braceros more than attests to the fact that the 10 percent savings program was just the tip of the iceberg in the ways that their rights were consistently violated and how they were cheated out of wages and subject to illegal deductions. At this point the biggest barriers are silence and historical amnesia. Placing the claims of former Braceros into public forums might break the silence in the United States.

Yet, the relative lack of consistent lobbying efforts certainly makes the Braceros reparations case much less tenable. The major Latino serving organizations have been duly silent in their support for Bracero claims. The largest U.S. organization representing Latinos, the National Council of La Raza (NLCR), has offered letters in support of local Bracero justice campaigns but a full brief and a commitment to the issue is to date still lacking. Other organizations, such as the League of United Latin American Citizens (LULAC), can certainly do much more to rectify its historical neglect of Mexican immigration issues and improve its service and credibility to more than Hispanic middle and upper class by lobbying on behalf of Bracero claims. The Congressional Hispanic Caucus needs the support from Latino lobbying organizations as well as coalitional support from civil rights and immigrant rights organizations. This would help to focus the issue on larger human rights concerns.

At this point, the U.S. immigrant serving organizations have been looking to Mexico for relief rather than efforts focused on the United States. *Union Sin Fronteras*, headed by Coachella Valley labor organizer Ventura Gutierrez, has been a driving force behind one of the largest grassroots mobilization of ex-Braceros in Mexico's border cities. The efforts of *Libreria Del Pueblo*, a nonprofit immigrant-assistance organization in San Bernardino, have focused to date on the Mexican consulates and a letter-writing campaign pressuring the Mexican government to reopen the verification lists of ex-Braceros for monetary redress. The Latino-serving organizations in the United States must understand that the contemporary immigration debate is built on the shoulders of former Braceros' plight and a project of historical memory recovery is essential to recasting the immigration debate as fundamentally a human rights issue.

Unquestionably, the grassroots mobilization by former Braceros themselves represents the most important impetus for igniting this issue into the public consciousness of not only Mexico but also the United States. It is only by comparing the recent life stories collected by respondents participating in the Bracero justice movement that we see how it is possible to dislodge prior role expectations and in solidarity, learn new ways of viewing the past. A sense of the Mexican and U.S. government's absconded role in enforcement, the brutally oppressive racial and class struggles that shaped their experiences in the United States, and the ways in which growers mistreated Braceros are now being discussed and shared in this, the twilight chapter of the Bracero Program. Former braceros met weekly in Hermosillo, Tijuana, Cuidad Juarez, Mexico City, and Zacatelco (Tlaxcala) to name a few locales, and publicly discussed how they were cheated out of wages by schemes such as the mandatory savings program. They are beginning to place blame where it squarely belongs: on the actors who made the decisions from above to construct the Bracero Program in a way that systematically denied the rights and dignities of contracted workers. *Alianza Braceroproa*, National Assembly of Ex-Braceros/*La Asamblea Nacional de Ex-Braceros*, and the Binational Union of Former Braceros are the more prominently recognized of the social movement organizations placing pressure on the Mexican government for monetary redress. In the process of organizing for restitution, they are beginning to share their experiences of the most repressed and humiliating aspects of the medical examinations, how growers and their intermediaries treated them, and the deleterious health effects of stoop labor. The Braceros I interviewed in 1997 did not have the same access to these shared, collective conversations, so if this book continues the conversation and opens the parameters of discussion, the last twenty years of my life were worth every difficult tribulation.

At the turn of the century, Braceros mobilized in California's Coachella Valley with the assistance of labor organizer Ventura Gutierrez. In Mexico, a march on the capital of Mexico City first brought the savings program issue to the Mexican public (who are much more cognizant as a whole of the abuse that Braceros endured from 1942 to 1964). A more recent pilgrimage to the border, like the former march to the original soccer stadium where Braceros were processed during WWII, followed the earlier tracks north to the border recruitment centers. Though the number of protestors at the time was small, a critical mass is crucial to the success of social movements in not only organizing communities but also shedding a public eye by requiring increased media attention on this historical wrong. "For instance, on April 7, 2003 more than 400 members of the organization *Alianza Braceroproa* and their families blocked the entrance to the Congress and proceeded to the President's house to again insist that the government compensate for its negligence during the bracero program" (Driscoll de Alvarado 2003). Well covered in Mexico's *La Jornada*, the only U.S. media coverage of the Bracero redress movement has been isolated to individual newspaper stories and a brief national mention of the Mexico City soccer stadium march. There is no question that Braceros will persevere; my only hope is that they finally receive the redress they seek and their struggle will be recognized as part and parcel of the larger struggle for racial and economic equality in Mexico and the United States.

The main means of organizing is to get ex-Braceros together, on a weekly basis, to begin the conversation about their shared experiences. Most of the public conversations have centered on the humiliating aspects of the processing centers. Quite predictably, the recent interviews conducted have extensive public recollections about the STD and hernia examinations and the delousing ordeal. The most plausible explanation as to why those interviewed in 1997 only confirmed details but preferred to stay silent about the processing centers, and why each respondent in 2005 spoke at length about it, seems to be specifically tied to the redress movement and the space it has created to share some of the more unfavorable and humiliating aspects of the program. Regardless of whether a monetary settlement is extended to all aggrieved parties by the Mexican government, the main contribution of collective action to this point seems to be the shared recognition of past wrongs and ways of remembering, thinking, speaking, and acting that completely counter the role expectations of the Bracero Program.

In 2007, the Mexican national government agreed to a settlement where they would not reimburse for the 10 percent deducted, but would provide every ex-Bracero who could prove his contract status with a cash "assistance" payment of approximately US$3,700. Nearly 30,000 Braceros provided the necessary documentation to their local government office in Mexico and received monies in 2007. Approximately 400,000 surviving Braceros were left out of the process because they either did not have documentation in their possession or they lived in the United States and could not get to Mexico to file a claim. "But only 28 braceros in the United States—including nine in San Bernardino and Riverside counties—got paid, said Ramon Vera, coordinator of an alliance to help former braceros in the region. Vera works for *Libreria Del Pueblo*, a nonprofit immigrant- assistance organization in San Bernardino" (Wall 2008). Current grassroots efforts are aimed at reopening the application process and allowing former Braceros to file claims at Mexican consular offices in the United States.

This problem was partially addressed in late 2008 when Judge Breyer revisited his decision to dismiss the case on statute of limitation technicalities in light of the recent cash payout by the Mexican government. All claims had to be filed within a two-and-a-half-month window at a Mexican consular office. Breyer released the settlement terms on October 12 and gave those eligible between October 23, 2008, to January 5, 2009, to file for the approximate payout of US$3,500. The ruling only applied to those with Mexican citizenship and the only class action defendant who was implicated in the decision is the Mexican federal government. The requirement was all forms by Braceros or their immediate relatives (if deceased) be submitted in person to one of the forty-eight Mexican consular offices located in twenty-four states and the District of Columbia. For many potentially eligible claimants, the time restriction and paperwork requirements most likely barred them from recovering the funds. "On a daily basis we receive about 300 phone calls from ex-Braceros or their families who have asked which of the required papers are needed to reclaim lost monies and many of them cannot find their documents," indicated a paralegal in Chicago (see *La Gente*, 11/26/2008).[8] Yet, it is most relevant that no culpability or wrongdoing has ever been admitted in any of these legal decisions and the cash payout is simply in response to the demands for reparations, not reparations per se.

Part of the pressure on then-President Vicente Fox and the National Congress was placed when the Zapatistas officially recognized the redress campaign of ex-Braceros. The "Other Campaign" seeks to bring the various subordinated constituencies within Mexico and abroad into a shared struggle against the Mexican government and its policy of neoliberalism. By reaching out to striking teachers in Oaxaca, former Braceros of Tlaxcala seeking redress, maquiladora workers, flower growers protesting Walmart in Atenco, sex workers, university students, and indigenous tribes throughout Mexico, a broad-based network of "others" who seek democratic transformations in the global social order are beginning to cohere under the Zapatista umbrella of autonomous self-organization and popular education. The Zapatistas' philosophy of challenging neoliberalism wherever you are invites organizers to bring local struggles into relationship with the broader global justice movement, to build transnational networks for social change.

When one ex-Bracero was asked in 2005 why he participated in the weekly get-togethers and paid his dues to join a former Bracero organization, he talked about how he might spend the money he most likely received in 2007.

> Don Baldomero: Well I decided to sign-up for the very poverty. To see what there was there. In the hacienda you know that they did? We left the hacienda because we did not want to work one Sunday. There, there is no festive day, there is no Sunday. A person has to have even if it is one day of rest.
>
> Int: If they returned the money that was owed to you when you worked as a bracero what would you do with it?
>
> Don Baldomero: Well I would first of all fix my home. It is my desire to fix my home up. I have never been able to fulfill my property. That is what I want to fix up my home for the rest of the days that I live.

The Braceros' deplorable experiences will be best rectified if the movement moves beyond just the savings program and sheds light on all the ways in which the rights of Braceros were systematically denied. The redress movement seems to be most effective in creating a space for the Braceros to publicly reject the role expectations of the Bracero Program and collectively identify the shared past wrongs they were forced to endure. The historical memory of the Bracero Program is for the first time being publicly identified by redress members and leaders as exploitative of former Braceros primarily in terms of Mexican and U.S. state culpability, though Mexico is slightly more willing to accept culpability than U.S. actors. The mandatory savings debacle and the degrading treatment in the processing centers are the main sources of contention and memory reconstruction. As soon as these two issues are identified as part of a larger process of dehumanization, exploitation, and racial subjugation, it will only be then that the Bracero Program will be understood in all of its forms as a program designed to marginalize workers, by creating the conditions of powerlessness, to meet the labor needs of U.S. agribusiness.

Nevertheless, the former Braceros' willingness to talk openly about the most humiliating aspects of the processing centers points to the potential for social movements in countering the role expectations of subservient, fearful acquiescence that Goffman (1961) thought total institutions were so successful in entrenching. One of the lessons learned from viewing the Bracero total institution within its specific context is that relations are never as total as they seem. The amount of work required to deploy the cunning of authority in nearly every aspect of the Braceros' interactions with authority figures was most often countered by Braceros skipping or deserting the contract. Most recently, it has been effectively countered when Braceros reconvene at the grassroots level to share their individual stories and see how their individual life stories are part of a much larger collective experience that was shaped by power relations duly influenced by racial oppression and class exploitation.

The roots for successful redress claims have taken to Mexican soil much more fruitfully than U.S. soil precisely because the Bracero Program is in the national consciousness of Mexico whereas the roadblocks of invisibility and intentional collective amnesia in the United States persist. The inability to recognize Bracero claims in class action lawsuits, restorative justice bills that are ignored in Congress, and a less than vibrant Latino lobby are all failing to take hold in an ahistorical context of the contemporary immigration debate. The historical memory about the Bracero Program, located within the citizens of Mexico, has not been seriously considered in academic accounts of Mexico-U.S. relations. As mentioned in the discussion of "Harvest of Shame" in the "Introduction," the *U.S.* historical memory of the Bracero Program is largely absent because even during the program's existence, the majority of U.S. citizens did not know what was happening in the agricultural fields of the United States. Americans rarely consider who is picking the crops that are eventually found on their dinner tables.

The very act of transforming the words of former Braceros into text challenges conventional history and gives some visibility and voice to this group that has been largely ignored. The contributions of explicitly theorizing class and race in the formation of the particular experiences of these respondents offers important analytical tools for the study of Mexican migration to the United States. This study is particularly significant at a time when an implementation of a guest worker program in the United States is being currently debated on Capitol Hill as part of comprehensive immigration reform.

With the end of the U.S.-Mexico Bracero guest worker program in 1964, and current political appeals in Washington, DC, and high immigrant-receiving states for a new temporary worker program, one would think that the United States did not have temporary worker programs in place. But in reality since 1965, the U.S. government has continually provided a mechanism for, most often agriculture but other industries, access to employ temporary immigrant laborers. Three major programs (H-2A, SAW/RAW, and H1&2-B) have served as the major conduits for U.S. employers to employ predominately, but not exclusively, Mexican immigrant labor. The H-2A and H-2B temporary worker programs have become a common, though relatively unknown, feature of immigration law. Both visa classifications ensure growers and non-agricultural employers that should the labor demand arise, the U.S. government will again be in the service of capital in securing its labor force and subsidizing its most important input in the profit equation (labor). Finally, current proposals for a re-installment of a large-scale Bracero program will be addressed.

With passage of the Immigration and Nationality Act of 1965, one provision extended the Bracero Program with the development of an H-2 temporary visa program. The H-2 (after 1986, the H-2A) program served largely as the safety valve for large-scale agribusiness and its seemingly unending desire for cheap, pliable, temporary labor. The H-2 program was severely underutilized because the other less bureaucratic option, hiring undocumented immigrants, was never deemed illegal or worthy of sanction until the 1986 Immigration Reform and Control Act (IRCA), for the first time in the history of the nation, held employers responsible for knowingly employing undocumented labor.

Additionally, the H-2A program was reauthorized through IRCA, and was also expanded to include H-1B (specialty occupations) and H-2B (wage-shortage industries) temporary migrants as well. In the early 1990s, three major firms utilized the temporary agricultural worker program. Although the sugar cane industry in Florida had by and large mechanized, one company, U.S. Sugar, still required manual labor to harvest cane. U.S. Sugar received H-2A workers from the West Indies (whose plight has been eloquently captured in "H-2 Worker" by the Jamaican reggae artist Mutabaruka). Sheepherders in Montana and apple farmers affiliated with the New England Apple Council were the only other employers of H-2A workers. Employers complain due to the several requirements when employing H-2A workers. These requirements are that recruitment efforts in local labor markets must first be exhausted; and that wages must match the state's adverse effect wage rate (2015 rates ranged from $10.00 in Alabama, Georgia, and South Carolina to $11.61 in Illinois, Indiana, and Ohio, to $13.59 in Kansas, Nebraska, North Dakota, and South Dakota). In addition, they must provide workers with free housing, free transportation, meals provided at a preestablished state rate, free and reimbursed transportation, workers' compensation insurance, free tools and supplies, and three-fourths of the workdays guaranteed. Moreover, workers cannot be used to replace striking or locked-out domestic workers. Employers must also provide pay records and work contracts and pay an employer certification fee (maximum amount $1,000).

Based on U.S. Department of Labor data released in FY2014, the H-2A has ballooned to a 116,689 person program utilized by nearly 6,500 U.S. companies in all fifty states. Tobacco cultivators are increasingly relying on H-2A workers, which explains why 12 percent of all workers were contracted in North Carolina. Today the majority of H-2A workers are employed by the North Carolina Growers Association.

The vast majority of temporary workers come through the H-1B program, which included 946,293 positions certified in FY2014. The social scientist Rafael Alarcón refers to these specialized workers, primarily computer engineers, financial services, and scientists, as *cerebreros* (mental laborers) due to their recruitment for mental labor. A small, but significant, contingent of Mexican citizens have entered the United States on H-1B temporary visas, but the majority of recipients are from India, China, and Great Britain. In FY2014, the five largest employers of the H-1B *cerebreros* are Pricewaterhouse Coopers, Cognizant Technology Solutions Corporation, Deloitte Consulting, Wipro Limited, and Tata Consultancy Services.

The H-2B program is the category left for temporary entry as long as an employer demonstrates no native workers are willing to take the jobs at prevailing wage. Landscaping, hotel cleaning, forestry, and other seasonal occupations, which traditionally rely on undocumented Mexican labor, comprise the majority of the 93,649 positions certified. Department of Labor reports identify that in FY2014 the laborer/landscaper position accounted for 37 percent of all H-2B certified occupations.

Long, intractable political debates on immigration at the national level have called for an expansion of temporary worker programs. The debate is not about whether temporary worker programs will be a part of comprehensive immigration reform. Democrats tend to lobby for increasing the number of visas allocated through existing, orderly programs. Republicans tend to call for large-scale programs more akin to the Bracero Program with significantly less bureaucratic oversight. Temporary worker programs are certain to be an integral component of U.S. immigration policy well into the future.

Guest worker programs have been introduced by anti-immigrant politicians such as former Governor Pete Wilson (R-CA) in his "Amigo Program," his attorney general and former gubernatorial hopeful Dan Lundgren (R-CA), Senators Phil Gramm and Lamar Smith (R-TX), Senator Bob Smith (R-OR), Senator Bob Graham (D-FL), and most recently Senator Saxby Chambliss (R-GA), who have proposed temporary worker programs with predominately the interests of agribusiness in mind. Former President George W. Bush attempted to make immigration a very visible aspect of his political platform. When the administration leaked its interest in pursuing a legalization program for undocumented immigrants residing in the United States, the immediate negative reaction it received certainly put an end to that discussion. Most likely this was at the behest of the Mexican government with former President Vicente Fox and his desire to address Mexico's immigration dilemma by regularizing the migrant flow with either legalization and/or temporary guest worker arrangements. But in the 2004 State of the Union address, Bush stated:

> I propose a new temporary worker program to match willing foreign workers with willing employers when no Americans can be found to fill the job. This reform will be good for our economy because employers will find needed workers in an honest and orderly system. . . . I oppose amnesty. . . . My temporary worker program will preserve the citizenship path for those who respect the law, while bringing millions of hardworking men and women out of the shadows of American life.

What was left out of the political rhetoric was the Bush temporary worker plan seeks to bypass "the orderly" temporary programs already in place and put in its place a mass program with little administrative oversight and few employer obligations. The most egregious aspect of the original Bracero Program was a percentage of workers' wages was withheld and could only be claimed at Mexican national banks. When workers returned, they found their money was gone and this eventually spawned lawsuits in Mexico and the United States to recoup lost wages. The Bush plan proposed this exact same provision. In many ways, we have returned to the 1950s in our current thinking on guest workers and immigration law. With the current anti-immigrant diatribe espoused by Fox News, CNN's Lou Dobbs and Glenn Beck, and presidential candidate Donald Trump and other nativist politicians, the biggest fear is we are returning to 1954 and initial calls for mass repatriation are emanating from the far right. In 1997, Don Jorge was framing the basic question that is off the charts of the anti-immigrant mood in the United

States. He identified the hypocrisy of calls for mass temporary worker programs at a time when immigrants are so vilified.

> Don Jorge: The question I wanted to ask you is that I don't know why the government wants to bring people, wants to bring Braceros if the people are here. Here there are people with papers but without work. So what is the objective of bringing people contracted if here we are for that, to work, to help the country, to lift up the harvest and everything. That is what we are. We come to help you. They pay us, but here we are. We are slaves of work because we need work.

NOTES

1. This class was familiar with my research interests and I was originally in the class to locate former Braceros for possible inclusion in the study. The conversation among class members seemed to arise spontaneously from simply my presence in the room.

2. Historical memories elucidate the complex relationships between conflict and consensus, hegemonies and counterhegemonies, historical blocs and transformative social action, past and present, and the politics of remembering, forgetting, and silencing.

3. The documents submitted included: Mize (2000), Mize (2004). Court Affidavit Filed on Behalf of Plaintiff, (2002) *Jimenez de la Torre v. U.S. Federal Government, Republic of Mexico, Wells Fargo Bank, Banco de Mexico, Banco de Credito Rural*.

4. See Robert Sadamu Shimabukuro's (2003) *Born in Seattle* for a contemporary account of the grassroots mobilization of Japanese Americans in Seattle seeking redress. Shimabukuro's account of grassroots mobilization certainly informs the backdrop to Yamamoto's tripartite proxy, but I think grassroots mobilization must be fully recognized and theorized in terms of its central importance as the role of popular pressure in the form of social movements cannot be underestimated.

5. *Isidro Jimenez de la Torre v. United States, Attorney General, Secretary of Labor, Secretary of Treasury, Secretary of State, Immigration and Naturalization Service, Secretary of Defense, Secretary of Agriculture, Republic of Mexico, Ministry of Foreign Affairs, Wells Fargo Bank, Banco de Mexico, Banco de Credito Rural*. Two similar class action lawsuits (*Chavez, et al. v. United States of America, et al.* and *Barba, et al. v. United States of America, et al.*) were moved from Eastern District Courts with de la Torre and consolidated in March 2002 with *Senorino Cruz v. U.S. et al.* to be heard in Northern California District Court by Judge Charles R. Breyer.

6. See media accounts, that is, James Smith March 15, 2001. "Ex-Migrants Sought for Class-Action." *Los Angeles Times*: Los Angeles, CA. Sergio Bustos (2002) "Braceros Seeking Release of Funds." *Arizona Republic*: Phoenix, AZ. Deborah Kong. (September 4, 2002). "Former Mexican Guest Workers Call for Wells Fargo Boycott." *La Prensa*. Toledo, OH. http://www.laprensatoledo.com/PDF/2002-5/September%204,%202002.pdf.

7. All oral comments in district court are based on email communications with Patricia Ryan, Esq. Plaintiff Co-Counsel.

8. Nosotros a diario recibimos como 300 llamadas de ex braceros o sus familiares que nos preguntan cuáles son los requisitos para reclamar el dinero y muchos de ellos no encuentran los documentos," indicó el asistente de abogados de Chicago (*La Gente*, 11/26/2008, accessed July 10, 2015. http://www.radiolaprimerisima.com/noticias/inmigrantes/42393).

Appendix I

The Articulation of Race and Class in the Making of the Bracero Total Institution

The making of the Bracero total institution brought the forces of racial oppression and class exploitation together in the formation of a system of total control (or at least that was the attempt at the time as no control is ever total) that maximized worker efficiency to increase profits while maintaining racialized institutions and Anglo racial frames that legitimated inequalities by characterizing Mexican Braceros as inferior, yet uniquely suited for stoop labor. Racialized labor markets combined with a temporary worker program that maintained hierarchies across the U.S.-Mexico border. The construction of the Bracero Program as a males-only affair separated men from their families, while creating the ideal workforce according to agribusiness interests. In this appendix, I will discuss the undergirding theories of race and class that explained the specific moment of World War II and post-war era United States and how Mexican Braceros were subjected to Anglo racial frames that cast them as invisible workers.

A number of theories have arisen to account for the persistence of racialized logics and institutions in contemporary societies that are assumed to have moved beyond the race "myth" (Bonilla-Silva 2014, 2001, Cobas, Duany, and Feagin 2009, Feagin 2010, 2006, Fields 1991, Frankenberg 1995, Goldberg 1990, 1993, Lipsitz 2011, 2006, and Omi and Winant 2014, 1993). The major division is between those theories that accept the premise that race is a myth[1] and therefore non-existent and those who view race as not a biological but a social construction (see Omi and Winant 1993). Viewing race as socially constructed eschews ontological claims about the status of race categories as either fixed, static, or absolute. Rather, the basic premise is that which people perceive to be real is real in its consequences. Furthermore, that "reality" changes over time and place. Whether or not there is a scientific biological basis for making distinctions based upon race, when a group commits to a certain racial logic and has the power to impose their definition of the situation on subordinated groups, those logics can have very real effects on the lived experiences of those involved.

By defining class in terms of the practices of work and everyday life, my analysis shifts away from treating class as a static category, an entity all unto itself, or as an artifact of our theories that has no reference to social conditions outside the realm of the academic's limited discursive definitions. To define class in terms of work, I revise the Marxist literature on the capitalist labor process to deal with the specificities of capitalist agricultural labor practices. In addition, a more expansive view of class in terms of class cultures captures those elements of a group's lived experiences that encompass ways of living not necessarily reducible to the capital-labor relation. Utilizing this definition of class enables me to examine how processes that form class inequality can articulate with other forms of inequality. Specifically, the close articulation between race and class in the lived experiences of former Braceros developed a particular set of social relations that can best be described as a total institution. The point is to elaborate upon the relations that represent the range of raced and classed experiences as remembered by former Braceros and represented in the supplementary materials of the life histories.

CONCEPTUALIZING RACE AS RACISM

Drawing on relevant components of these previous theories, I seek to develop a theory of race specific to its relationship to racism. I contend that it is a disservice to divorce the race concept from the social conditions that construct races. Race is a product of racism. It is a category that belies the Black/White binary. Though race is historically variant, groups that face racism today in the United States have experienced racism for a better portion of the nation's existence. Discussions about the "new" racism or "new" nativism disregard the historical roots of racial oppression. When race is defined in terms of racism, identities are imposed from those who view themselves as superior. New terms must be employed in order to articulate the active resistance from those deemed inferior in the racialization process.

In complete agreement with the finding that there is a lack of clearly definable phenotypes that could define race as a set of universal categories, I contend that racist logics are stereotyped representations of groups (rooted in biology to be sure but also in cultural explanations). They represent a set of power relations where a dominant group imposes definitions on subordinate groups to construct and defend unequal lived experiences. When a group is essentialized to its set of perceived common racial characteristics, it is quite appropriate to talk about race in order to challenge that racism. Rendering racial groups invisible, by denying the use of the term "race," is not a particularly viable solution for the representations of Braceros, Chicanos, or any other group that experiences racism. It is from this theorization of race as racism that we can begin to understand how the concept of race is deployed in the lived experiences of Chicana/os generally and specifically Braceros.

A more expansive view of race and its social construction is offered by theorists who specifically work from the vantage point of non-White groups that do not align along the Black-White color line. Frankenberg (1995, 2) "views groups who are currently targets of racism—Native Americans, Latinos, African Americans, and Asian-Pacific Americans, as well as other nonwhite immigrants—as being racially different from white people, and from each other." It is not necessarily the characteristics of the racialized group that define race, but rather the perceptions by Anglos that define other racial groups.

Racism is embedded within specific histories that relate to specific subordinate groups. The historical process of the racialization of Chicanos differs considerably from African Americans in the United States and their experiences of slavery, Chinese and Japanese immigrants and their shared indentured servitude and the latter's internment during World War II, and the genocide of Native Americans. The history of racialization for Chicanos begins with the Spanish conquest of the native peoples of Mexico. The formation of the mestizo population and the northward expansion accompanying the mission movement tended to reinforce the *indio-hispano* "color" line. When the United States came to the northern frontier of Mexico starting in the early 1800s, those racial lines were irrelevant to Anglos who raced Mexicans, more or less, based on the labor needs of local regions of the U.S.-Spanish frontier (Montejano 1987).

Viewing race as racism predisposes one to view racial identities as imposed upon sub-groups. In fact, the construction of races is embedded in specific unequal relations that require a rationale for explaining why particular "communities" live, work, and even die in relative affluence. It is especially important in demonstrating how that relative affluence is at the expense of other groups who are subjected to dirty, dangerous, difficult, and undesirable jobs; expected to live in urban and rural ghettos; and at certain times in history murdered, buried in mass-unmarked graves, their corpses burned *en masse*, or not allowed to be buried in certain cemeteries. Living, working, and dying with dignity are markers of privilege, not basic unalienable rights, as evidenced by the history of racialization in the United States.

Resistance to racism by subordinate groups requires a new set of terms that transcends "race." We may talk of "strategic essentialism" or "reverse racism" to explain how solidarities or reactionary politics are formed to mount a resistance to the imposed definitions to which sub-groups are subjected. But rather than saying members of sub-groups do not think in racial terms, my contention is solely that the effect this has is qualitatively different than the effects of Anglo racial frames. Anglo racism is linked to a system of privileges. The benefits of the system are not equally shared by everyone marked by whiteness, but the system certainly furthers the enjoyment of privilege by a few.

The forms of racism, which each sub-group actively resists, differ at the *level* of discriminatory practices. As Omi and Winant (1994, 56) point out, race "is a matter of both social structure and cultural representation." In a separate essay (1993), they demarcate two dominant trends in "race" theorizing that view race as an ideology or race as an objective condition that they juxtapose to their racial formation thesis. Rather than saying the formation of racial groups (i.e., racism) is this or that, for Omi and Winant the reason why racism is so naturalized is that it works at multiple levels. Racism is a set of ideological beliefs; a way of thinking about the world in terms of superior and inferior groups that justifies unequal social conditions. Racism is also an institution that patterns racial segregation in housing, employment, health, and leisure activities. Racism is also a set of attitudes and actions that are deployed on the level of interpersonal relations and have very real effects on how people deal with one another. It is at all these levels that the term racism is appropriate to describe why racially defined minority groups are systematically excluded from the benefits of U.S. capitalist society.

CONCEPTUALIZING CLASS: FROM THE LABOR PROCESS TO CLASS CULTURES

The capitalist labor process literature has carried on a tradition of understanding factory production as the archetype for workplace relations (see Braverman 1974 and Burawoy 1985, 1979). Harry Braverman's (1974) classic *Labor and Monopoly Capital* can be viewed as almost singly responsible for resuscitating a Marxist analysis of the capitalist labor process. As Braverman notes in his introduction, nobody since Marx had seriously studied the labor process. Those interested in Marxian political economy tended to foreground the general theoretical concepts to the neglect of the historical details in Marx's writing. Braverman was interested in how the monopoly form of capitalism gave rise to the de-skilling of workers through the application of scientific management techniques that further alienated workers from the means of production (the Taylorization of the workplace). Alienation consisted of the separation of conception from execution, mental from material labor, and the product from control by those who produced it. Michael Burawoy's (1979) *Manufacturing Consent* sought to extend the analysis resurrected by Braverman but the central question for Burawoy was why factory laborers worked so hard in the process of conceding to their own exploitation, that is, how in fact is hegemony manufactured?

The few examples of analyzing the capitalist agricultural labor process (see Thomas 1985 and Wells 1996) utilize Burawoy's hegemonic model to examine agricultural labor in California, but each limit their respective analyses to the lettuce/tomato and strawberry industries. Thomas (1985) looks for similarity between contemporary agricultural and industrial sectors in the U.S. economy to challenge agrarian exceptionalism claims. By acknowledging agriculture's uniqueness as a form of production, one does not necessarily further growers' interests. The exceptionalism of post-war U.S. agrarian production is, in the end, what makes it so much like other particular forms of capitalist industrial production. Yet this comparison is incongruous due to the unique place of agriculture in the history of U.S. labor laws and the unique characteristics of agricultural production. The similarities of the post-War U.S. agricultural labor process are more in line with Marx's "despotic regime" of the country and time frame that gave birth to the capitalist industrial process than the late capitalist production processes of the contemporary U.S. economy. For me, an elucidation of the labor process in Marx's *Capital, Volume I* became most applicable to the U.S. capitalist agricultural labor process. Certain workplace arrangements begin to look similar across industries, times, and places, as there is still an increasing drive toward specialization and repetition in particular sectors that have not seen the need for flexible, post-Fordist modes of production.

Work is one way of defining class and as my presentation of other academic accounts has shown, one can specify the dynamics within economic sectors to characterize the nature of the job tasks involved. But work is not the only element that should be considered when defining class. When the work day ends and people become involved in the other aspects of their lives, that are often referred to as either "leisure" activities or consumption practices, the issue of class does not suddenly cease to be relevant. Work practices are completely germane to understanding the nature of class relations, but they do not encompass the totality of class relations. Everyday practices are thoroughly classed and just as important as work practices to an understanding of class relations.

By surveying the formation of British cultural studies and the early work that culminated in Paul Willis' (1977) explication of class cultures, I develop a set of theoretical expectations as to the oppositional content of everyday practices. In the U.S. context, the interpretation of class cultures by Doug Foley was key to "talking about social classes as distinct everyday ways of life" (Foley 1990, 163). He goes on to state that class cultures are "a way of focusing class analysis on the cultural politics of how economic classes are culturally reproduced and resisted" (170). What always struck me as a fundamental shortcoming with Foley's theoretical appendix is that for all the talk of Marxian theory, class, and political economy, what he left un-theorized in his rich ethnography was the racial and gender dynamics playing out and their articulations with class dynamics. In his recent update (2010), a thoroughly reworked book still has a major disconnect between a deep ethnography of intersectional lived experiences and a theory focused on class reproduction and resistance.

I brought these expectations to the study of the former workers of the Bracero Program. As a result, we get a much fuller account of what these simultaneously raced and classed cultures of resistance begin to approximate in the U.S. context and an account of the key manifestations of opposition. Finally, I present a thorough discussion of the mechanisms in which race and class articulate and how Erving Goffman's ideas on the "total institution" apply to the case of the lived experiences of Braceros.

The origins of British cultural studies tend to be traced back to three authors and their central texts. Raymond Williams' (1958) *Culture and Society*, Richard Hoggart's (1957) *The Uses of Literacy*, and E. P. Thompson's (1968) *The Making of the English Working Class* are considered the major works that launched the approach that eventually found its institutional home in the Birmingham School of Contemporary Cultural Studies.[2] It is the experiences that comprise working-class ways of living that Thompson, Hoggart, and Williams sought to valorize, in the positive sense, by giving them a legitimate place in the area of academic study.

It was Thompson who sought to critically interrogate class. While surveying the field of class analysis during his time, Thompson (1968) found it demarcated by two dominant tendencies. Those who tended to view class as a *thing*, marked by a real mathematical, or quantifiable, existence, that assumed what the consciousness of the working class ought to be. Therefore, the party or theorist could impute the proper consciousness based upon the relations of production. Conversely, Thompson found a second tendency that represented its polar opposite. Viewing class solely as a *theoretical concept*: a way of looking at the world, but one that does not have a relation to what people go through on a day-to-day level. Those opposed tendencies set up the terrain of class analysis as either vulgarly materialist or vulgarly idealist. Either one treated class as an object or as an idea with no material basis. Not unlike later propositions by Bourdieu (1985), he called for a concept of class that is relational; that which is historically constructed within patterns of relationships, ideas, and institutions into which people involuntarily enter or are born into. For Thompson, the relationship to the means of production is not a mathematical formula from which we can impute a real or true class consciousness. Class is embedded in the social relations people actively live out in everyday experiences. These social relations shape and are shaped by institutions so that people do in fact make their own history, but not fully of their own choosing.

The major contribution of Hoggart and Williams was their focus on redefining culture. Yet, it was not as if these authors ignored class issues. Rather, they sought to define class on its cultural terrain and not necessarily in terms of production that Thompson relied upon. When the whistle blew or the timeclock struck five, a whole set of shared lived experiences were enacted outside the factory gates. But rather than directly engaging the primacy of the social relations of production in Thompson's analysis, the object of debate, at least for Williams, was the literary history of defining culture in the British context. In *Culture and Society*, Williams (1958, 325) states that culture "is not only a body of intellectual and imaginative work; it is also and essentially a whole way of life."

But it is in *The Long Revolution* that Williams defines culture in its fullest form. In the analysis of culture, there are three central categories to defining cultures. First, the ideal category is viewed as a state or process of human perfection, in absolute, or universal values. Second, the documentary category is the ways in which a body of intellectual and imaginative work, human thought and experiences are recorded. It defines the study of relationships between elements in a whole way of life (1961, 46). It is at this point that Williams demarcates three sub-levels of culture: the lived culture of a particular place and time, the recorded culture of everything from art to everyday facts which designate the culture of the period, and a selective tradition that connects lived and period cultures. The third category of culture is its social definition "in which culture is a description of a particular way of life, which expresses certain meanings and values not only in art and learning but also in institutions and *ordinary* behavior" (Williams 1961, 41).[3]

The culmination of this tradition of fostering a better understanding of working class culture by reconceptualizing both class and culture is represented by Paul Willis' (1977) *Learning to Labour*. Not necessarily dismissive of the productive relations that Thompson placed his stock in and certainly indebted to the Williams' definition of culture, *Learning to Labour* can be read as a mediation of this split in cultural studies. Most scholars who view class cultures as shared lived experiences (in particular see Willis' 1990, *Common Culture*) seem to have sacrificed the workplace as a potential site of resistance. Work seems to be assumed to be too alienating to put up a fight against or the workplace is simply dismissed as a site of resistance, reproduction, or ideology formation.[4] The notion of class cultures represents Willis' attempt to understand that the major, non-production based institutions of capitalist society play a major role in the reproduction of class relations. "The informal and formal processes of the school are obviously vital in preparing labour power in a certain way, but the home, family, neighbourhood, media and non-productive working class experience in general are equally vital for its continuous reproduction and daily reapplication to the labour process" (Willis 1977, 106).

In particular, Willis's starting point is the British state education system and the importance of schooling in preparing working class students to eventually become workers for life. The entire book is an elaboration of the concept of class cultures but the following statement summarizes the key facets of the notion.

> The products of this independent ability of the working class—profane testing of the formal, sharp un-reified language, oppositional solidarity, and a humorous presence, style and value not based on formal job status—are no less the product of the capitalist era for their subversive, or potentially subversive, forms. Though these things must not be exaggerated or romanticised or seen out of proportion to the minimal real freedom and material base which allows them, they arise nevertheless not from a mere suffering of, but from a creative response to, the demands of capitalism (Willis 1977, 132).

Willis applies a necessary corrective to Williams' conceptualization of culture as ordinary, lived experiences to examine how working class "lads" embodied resistance to their immediate oppressor. This "opposition to authority" within counter-school culture gives agency back to working-class actors in their resistance to a curriculum designed to prepare them for working-class jobs. But Willis does not romanticize these "penetrations." "It is quite wrong to picture working class culture or consciousness optimistically as the vanguard in the grand march towards rationality and socialism. If anything—the central case in this book [*Learning to Labor*]—it is these elements of rationality and of the future in working class culture, and particularly in that of the school, which act finally in their current social form and in complex and unintended ways to prevent precisely that" (Willis 1977, 122). It is these very cultural forms, in opposition to domination, that eventually result in class reproduction. "The class culture concept is a way of focusing class analysis on the cultural politics of how economic classes are reproduced and resisted" (Foley 1990, 170).

Opposition to authority, in the case of the Bracero Program, was met with fierce repercussions such as job task reassignment, refusal to re-contract, even deportation. The looming threat of violence and death was present in the recollections of at least two Braceros I interviewed. The main means of resistance was to skip or desert before contracts expired.

On the surface, this seems to fit a dominant Marxist position of viewing the working class as masses duped by commodified culture, best represented by Horkheimer and Adorno's (1972) delineation of "The Culture Industry," which stated:

> The consumers are workers and employees, the farmers and lower middle class. Capitalist production so confines them, body and soul, that they fall helpless victims to what is offered to them. As naturally as the ruled always took the morality imposed upon them more seriously than did the rulers themselves, the deceived masses are today captivated by the myth of success even more than the successful are. Immovably, they insist on the very ideology which enslaves them. The misplaced love of the common people for the wrong which is done to them is a greater force than the cunning of the authorities (Horkheimer and Adorno 1972, 134).

Even as farm *workers* fall out of the Frankfurt School frame, their reinsertion identifies both the economic and cultural forms of class. Crude Marxist notions of false consciousness fit well with the mass culture thesis. It assumes that the working class is so thoroughly dominated that its own collective subjectivity is a mystification or mass deception. According to Horkheimer and Adorno, it is not a matter of depth to which definitions of the situation are imposed from above (i.e., the cunning of authority). The lack of oppositionality or resistance by the working class is squarely rooted in the collective mindset of working class culture.

Rather than *assuming* that minority working class cultures are either expressive or dominated cultures, regardless of time and place, I began this study with the intention of uncovering the "hidden transcripts of resistance" (Scott 1990) in the life stories of former workers of the Bracero Program. I was aware, thanks to the established literature on the program, that growers did in fact have a good deal of control over the actions of workers (Galarza 1964, 1956, Kirstein 1977). I was also aware of the acts of resistance, in the form of work stoppages and strikes, which Gamboa (1990) documented in the Pacific Northwest. But what I was not prepared for was the almost total degree of control that growers had over both the work and non-work practices of the Braceros I spoke with.

The "cunning of authorities" actually became central for understanding what I refer to as the Bracero total institution. The Bracero total institution is an institution specifically distinguished by its lack of resistance and opposition to authority. The hidden transcripts of resistance, which I initially expected to uncover, did not surface, nor did the mass culture of domination thesis fit with the life stories of former Braceros. By looking for resistance, I found domination, but within a context that silenced discontent and required obedience to authority as a *pre*condition for work. It was specifically how class and race related in the formation of the experiences of the Braceros that enabled this situation to take root in the first place and grow into a web of state and labor controls that spread well beyond the confines of the fields.

RACE AND CLASS IN ARTICULATION

Rather than fully theorizing the race-class question, the theoretical work of Stuart Hall provides the necessary elements for thinking about the relationship. "Articulation" is the distinguishing feature that enables us to ask in what ways and to what extent do class and race cohere.

> An articulation is thus the form of the connection that can make a unity of two different elements, under certain conditions. It is a linkage which is not necessary, determined absolute, and essential for all time. Thus, a theory of articulation is both a way of understanding how ideological elements come, under certain conditions, to cohere together within a discourse, and a way of asking how they do or do not become articulated, at specific conjunctures, to certain political subjects (Hall 1986b, 53).

The degree of autonomy of spheres is a historically produced question, not a built-in assumption. Whether the spheres are separate or mutually constitutive is a question that can only be addressed by studying real-world contexts. For working-class "minorities," the degree of autonomy between class and racial oppression is, more often than not, extremely low. As Gaventa (1980, 260) explains in his study of power relations in the Appalachian Valley: "The institutions that affect the valley—corporate, governmental, communications, labor—may appear at the top diverse, relatively unconnected, even competing but when the same institutions are viewed from the bottom, i.e. from the perspective of the non-elite of the community, they appear unitary in nature."

Rather than personally constructing the general theory of race and class, Hall points to Gramsci for offering the most relevant insights into the relationship. This rather long passage is the formative text for understanding how Gramsci enables us to understand the interconnections without reducing race to class or vice versa.

> I would underline the non-reductive approach to questions concerning the interrelationship between class and race. This has proved to be one of the most complex and difficult theoretical problems to address, and it has frequently led to the adoption of one or another extreme positions. Either one "privileges" the underlying class relationships, emphasizing that all ethnically and racially differentiated labor forces are subject to the same exploitative relationships with capital; or one emphasizes the centrality of ethnic and racial categories and divisions at the expense of the fundamental class structuring of society. Though these two extremes appear to be the polar opposites of one another, in fact, they are inverse, mirror-images of each other, in the sense that, both feel required to produce a single and exclusive determining principle of articulation—class or race—even if they disagree as to which should be accorded the privileged sign. I believe the fact that Gramsci adopts a non-reductive ap-

> proach to questions of class, coupled with his understanding of the profoundly historical shaping to any specific social formation, does help point the way towards a non-reductionist approach to the race/class question (Hall 1986c, 24; reprinted in Morley and Chen eds. 1996, 435–36, for a similar critique in the language of the "economic" and "sociological" views of race and racism, see Hall 1980).[5]

The relationship between race and class is not one that naturally coheres or one where absolute distinctions can be drawn. It is a matter of degree that we must clarify in each historical instance with each racialized sub-group. It requires a great deal of articulatory work, on the part of elites, in the ideological and material realms to sustain a conjoined system of oppression. The degree to which racial and class oppression work in concert is fundamentally a question concerning how classed the race category and how raced the class category are in any particular context.

As Hall (1978, 394) elaborates the relation in an early essay:

> Race is intrinsic to the manner in which the black labouring classes are *complexly constituted* at each of those levels. Race enters into the way black labour, male and female, is distributed as economic agents on the level of economic practice—and the class struggles which result; and in the manner in which that class is articulated as the collective and individual "subjects" of emergent ideologies and forms of consciousness—and the struggle over ideology, culture and consciousness which results. This gives the matter of race and *racism* a theoretical as well as a practical centrality to all the relations and practices which affect black labour. The constitution of this class fraction as a class, and the *class relations* which inscribe it, function as *race relations*. The two are inseparable. Race is the modality in which class is lived. It is also the medium in which class relations are experienced. This does not immediately heal any breaches or bridge any chasms. But it has consequences for the *whole class*, whose relation to their conditions of existence is now systematically transformed by race. It determines some of the modes of struggle. It also provides one of the criteria by which we measure the *adequacy* of struggle to the structures it aims to transform.

Hall squarely theorizes the Black-White binary so historical, contextual, and spatial work must be conducted to situate race relations beyond the binary. For me, the idea of an Anglo racial frame, as adapted from Bonilla-Silva and Feagin, allows one to specify the social groups that shape and respond to Anglo-Mexicano relations. Foley (2010, 1990) problematically asserts a class-first approach that leaves little room to theorize gender and race, but he never opens up a full theorization of class as part of intersectionality, and thus winds his way to Goffman's ethnographic explorations of the self to distinguish class cultures.

The dramaturgical model, often associated with the microinteractionist tradition (see Collins 1994: 218–19, 276–83 for counterevidence), as embodied in the work of Erving Goffman (1959, 1961), on the surface seems to belie a serious engagement with power. Foley (1990) posits that the everyday interaction studies of Goffman are indicative of Habermas's instrumental speech acts but that seems to ignore Goffman's institutional analysis. Viewing life as theater and the small-scale interactions it seeks to comprehend were complicated with Erving Goffman's analysis of mental hospitals in *Asylums* (1961). The institutional setting of the mental asylum necessarily complicated the presentation of self. Whereas *The Presentation of Self in Everyday Life* (1959) seemed to posit a universal and uniform stage for interactions (through the metaphor that life is theater), *Asylums* was steeped in the logic that context matters and power relations are constitutive of certain forms of interaction. To thoroughly contextualize and historicize Goffman's theory, it must be noted that *Asylums* came out at a time when those in charge of large bureaucratic holding facilities were completely convinced that they could exert total control over those assigned to the facilities. Studies of total institutions have been limited, even to today, to observing prisons, mental hospitals, and the military (Braswell, Dillingham and Montgomery 1985; Brissett and Edgley 1994; Goffman 1961; Watson 1980). A very problematic application of slavery as a total institution (Elkins 1959) is important to note for all of its essentialist and stereotypical representations of slave mentalities. The pitfalls associated with reducing agency to the whims of the institution are fully noted and a more nuanced perspective is applied here.

Stanley Elkins (1959) analysis of slavery as a total institution can be credited, albeit most unintentionally, for sparking the new social history of slavery research tradition. Historians such as Eric Foner, Herbert Gutman, and Eugene Genovese wrote some of the most widely accepted analyses of slavery in part to discredit the claims of Elkins. The dubious hypothesis that Elkins sought to verify was that the peculiar system of U.S. chattel slavery caused the Sambo social psychology of slaves.

> Sambo, the typical plantation slave, was docile but irresponsible, loyal but lazy, humble but chronically given to lying the stealing; his behavior was full of infantile silliness and his talk inflated with childish exaggeration. His relationship with his master was full of utter dependence and childlike attachment: it was indeed this childlike quality that was the very key to his being (Elkins 1959, 87).

Elkins never empirically verifies that "Sambos" existed but assumes their presence. The following generation of historians effectively challenged this assumption with a body of research that has found U.S. slaves to be much more contentious, purposive as actors fighting for social change, and their strength in maintaining family and cultural ties in spite of oppressive social conditions.

The subsequent scholarly focus on resistance to total institutions, inspired by the 1960s protest era of prison rebellions, public outcry over sanitariums and the closing of the asylums, revisionist literature on slave rebellions, and labor organizing of migrant farmworkers by the United Farm Workers all led to the eventual discrediting of the aims and theoretical basis of total institutions (Blassingame 1979, Blight 2006, Braswell, Dillingham and Montgomery 1985, Griswold del Castillo and Garcia 1995, Matthiessen 2000). It is important to note that the time frame after the Second World War until the 1960s protest movements was a time when it was assumed that the best way to deal with an unwanted population was to separate them from mainstream society and place them under the control of total institutions. When the scope of the atrocities associated with the Nazi Holocaust came into full view, it was patently clear that those in power had learned the lessons of total control from the Nazi regime and were deploying them with regularity on those deemed undesirable. The 1960s protest movements provided a worldwide response and challenge to those in power who sought to perpetuate inequality through the means of social control.

The precise nodes of conflict and resistance came from the places that were completely un-theorized in the total institutional framework. Had Goffman paid particular attention to gender, he would have noted how thoroughly gendered the mental health system was and still is to this day. He would have noted that "women's" illnesses labeled hysteria and medical model solutions to their Freudian invoked "instabilities," such as the surgical practice of hysterectomies to remedy assumed inadequacies, were part and parcel of larger gender hierarchies. Gendered power relations resulted in a much larger percentage of the female population labeled as mentally ill than their male counterparts (Chesler 1997, Turner and Edgley 1983). As Goffman (1961, 3) notes, ". . . to learn about one of these institutions we would be well advised to look at the others." For the present purposes, looking at the managed life of men during the Bracero Program can further illuminate the racial/class inequalities codified in the total institutional framework.

After a brief delineation of the total institution framework as theorized by Goffman and Foucault, I will explain how the workings of the Bracero Program served as an attempt at total social control. Rather than rooting control strictly in the labor process, a place where one expects growers or employers to enforce power relations, I came to understand the entire Bracero experience as part and parcel of the total institution. Most scholars who study the elements of everyday life, beyond the confines of work, assume that leisure time provides the space for counter-hegemonic or oppositional practices (de Certeau 2002, Fiske 1989a, 1989b, 1993, Hall and Jefferson 1976, Lipsitz 1990, and Scott 1990). But for Braceros, what became much more salient was the "cunning of authority"—a concept dismissively introduced by Horkheimer and Adorno (1972) in their defense of the culture industries thesis. In the case of the Bracero total institution, the cunning of authority, which consisted of the state agents and growers' ability to use various means to dominate and control the workforce, was a much more salient explanation than viewing everyday practices solely as acts of resistance. Simultaneously, it was also a cunning of Anglo authority that presumed racialized men in their totality could be reduced to simply labor inputs. The work demands placed upon the workers dictated their lived experiences in almost every realm of interaction—both mental and manual. The recent attempts at Bracero reparations provide a window into how the role expectations of the total institution can be countered by public movements and shared historical memory reconstructions.

GOFFMAN, FOUCAULT, AND THE BRACERO TOTAL INSTITUTION

Though they covered similar empirical terrain, they both came to the topic for similar theoretical interests in power, and they were both interested in the formation of asylums, the views of Erving Goffman and Michel Foucault on institutional power could not be more divergent.[6] On the one hand, Goffman had moved on to other topics by the time Foucault began writing about the origins of disciplinary institutions, and on the other hand, Foucault never cites Goffman in his entire corpus on institutions and power. If Goffman was in some ways challenging the American preoccupation with the universal self through pragmatist philosophy, Foucault was reacting to the trends in French leftist thought and the dominance of structural Marxism. As Foucault described the academic context of French social thought:

> The way power was exercised—concretely and in detail—with its specificity, its techniques and tactics, was something that no one attempted to ascertain. . . . This task could only begin after 1968, that is to say, on the basis of daily struggles at the grass-roots level. This is where the concrete nature of power became visible, along with the prospect that these analyses of power would provide fruitful in accounting for all that had hitherto remained outside the field of political analysis. To put it simply, psychiatric internment, the mental normalization of individuals, and penal institutions have no doubt a fairly limited importance if one is only looking for their economic significance (Foucault 1984, 57–58).

The base-superstructure economic reductionism of Althusser (1969, 1970) limited the terrain of analysis for left social thought in France. Foucault's intervention, in terms of the study of power, moved the epiphenomenal to the center. In particular, his concepts of bio-power and disciplinary institutions shifted the analysis of prisons and asylums to their historical origins, and then specifically rooted in the analysis of bodies in institutions. This is in marked contrast to Goffman's moral careers of mental patients and his argument that institutional contexts matter in the shaping of the mind or conceptions of self. Yet both men are positing total power as much more universal than I would advocate and looking at the specificities of the Bracero labor camps, in its socio-historical context, would serve the field well by limiting its over-generalizing claims. There is a presentist drive always already present in Foucault's analysis of the origins of institutional power. Goffman's ahistorical ethnographic approach roots his presentist concerns similarly in what seems to be posited as a universal total institution that does not take the specific post-war U.S. context seriously. Arguing against Foucault's universalism in institutions and Goffman's limitations based on a non-fully specified context, I posit that power must be explored in its specific socio-historical and spatial contexts, as this is where power is deployed. It is not enough to delimit contexts to historical periodizations. Specific institutional arrangements are shaped by their historical contexts to be sure, but the specific configuration of power relations are best understood when examining how inequalities are constructed and legitimated by those in power and experienced by those how are powerless, to a lesser or greater extent.

Interested in the origins and machinations of power, Foucault's intellectual progression was rooted in a revisionist approach to the origins of modernity, away from deeming issues of bodies, control, and the birth of disciplinary institutions as epiphenomenal interests and centering what he marks as the "beginning of an era of 'biopower'" (Foucault 1990, 140).

> If the development of the great instruments of the state, as *institutions* of power, ensured the maintenance of production relations, the rudiments of anatomo- and bio-politics, created in the eighteenth century as *techniques* of power present at every level of the social body and utilized by very diverse institutions (the family and the army, schools and the police, individual medicine and the administration of collective bodies), operated in the sphere of economic processes, their development, and the forces working to sustain them (Foucault 1990, 141).

As Foucault identifies the origins of prisons, mental asylums, and medicine in their institutionalized forms, he intentionally asks the Bentham-inspired question in a circular fashion: "Is it surprising that prisons resemble factories, schools, barracks, hospitals, which all resemble prisons?" (Foucault 1977, 228).

The high degree of social control is not only secured by physical structures such as the panopticon but also specific techniques of treating the institutionalized that ensure the place of those in power as well as those who are deemed the "other." "Fear appears as an essential presence in the asylum" (Foucault 2001, 232). As Foucault discusses one of the original designers of the Quaker asylum, William Tuke, he notes:

> The asylum no longer punished the madman's guilt, it is true; but it did more, it organized that guilt; it organized it for the madman as a consciousness of himself, and as a non-reciprocal relation to the keeper; it organized it for the man of reason as an awareness of the Other, a therapeutic intervention in the madman's existence. In other words, by this guilt the madman became an object of punishment always vulnerable to himself and to the Other; and, from the acknowledgment of his status as object, from the awareness of his guilt, the madman was to return to his awareness of himself as a free and responsible subject, and consequently to reason (Foucault 2001, 234–35).

The use of fear and intimidation to both construct the "other" and put them in their place is extremely relevant for understanding the Bracero total institution. Viewing power as a set of social relations makes it less about the physical institution and more about how power is experienced by both those in and out of power. The presentist concerns in Foucault's analysis on the origins of modernity do not become clear until his work addresses the history of sexuality and its relationship to power. He notes "[t]he omnipresence of power: not because it has the privilege of consolidating everything under its invincible unity, but because it is produced from one moment to the next, at every point, or rather in every relation from one point to the other. Power is everywhere; not because it embraces everything, but because it comes from everywhere" (Foucault 1990, 93).[7] His analysis of the origins of modern power has a much more universal reach to Foucault than his historical analysis would seem to allow. Yet the idea that power is everywhere in some ways renders the different levels of power to be conflated into one abstract, omnipresent origin and thus the idea that different forms of power are more insidious, and downright deadly, than other forms of power seems to belie a much more historically contingent analysis. A more historically limited application of the birth and maintenance of asylums would have to ground those total institutions in their specific socio-historical and spatial contexts. I would contend that in order to understand the eventual decline in total institutions and the specific context that led to them (see Mize 2004, 134–35), it is important to note Habermas's view of the twentieth century as a time of repression and total war. This context goes beyond just the institution itself and explores both the mindset and the lived reality of the post-war U.S. context. As Habermas (2001, 45) states,

> . . . the gruesome features of a century that "invented" the gas chamber, total war, state-sponsored genocide and extermination camps, brain-washing, state security apparatuses, and the panoptic surveillance of entire populations. The twentieth century "generated" more victims, more dead soldiers, more murdered civilians, more displaced minorities, more torture, more dead from cold, from hunger, from maltreatment, more political prisoners and refugees, than could ever have been imagined.

Goffman's Total Institution

"A total institution may be defined as a place of residence and work where a large number of like-situated individuals, cut off from the wider society for an appreciable period of time, together lead an enclosed, formally administered round of life" (Goffman 1961, xiii). The physical structures that represent this separation are as much symbolic as utilitarian. "Their encompassing or total character is symbolized by the barrier to social intercourse with the outside and to departure that is often built right into the physical plant such as locked doors, high walls, barbed wire, cliffs, water, forests or moors" (4). Goffman lists five types of total institutions that represent the degree of differentiation in characteristics.

> 1. Institutions established to care for persons felt to be both incapable and harmless (homes for the blind, aged, orphaned, or indigent).
> 2. Places established to care for persons felt to be both incapable of looking after themselves and a threat to the community (TB sanitaria, mental hospitals, and leprosaria).
> 3. Institutions organized to protect the community against what are felt to be intentional dangers to it, with the welfare of persons thus sequestered not the immediate issue (jails, penitentiaries, P.O.W. camps, and concentration camps).
> 4. Establishments designed as retreats from the world even while often serving as training stations for the religious (abbeys, monasteries, convents, and cloisters).
> 5. Institutions purportedly established to pursue some worklike task and justifying themselves only on these instrumental grounds (army barracks, *labor camps*, colonial compounds, servants' quarters of large mansions) (4–5, *emphasis added*).

The total institution is a nearly complete system of domination—or at least it is designed with complete domination as the ideal. From Goffman's research, the salient characteristics of the total institution are as follows:

> 1. All aspects of life are conducted in the same place and under the same single authority.
> 2. Each phase of the member's daily activity is carried on in the immediate company of a large batch of others, all of who are treated alike and required to do the same thing together.
> 3. All phases of the day's activities are tightly scheduled, with one activity leading at a prearranged time into the next, the whole sequence of activities being imposed from above by a system of explicit formal rulings and a body of officials.

4. The various enforced activities are brought together into a single rational plan purportedly designed to fulfill the official aims of the institution (Goffman 1961, 6).

Unfortunately, but for reasons that become obvious when one considers the general refusal to address larger systemic inequalities in early microinteractionist iterations, sociologists working in the Goffman-inspired dramaturgical tradition have not turned their attentions to life in labor camps. For the present purposes, the Braceros' memories of life in the total institution offer a unique perspective on the identities so diligently managed by their crew bosses, farm labor contractors (FLCs), and growers. According to Goffman (1961, 168),

> Each moral career, and behind this, each self, occurs within the confines of an institutional system, whether a social establishment such as a mental hospital or a complex of personal and professional relationships. The self, then, can be seen as something that resides in the arrangements prevailing in a social system for its members. The self in this sense is not a property of the person to whom it is attributed, but dwells rather in the pattern of social control that is exerted in connection with the person by himself and those around him. This special kind of institutional arrangement does not so much support the self as constitute it.

The performative aspects of the self are based upon a series of role expectations between inmates and staff (or in the present case, workers and bosses). "Each grouping tends to conceive of the other in terms of narrowly hostile stereotypes. . . . Staff tends to feel superior and righteous; inmates tend, in some ways at least, to feel inferior, weak, blameworthy, and guilty" (7).

The total institution represents a system of domination and coercion that relies on its subjects being physically and symbolically segregated from the rest of society. The managed character of the institution is designed to control the actions of those subjects twenty-four hours a day, seven days a week. In a potentially much more harmful way, the total institution is designed to impose its definition on the self-identities of inmates/workers. This has far-reaching consequences for how participants view themselves, and assess their prior experiences and future possibilities. The managed self is one of the most potentially destructive products of the total institution. For this study, research was conducted both prior to and after the Braceros reparations movement and found a vastly different set of recollections in terms of how the Bracero Program was directly experienced by the workers themselves. What I reconciled was how the Bracero social justice attempts at revisiting history and contemporary social movements provide a space for the collective recollection of memories silenced by the ensuing years of racial and class marginalization. Even if monetary claims are never received, it seems that the major contributions of social movements are shifts in consciousness and public memory making.

Bracero Total Institution

The delineation of the asylum as total institution by Goffman and Foucault respectively provides insights into how the self is constructed through institutional arrangements and how bodies are subjected to power relations for the purposes of social control and the construction of the other—in the present case to meet the labor demands of agribusiness. Unfortunately, both Goffman and Foucault are hampered by their location of the total institution within the confines of bounded physical structures. By looking at the Bracero total institution from those who were directly subjected to a set of social conditions not of their own making—the workers themselves—delineating the Bracero total institution required that attention be paid to experiences well beyond the confines of the labor camp. From the initial decision to migrate, every step Braceros took was within the shadow of the Bracero total institution. Paying to pass through the Mexican recruiting centers, enduring the U.S. processing centers, signing a name on the standard work contract, meeting the preconditions for recontracting, navigating the dangers of transportation, consuming institutional means according to a predetermined schedule, and finally living in the labor camps were part of a larger interrelated web of social relations that privileged U.S. agribusiness to the further detriment of Mexican Braceros. In other words, the Bracero total institution was more than a labor camp. It was an overall set of experiences rooted in racial and class inequality. The grower-defined role expectations impacted recollections of how Braceros publicly recalled their experiences. In many ways the role expectations that were so constantly and effectively hammered into their psyches often led to silences when publicly recalling the less salient aspects of the Bracero Program. In effect, the long-term effect of agribusiness's cunning of authority was the constant dehumanization and degradation of Braceros' self-identities and a demand for subservience as a precondition for receiving a contract. Growers rarely had to enforce this marginalization themselves because they had farm labor contractors, crew bosses, medical examiners, Mexican and U.S. state officials, and local communities doing most of the berating and dehumanizing for them.

Research conducted with participants in the Bracero redress movement points to the crucial role that social movements can play in countering this cunning of authority. At present, I have not collected the life stories of movement non-participants, so it is impossible to say if the Bracero redress movement has shifted public memory displays writ large or if the consciousness raising is situated solely within the movement. Nevertheless, the former Braceros willingness to talk openly about the most humiliating aspects of the processing centers points to the potential for social movements in countering the role expectations of subservient, fearful acquiescence that Goffman and Foucault thought total institutions were so successful in entrenching.

One of the lessons learned from viewing the Bracero total institution within its specific context is that relations are never as total as they seem. The amount of work required to deploy the cunning of authority in nearly every aspect of the Braceros' interactions with authority figures was most often countered by Braceros skipping or deserting the contract. Most recently, it has been effectively countered when Braceros reconvene at the grassroots level to share their individual stories and see how their individual life stories are part of a much larger collective experience that was shaped by power relations duly influenced by racial oppression and class exploitation. Understanding the post-war context, of reinforcing total institutions to keep the "other" separate from the public, benefits from the ethnographic research of Goffman (1961) and his extrapolation of the features of the total institution from the specific context of mental asylums. As Goffman (1961, 3) notes, ". . . to learn about one of these institutions we would be well advised to look at the others." It also benefits from a specific delineation of Foucault's general focus on bio-power, the other, and power relations as too often the stakes of the total institution have been a matter of life and death. To understand how power relations are deployed, it requires substantive insights from those deemed powerless as to their daily experiences with those in authority. The specific configuration of the cunning of authority most certainly needs to be understood from above but the view from below is most important if disciplinary power is to be effectively countered and those who are marginalized construct their own social justice aims to rectify past wrongs.

NOTES

1. "Myth" is used in theories accounting for race to signify the false nature of the claims of the existence of distinct, readily identifiable, and absolutist groups demarcated by their race. If natural scientists cannot prove the existence of races, it is assumed that thinking in racial terms, whether by academics or the general populace, is based on a false ideology and essentially wrong (see Fields 1990).

2. One originator, Raymond Williams (1989), took exception to this author/text-based description of the approach's origins in "The Future of Cultural Studies" and stressed that what brought cultural studies together was a shared vision of the role of education in promoting progressive social change. The authors, mentioned above, came together as a result of their common commitment to adult education. Even within cultural studies in Britain, this original impulse is often displaced in favor of the textual origins of the *study* of working-class life. Stuart Hall (1992) recently placed the origins of cultural studies in its political context of the New Left and its uneasiness with certain forms of Marxism.

3. It is interesting to note that W. E. B. DuBois embarked upon a very similar project that remains one of his central, substantive insights into the study of race, class, and culture. To DuBois, races are really "cultural groups" by which he meant:

> That 15,000,000 men and women for three centuries have shared common experiences and common suffering, and have worked all those days and nights together for their own survival and progress; that this complex of habits and manners must not be lost. That people sharing this experience formed a race no matter what their blood may be (DuBois [1948] reprinted in Gates and West 1996, 164).

4. Willis's views seem to have shifted more toward the study of exclusively "cultural" (i.e., non-work) aspects of the working class even though his early article on "Shop Floor Culture, Masculinity and the Wage Form" and *Learning to Labour* very effectively weave the work-based (production) aspects of class cultures with the "superstructural" or consumption-based aspects. In both studies (1979, 1977), Willis avoids treating work and "leisure" as unconnected, separate realms in a way that his later work (1990) and other cultural studies proponents promote almost exclusively.

5. In a particularly problematic passage where Hall equates immigrant labor with the Marxian industrial reserve army thesis and discusses his view of U.S. race relations, Hall's contribution to theorizing the race-class couplet falters when he shifts analysis away from Blacks in Britain. "For example, the position of black labour in the industrial North of the United States and of black migration to post-war Britain show highly distinctive patternings along racial lines . . . Yet it is clear that blacks are not the only division within the 'reserve army': hence race is not the only mechanism through which its size and composition is regulated. In the United States, white immigrants (e.g. European and Mexican) and women, and in Britain, both women and the Irish have provided a significant alternative element" (1980, 340). It should be clear from my analysis that Mexicans in the United States are a thoroughly raced sub-group and the similarities between European immigrants and their Mexican counterparts are more imputed than actual.

6. Both authors are clearly directly influenced by Bentham's writings on the panopticon. Both authors' beginning points are their shared criticisms of the rational-utilitarian drive behind this prescribed form of institutionalized social coercion and both aim to critically interrogate the resultant forms of social control that result from Bentham's normative assumptions about how populations he deemed worthy should be subjected to direct, constant surveillance. "No matter how different, or even opposite the purpose: whether it be that of *punishing the incorrigible, guarding the insane, reforming the vicious, confining the suspected, employing the idle, maintaining the helpless, curing the sick, instructing the willing* in any branch of industry, or *training the rising race* in the path of *education*: in a word, whether it be applied to the purposes of *perpetual prisons* in the room of death, or *prisons for confinement* before trial, of *penitentiary-houses,* or *houses of correction*, or *work-houses*, or *manufactories*, or *mad-houses*, or *hospitals*, or *schools*" (Bentham 1995, 34). But the intellectual contexts of Goffman (and his reaction to universalist views of the self as posited by pragmatism) and Foucault (and the dominance of structural Marxism in French social thought) in many ways shaped their divergent characterizations of total institutions.

7. As Foucault fully defines his approach to power, "It seems to me that power must be understood in the first instance as the multiplicity of force relations immanent in the sphere in which they operate and which constitute their own organization; as the process which, through ceaseless struggles and confrontations, transforms, strengthens, or reverses them; as the support which these force relations find in one another, thus forming a chain or a system, or on the contrary, the disjunctions and contradictions which isolate them from one another; and lastly, as the strategies in which they take effect, whose general design or institutional crystallization is embodied in the state apparatus, in the formulation of law, in the various social hegemonies" (Foucault 1990, 92–3).

Appendix II

Working in the Field

Historical Memory, Archival Ethnography, and Direct Accounts of Agricultural Migrant Labor

How people remember is related as much to their relationship to past experiences as their present context of recollection. The life stories collected for *The Invisible Workers of the U.S.–Mexico Bracero Program: Obreros Olvidados* maximized variation in the types of interviews conducted. In 1997, I conducted a focus group interview with four former Braceros, as well as a sister and a daughter of Braceros. The initial open-ended question allowed Braceros to identify with aspects of the program that resonated most with their recollections.[1]

> Int: Can you tell me about life working as a Bracero?
>
> Don Jose: I worked on a ranch in Kerman. Then we were told they needed about ten men to work in Fresno. I was chosen. I was picking grapes. About twenty people were working in Fresno and they all had contracts. You had to pay for the contract. In the association's camps, we would be chosen to pick grapes. There was a representative to assure working [conditions] and living quarters. We worked ten hours per day and were paid by how much we picked. We got piece work.
>
> Don Emilio: I tried to receive a contract three to four times. In the medical examination, I would get disqualified because I had a back operation.
>
> Don Jose: [Interrupting] It was the luck of the draw if you found work.
>
> Don Emilio: [Continues] I eventually found work picking tomatoes in Michigan. I picked lettuce and orange in California. But in oranges, I was injured and did not recontract.

Don Hector: It's the money, once you get used to having the money, it keeps you coming. I picked cotton in Texas. The work was hard. But I did not have problems. Everything was fine.

Don Jose: Yes, everything was fine. I have no reason to complain.

Int: All the time? You never had problems? I've heard from others that everything was fine. Most of the time it was? What was it like when it wasn't fine?

Don Emilio: Well, they had no beds for us. We slept on the concrete floor. We were given one meal a day. There were no bathrooms.

The notion that men either had either good or bad experiences was most often attributed to the "luck of the draw." This particular interview tended to be dominated by Don Jose as he had moved up the agricultural ladder to the position of farm labor contractor so he was vested in defending that subject position. The silencing of Don Emilio was only countered when a space was opened to talk about the mistreatment experienced. Don Emilio's detailing of the abuses he endured (fed only one meal per day, sleeping on a concrete floor, labor camps without restrooms) was a major breakthrough in 1997 when most of these men had rarely talked about the Bracero Program—even to family members—over the previous thirty years. The most consistent response I received from family members of ex-Braceros is that the Bracero Program was rarely, if ever, talked about in any detail. The standard answer was a minimal retelling of location, year, crop, and work tasks (harvesting, thinning, pruning, irrigating, etc.).

The detailed responses to certain aspects of the program's workings, elicited via further probing questions, confirmed the findings of the established scholarly literature on the Bracero Program. When asked generally about the food, housing, and other living conditions, I was most often told everything was fine or "*fue bien*." Once I asked specifically about wages, housing, quality of food and water in a way that did not implicate U.S. growers or other citizens, the details were much closer to what the literature on the program deems as the extreme mistreatment of Braceros (Anderson 1963, 1976, Cohen 2011, Galarza 1956, 1964, Gamboa 1990, Garcia 1980, Garcia y Griego 1980, 1996, Gonzalez 2006, Kirstein 1977, López 2010, Mitchell 2012).

The former Braceros I interviewed, when pressed for more detailed responses than *fue bien*, provided the details on the specific aspects of the total racial segregation they experienced, their insertion and maintenance into the bottom levels of the capitalist agricultural labor process and the attendant deplorable working conditions, and a set of lived experiences that could best be described as managed, controlled, even coerced. The silenced past experiences abounded but most often they centered around wages and deductions, the batch-handling of Braceros at U.S. processing centers, and labor camp conditions. Braceros stated that they did not remember how much was deducted out of their paychecks. In the 1997 first wave of interviews, the men rarely talked in depth about medical exams and delousing procedures they had to endure in order to enter the United States. They simply confirmed details when asked but did not elaborate upon the major themes that meet the legal definition of peonage.

When Don Daniel and Don Roberto were interviewed together in 1997, Don Roberto described his Bracero Program experience at the recruitment center. "In that time . . . we had to report in Sonora. There we didn't have to pay anything. We came in train to Calexico, to the U.S. There in Calexico, they checked your lungs and you signed the contract and then they came to leave with you with the boss where you were going to work" (Interview with Don Roberto 1997). He started to discuss the specific locales and crops he worked but I interrupted to ask him to confirm the DDT delousing to which they were subjected.

Int: Did they spray a powder? I don't know how to say a powder. Like sand? *(some blank looks and then they seem to understand)*

Don Roberto: Disinfectant. All over the body.

Int: The whole body.

Don Daniel: Spray.

Int: With other people or alone?

Don Roberto: Rain. Every one got in a line and they go . . . one by one.

Though he was subjected to the mass medical exam and subsequent delousing completely naked, he was not comfortable providing those details and would have skipped over the topic without the intervention.

However, the Braceros interviewed in 2005 on the U.S.-Mexico border were much more forthright about the details of the processing center and they often verified how uncomfortable they were made to feel. Since this treatment may have felt humiliating and degrading, it is likely that those who directly experienced it did not want to talk about it. The space created by the social movement to collect on the mandatory savings program was twofold in design. First, the social movement leaders spoke often about the degrading aspects of the recruitment process. Second, the coming together of former Braceros for the purpose of working towards a common goal based on a shared past meant that the lines of communication were now open. Both aspects meant that the Braceros were no longer viewing their experiences as "personal troubles," but were in fact larger "public issues" that helped developed a sense of solidarity (Mills 1959). This unity was in response to a collective understanding of how the personal abuses they endured was part and parcel of how they were collectively wronged, violated, and exploited. Unfortunately, the same discursive space for Braceros in late-1990s Fresno was simply not present.

The quality of housing, food, and wages was discussed as the luck of the draw. Braceros stated that some places were good, some were bad, and it was purely by chance that they personally enjoyed favorable conditions. The major complaints registered by the Braceros were the lack of availability of work or particular camps where food was rotten. But by and large, those aspects of the program, which scholars concur as the worst aspects, were not talked about by the Braceros I interviewed. We have to read the silences in order to understand why the non-issues are so relevant. For example, no respondent, even when specifically asked, broached the subject of the coercive labor practices of crew bosses, FLCs, or growers. One respondent in Mexico, Don Lupe, registered complaints about the *pocho* (assimilated Mexican American) foremen but most of the Mexico-based respondents did not elaborate on their experiences in the United States to the same extent that they focused on the recruitment process. The discursive space for talking about the unsalient aspects of the program still needs to be widened quite a bit. Most of the 2005 border respondents were still making sure that their worth as a worker, often defined by the number of boxes they filled, was defended.

From these subjective evaluations about the nature of their experiences in the Bracero Program, it becomes all the more important to focus on the poor conditions as detailed by the workers since it is these recollections that have endured in opposition to the imposed definitions of the situation from above. The role expectations placed upon Braceros severely curtailed negative evaluations about how they were treated in the United States. Any discussions that followed this negative line become even more important in the face of power relations, both within and beyond the research act, which imposed silence as the most favorable course of action. From these life stories and the secondary materials collected by the author, the remaining sections will focus on methods of inquiry that privilege the experiences as recollected by the Braceros to shed light on their treatment in the United States. In addition, it will explain how their place in a U.S. society that treated them as outsiders to be neither seen nor heard affected what they remembered and shared within the interview context.

My hope is that the people I speak with in this text are recognized for their unique experiences in their living out of the Bracero Program. But if this ethnography ends there, I think it's a failure. Finding the links between the migrant laborers of today, maquiladora workers along the U.S.–Mexico border, and workers across the global South in the export processing zones and informal sectors of our globalized economy will only be understood if the next generation of ethnographers avoid the paralysis of self-reflection, the narcissistic bent toward inward speculation and self-doubt, and put themselves out there to listen to what the globalized poor have to say, to document those experiences and find connections, and finally to share the hope that is imbued in so much sorrow and misery. Without hope, there is no resistance.

The methodological approach of this study is rooted in a fully developed life history approach. Though the life stories of individual Braceros are the centerpiece of this work, the life history method necessitates a context to understand these stories. The context provided is based in ethnographic, participant observation, and historical archival analysis. The methodological investigation of life histories has a long, yet sporadic, tradition in the study of migration. From Thomas and Znaniecki's (1918–1920) *The Polish Peasant*, American sociology has been particularly indebted to this methodological approach. While the life history approach has recently been resurrected, it has rarely been applied to the study of migration (see Bertaux 1981).[2] The study of lived social relations and the effects of class and racial oppression are of critical relevance to this study. As a leading contemporary exponent of the method argues: "It is one thing to reestablish the structure of power relations, the laws and customs governing some sector of social life in the past, another to imagine its consequences on the lives of people. Direct testimonies help chart the consequences" (Bertaux 1982, 102).

The first section of this appendix deals with the ethnographic research conducted in order to better understand the lived experiences of migrant workers. I will share my experiences working in the agricultural fields of California as well as my direct observations of migrant life in Wisconsin and Colorado. Secondly, I will discuss the archival ethnography approach and the appropriateness of the life history method for the study of migrants' experiences as well as a discussion of the sampling procedures, means of gaining access, types of interview settings, and the life story topics. Finally, the procedures for analysis will be discussed by detailing the relationship between social locations, form, and content in understanding how people remember.

The form that the life stories takes gives us insight into how particular contexts influence the determination of meaning. In this section, I engage the three relevant components of the formal aspects of the Bracero life stories collected. The focus is on how the stories are told in terms of their almost exclusively chronological story line, the positive subjective evaluations of past experiences, and the reliance on the common trope of "luck" to explain those positively viewed experiences. The various explanations available for why the life stories took the form that they did will consider factors internal and external to the interview situation. In addition, the source of meaning construction in the recollection of memories will focus on past experiences and present social locations of the Braceros interviewed. Four explanations—termed sedimentation, dialogical research acts, strategic manipulation, and imposed definitions from above—are delineated in order to account for why the life stories took the form that they did.

LOS FILES (THE FIELDS) AS A FIELD OF INQUIRY

Beginning in the summer of 1997, I embarked upon an eighteen-month venture into the field that was, quite literally, the field. I knew that I was interested in studying how Braceros experienced the program and I knew that the labor process would be extremely important given the overriding perception of Braceros that "we were here to work," as Don Daniel would tell me in a later interview. The field site for this project was the agricultural fields in Wisconsin, Colorado, and California, and I explicitly sought to work in agriculture to have more first-hand knowledge of what it felt like, for instance, to pick grapes for a paltry day's pay (though I worked for free as a precondition of employment).

For a kid who grew up in urban Denver, Colorado, with allergic and asthmatic reactions to all things organic, the idea that farm work intrinsically shaped my family history did not automatically resonate with me for a good portion of my life. My father, whose own father passed away when he was twelve, moved a number of times in his adolescence and spent time in Goodyear, Arizona, working the cotton fields with his stepfather, mom, and three brothers. They definitely did not evoke "happy memories" or "good times" which is one of the reasons he did not talk much about it to his kids. As the only Anglo family working the fields by a corporation that recruited Mexican-American laborers, my dad's life story offered a much more critical and damning retelling of life on the Goodyear farms of Litchfield Park than an older generation of Mexican Americans recalled (see Cuadraz 2005–2007).[3] Ironically, the home my parents bought to retire in is approximately five miles north of the original location of the Goodyear farms, a squalid state and city he swore he'd never return. As we trace more of the Mize family geneology, we find a long line of Kentucky and Ohio small farms in the holdings of the Mize/Eldridge/Jackson ancestors. I certainly can sympathize with the Braceros' reluctance to share the worst aspects of their Bracero Program experience for exactly this reason.

On my mother's side, the Herrera/Otero line has been farming (either as landowners, *peones*, or hired hands) for at least as long as the Spanish colonial government kept records on New Mexico. Summers for my mom were spent as a *betabalera* (sugar beet harvester) with her two sisters, two brothers, and mom. My grandpa was employed full-time in the CF&I owned iron pit mine in Sunrise, Wyoming, but his pay was never solely sufficient to afford the company-owned housing, the company-store purchased items, or the amenities (such as the YMCA) that the company owned and controlled.

So as the first generation in my family that has not had to work the fields, I embarked on my participant observation of the capitalist agricultural labor process with a certain disconnect from my family history and also from the direct experiences of the Braceros I would soon be interviewing. But there is nothing like a little on-the-job training to get the feel for the arduous nature of manual labor, to feel the aches and pains, to listen quietly while the crew boss chews your ass out for a misstep, and the disappointment felt at the end of the day when so much toil returns so little monetarily.

My first foray into the agricultural fields as a field of research inquiry actually began two years prior in rural Wisconsin. Beginning the summer of 1995, I received the opportunity to interview migrant farmworkers in Wisconsin as part of a pilot study, sponsored by the National Cancer Institutes, that examined the long-term health impacts of pesticide exposure. As part of the interviews conducted, I and two interviewers visited the labor camps in Wisconsin's Christmas tree, cucumber, and truck farm industries. Wisconsin is one of the states that prides itself on the quality of migrant housing mandated by state law, the regulation of pay and work hours, and general medical, social, and educational services for migrant families. I was constantly reminded by the study director, Dr. Doris Slesinger, that what I was witnessing was the best of conditions for migrants. The conditions I observed seemed to be based on the philosophy of "good enough" for poor Mexican immigrants but certainly not the standards that most U.S. citizens, regardless of their class status, are accustomed to.

During this research, I had less access to the labor process because we interviewed respondents at the end of the work day. What I did get much more direct exposure to was life in the labor camps and what I viewed as deplorable housing conditions. The ramschackle housing seemed to be universally marked by large gaping holes in window screens (large enough for any living thing with wings to pass through) and doors that rarely fit squarely in their jams which allowed all flightless insects easy entry. If a family decided to spend their own money, you might find fans, but the heat and humidity coupled with the lack of grass lawns, rocks, or landscaping of any kind meant houses always felt like dirty saunas. Most rooms were probably six by six feet and always served more than one function so you were either in the kitchen/bedroom or efficiency style living but for multiple families. Because most living quarters on growers' land are designed to maximize crop space, you never found yards and homes were always abutted to the crop at the legally mandated distance—never farther than the mandated 250 feet (Wisconsin Administrative Register 2004).

There always seemed to be a fresh stench of pesticide and though rules were obeyed in terms of staying out of fields after a fresh spray, the drift into the labor camps was a regular and inevitable occurrence. If there was a regular finding in all of the labor camps we visited, it always centered around the fact that there were too many families and strangers living together in single-wide trailers or three-room bungalows designed for one single family. Overcrowding was often a necessary strategy to keep rents low enough to afford, but the result was always that these cramped quarters felt much like the jobs themselves—dirty, dangerous, and undesirable.

In some of the labor camps visited, there were communal washing and bathing facilities because some homes were not equipped with running water. The appliances provided were the cheapest, crappiest, and of course dirtiest one could find. In one cucumber labor camp, we were allowed into one home where the linoleum was coming loose, exposing the dirt floor below. The stove had acquired about fifteen to twenty years of cooking experiments gone bad so that the entire surface of this once white stove was a solid black charred remnant of past meals approximately two inches thick. Directly next to the gas stove was one cot, and two more beds could be found in the kitchen, but chairs or a table were noticeably absent. In addition to cramped quarters that often meant sleeping quarters next to a gas stove, all personal contents were out for everybody to see because there was no storage except under the cots. One teenager we interviewed stated he no longer kept his personal property under his cot because the mice would then find a place to hide and eventually burrow into the mattress. He stated he did not like mice.

It is interesting to compare the experiences of the workers to one farm labor contractor (FLC) we met on a Christmas tree farm. The FLC-crew boss (he took on both roles) had satellite television, street rods, a large enclosed trailer for transporting his cars, and a double-wide to himself and his immediate family (three persons total). Even during times when nobody was in the house, his big screen TV was always on and heard blaring through an open window. His family was doing quite well by all accounts and he owned property and a home in South Texas where he recruited most of the workers to come up for the summer. His opulence was only shared by a brother who did some of the bossing around (his immediate family had a single-wide trailer to themselves). The workers' trailers we visited were always inhabited by at least two families sharing one trailer which meant two or three bedrooms and a shared kitchen/living area/bathroom. Most often, the families then rented out a portion of the living area to a single unattached male worker or two so that one trailer we visited had six adults and four children sharing this approximately 800-square-foot, three-room trailer. As the FLC lived like a king and often postured himself in such a manner, the rest lived like rats in cages.

For the vast majority of workers in the labor camps, they experienced a complete lack of privacy. Communal bathrooms and showers were key to this but also the cramped living quarters meant that workers were always in each other's personal space. On the rare occasion that people left the labor camps, they often had to drive at least ten to fifteen miles before reaching the closest small towns. Nothing was within walking distance and the few times migrants visited the local gathering places and shops, they often felt quite unwanted and those that had picked up enough English knew that the nasty looks they received were also followed up verbally by questions such as "what are *those* people doing in our town anyway?" Our research team (all Latino) witnessed this behavior in the local towns every time we took a break to fill up the gas tank or eat a meal. Lots of "there goes the neighborhood" quips were thrown our way. Unless absolutely necessary, most migrants only ventured into the local towns to pick up supplies and often tried to either get to bigger cities an hour or two away or visit stores in the late evenings or off-hours to avoid the stares and snide comments.

The one finding that seems to hold from the Bracero Program days that Ernesto Galarza identified was that the migrant housing in most public view would always be in the best condition, whereas camps off the beaten path, out of view, and hidden deep on growers' property would exemplify the most deplorable conditions. What seemed to differ is that the long, ardous work days seemed to be limited as most work I observed was based on an eight hour workday that normally started around 5:30 or 6:00 am and ended by 2:00 or 3:00 o'clock. This helped workers really miss the heat of the day during the hot and humid Wisconsin summers. We did find a general mistrust of growers to the UW–Madison research team (probably fearing that we would actually share what I am writing in this chapter). We often were forced to listen to grower complaints that migrants live better than the growers do as a condition of gaining access to respondents housed on growers' property. We also heard about window screens as the biggest complaint from growers because they hated replacing them and felt that workers constantly broke the screens themselves, but the only broken screens I witnessed were in the migrant housing, never the big house of the grower, and unless people were throwing large objects through screens and somehow wearing them thinner at the same time, it seemed that most of the screens were suffering from being too old and wearing out. Growers could be fined by state housing inspectors and the screen issue seemed to be the main tool for citing housing as not up to code. We often listened to complaints and lectures about how migrants get everything for free, particularly medical coverage, but the growers have to pay their own. Often interviews could only happen if growers were assured that the migrants would be getting nothing out of it.

As important as these observations of Wisconsin labor camp conditions, I really did not begin the participant observation component of the research until two years later when I set out to interview Braceros in Colorado and California. In the spring of 1997, I embarked upon a field research project that enabled me to connect not only my personal past and present but also the history of the Bracero Program to the contemporary capitalist agricultural labor process. During that time, I freely offered my labor to the factories in the field owners in order to learn firsthand about the nature of work in agriculture and what the Braceros endured while toiling in the fields.

If we walk through a normal working day, one gets an idea about the ardous nature of agricultural labor. I use the example of picking potatoes in the San Luis Valley of Colorado and I rely upon the testimony of an anonymous respondent who walked me through a normal day of operations that she worked as a child in the 1960s. I later observed the large potato operation that is still in operation in the center of the county seat. The respondent was one of the former migrant and seasonal workers that made it out of the fields and went on to become an advocate for migrants' rights. She, at the time of the interview, worked for a migrant services agency and detailed the effects of agricultural work on one's body. Sunrise usually means that work is already under way in the majority of factory farms across the United States. The respondent worked in the valley's potato harvest as an adolescent. "You get a terrible sunburn on your neck and back if your shirt exposes skin. You couldn't wear the gloves to pull the potatoes since you were sweating too much. . . . You had to carry the bags of potatoes to the end of the row when you filled them up and I would get blisters on my leg where the bag rubbed up against me" (Interview with Doña Isabel 1997). The respondent conducted work during her teenage years, so carrying fifty-pound bags on her shoulder, while stooping over to pick up potatoes, was particularly grueling on her body.

At the time, her work was paid as part of a family wage, so her output was included with the rest of her family's and pay would be lumped into one check. She stated that even though she was young, if she didn't fill the potato bag to the top, the person weighing and keeping track of how many bags a person filled would dump the potatoes on the ground and require her to start again. Often she and others overfilled the bag to make sure they received full credit for each bag—given that they were paid per bag (about 15 or 20 cents per bag as she recollected). Because they were paid on a piece rate, breaks were minimized and she stated her family did not earn enough to pay for lunch on some days but if they wanted food or drink, they brought it when they could afford to and ate it as quickly as possible. After the bags were filled, they were transported via trucks to the packing shed where another crew would first inspect and then place the potatoes in bags to be shipped to market. It is interesting that the major organizing features of the capitalist agricultural labor process do not differ significantly in terms of temporal and spatial contexts.

With all of these observations at hand, I was ready to embark upon more direct participant observation once we settled into the city of Fresno in the late summer of 1997. When my family and I first arrived in Fresno, our search for housing was assumed to be separate from research matters. What we quickly discovered was that Fresno was an extremely expensive city to reside in, and our limited income would only allow us to live in the concentrated low-rent areas of town. Most of the rental housing was constructed in the post-WWII housing boom that built the California economy. Some of the Braceros I interviewed lived in the same neighborhood. I, and unwittingly my family, would be much more ensconsed in the participant observation component of my research than we ever intended. What we also discovered was that in the high times of the 1990s California and national economic boom, we were moving to a community with an unemployment rate of approximately 13 percent. Fresno is a city with no significant industrial base, and given the fact that Fresno County is the most profitable, highest-producing agricultural county in the United States, the city's minimal economic infrastructure is almost completely steeped in agriculture. Unlike the coastal metropoles, the central valley of California has remained primarily a one-trick pony with agriculture firmly rooted as the nearly exclusive base of the economy. Though the temperate climate allows for several production cycles and year-round land usage, the work associated with agriculture is highly sporadic and seasonal in nature. Non-harvesting, low labor intensive times of the growing cycle meant unemployment might rise to something closer to an unofficial 25 percent.

So we eventually selected a charming, little bungalow that had two bedrooms, allowed pets, and fit our budget. Little did we know when we selected the home that we would experience a year that included cockfights, our house nearly burnt down, prostitution deals gone awry outside our bedroom window, Fresno as seen through the eyes of heroin addicts, the nightly visits of "ghetto birds," and New Year's Eve under the hail of gunfire. We selected a home on a dead-end street that abutted up against the canal. In the days of the Bracero Program, the canals were irrigating a larger number of farms within the city limits in what are now residential areas. The canals seem to be the place where illicit activities thrive. The reasons are twofold: (1) getting an automobile (i.e., cop car) onto the canal pathways is almost impossible and (2) the nearby yards make for great hiding places. Illicit activities including heavy drug use, theft, and prostitution seemed to be the main deviant means of coping with life in a city with 25 percent unemployment during the boom-boom economy circa 1990s era.

In the year we lived along the canal, we had the next door neighbor's abandoned garage burned to the ground. We were awakened by our dog, Puck, barking at the bright orange glow in the window that signaled our fence, trelliced deck, and tree that hung over our home was on fire. It was the only night that we were glad to see the Fresno police helicopter with its search light shining in our backyard. Every other night we were guaranteed to be spotted, with the lights shining down on us, whenever we let our dog out, sat in our backyard, or stepped outside of our home. Living on the canal meant we were in the direct path of the police surveillance apparatus. The other event that brought inner city living to this farm town too big for its britches was the regular practice, largely ignored by Fresno's finest, of street prostitution. We lived a block off Blackstone Avenue which was home to the rundown mall, Denny's, and sex workers. The fact that we lived off the canal on a dead-end street meant that we were the regular stop for the consummation of john-prostitute exchanges. We learned to deal with it, but the uneasiness of it all happened one night with an exchange gone badly (directly outside our bedroom window) resulted in a woman screaming at the top of her lungs while running half-naked through our front yard and a car speeding off first towards the woman and finally down another street and away from the scene.

My partner Chris was one of the few city residents, not employed in agriculture, who was able to find steady employment while I conducted research and drained the family's financial reserves (ok we had no reserves, let's say pushed the credit cards to their limit). Chris was employed by the local methadone clinic as a drug counselor. Understanding the city from the sizable clientele of Fresno's heroin addicts, Chris was introduced to many of the ways that people cope with an obscenely high standard of living coupled with severely limited economic opportunities. Her clients ran the spectrum that the city had to offer: prostitutes, homeless, bank managers, agricultural laborers, farm labor contractors, housewives, veterans, small business owners, truck drivers, and creative entreprenuers. We probably bought every handcrafted item that her clients were offering for sale and heard about every descent into addiction story that always seems amazing that people have the will to live given such horrendous life circumstances.

On the days when I had my daughter and she needed a walk, we often used the canal (much less activity during daylight hours) to explore the city and see what people threw into the canal this week. Tori's favorite item was shopping carts; local television news' favorites included stolen cars and dead bodies, but luckily our discoveries were tame and mildly amusing. Rarely did life on either side of the canal come into direct contact with one another but once in awhile we would cross the street bridge to explore the "other side." Tori was thrilled one day when she discovered roosters, lots of roosters ornately decorated, stored in cages, and some walking around freely in the yard. Farm animals in the middle of the city, now I've seen everything, was my first response, but when we heard about the cockfighting ring that had been uncovered and shut down a few months later, we returned to find the house boarded up and no more chickens.

Rarely did we find ourselves feeling like we were in direct danger and definitely the best neighbors and landlord we have ever had lived in Fresno. In fact, the kids who were getting high in the abandoned garage and accidentally lit it on fire were the same kids who ran over to our house and attempted to put out the fence/deck/tree fire with our garden hose, before the fire rescue and police arrived. It was New Year's Eve that put personal fear into random acts of violence. Fresno, when the new year arrives, is like any other city with some people partying in bars, most at home watching Dick Clark and the ball drop, but the added touch of distinction happens at midnight when anybody who owns a gun loads it and fires it into the air. It was the only night when the ghetto bird was not flying, which I took notice of when I went out with the dog and wasn't blinded by the police helicopter searchlight. A hail of gunfire erupted and the sounds of AK-47s and other automatic weapons drowned out the single shots of handguns and shotguns. Unfortunately, the recognition that gunshots must inevitably come down seems to be lost on the celebrants, and every year, there is a story of a child asleep in his or her bed is hit by a bullet that penetrates the roof of a house. The new year we experienced resulted in one child shot to death by raining gunfire that pelted neighbors' roofs but the single shot that hit the young boy's house traveled through the roof, crawlspace, and embedded into the head of the sleeping child, killing him instantly. The night the Fresno police were too frightened to go out was enough to strike fear in this family that had already survived fire, tricks gone bad, drug addicts, and several other illicit incidents.

But the main reason for moving to Fresno was to interview Braceros and get a firsthand feel for what it was like to perform agricultural labor. With initial contacts established by Professor Andy Alvarado at CSU-Fresno, I began working in the grape fields near the end of the summer harvest. Accompanied into the fields by the FLC contact who was nice enough to employ me without grower permission, I began my firsthand accounting of the contours of agricultural labor. An excerpt from my field notes should suffice in describing how the contemporary agricultural labor process is organized.

> September 23, 1997. *First Day on the Job*: I arrived late and everybody had already begun. I parked off the highway and the FLC drove me to the growers' field. Arriving in the big blue Ford Torino (not the *qué chévere* Starsky and Hutch model, more the mid-80's boat on wheels with white vinyl seats), the car immediately attracted the attention of the workers. The female crew boss automatically put down her tools and met the car near another worker's parked van. People knew that the FLC had arrived and a few quick glances to survey the situation did not seem to slow the pace of work. I was told that the heavy rains were molding the second run through so I would have to clean each bunch to remove moldy grapes and vines. I was given a plastic tray (a 2x2 foot square about 6 inches deep) to place the good grapes. The FLC asked if I had pruning shears, my answer was no, so we went back to the back of the Torino to get the necessary tool. In this field of Emperor table grapes, each row was about one-quarter mile long and there were at least fifty rows. A large extended family (aged about six to sixties) worked on one row and I was placed with a single, unattached male in the next row. He never spoke with anyone

the entire day and seemed new to this work crew, but certainly not to the job task. He moved quickly and easily doubled my output.

Starting in at 9:00 am, it wasn't too hot though the sun never seemed to offer any relief. One quickly began to hope for a breeze or a even a small, wispy cloud to interrupt the direct rays. Each row was created with 2x4's that were shaped in Y's to create a row of grapevines on each side. The vines grew at eye-level so most of the day one's arms are lifted up to pull the bunches off the vines. Many of the grapes had spoiled, the best ones picked in the first run. The full work day would mean I completed about ½ of a row, whereas the good workers completed about one and one-half to two rows. Every 30 minutes or so the tractor would come through the rows (each row was spaced to fit the tractor on the muddy path between them) so by watching my fellow worker, I saw him place his body under the vines and pull his head into the vines to make sure he avoided the six foot in diameter tractor tires. After a few close shaves with the tire coming close enough to my face to feel the displaced wind, I figured out the trick (so much for unskilled labor). With a tractor driver and one helper, we waited until the tractor pulled makeshift trailer passed and lifted our filled trays to the helper. I didn't find out until the end of the day that I was paid by the number of crates filled (certainly I numbered less than 10 with all the cleaning and pruning that was needed). Subsequently I find out from crew boss that the first run usually paid an hourly wage and it was easy to fill fifty trays on the days when the picking was good.

During a quick break, the crew boss asks why I am here. I explain my research and she tells me she's taking college classes in addition to her work. She's the only English speaker in her family so our conversation remains between the two of us. Everybody has brought their own Diet Pepsi's to drink and a quick snack of a burrito wrapped in tin foil or a bag of chips. Only the single worker and I have nothing to eat or drink. Wanting to get the full experience, I visit the portable toilet (about 10 rows down from where we are working) With UFW and ALRB [United Farm Workers and California Agricultural Labor Relations Board] advances in the safety and protections of workers, I decided to take advantage of the mandated facility within 150 feet. Quick realization: workers don't use the portable facilities, they seem to have figured out the liquid intake and sweat expulsion ratio to avoid the need to empty the bladder. This porta-potty has never been cleaned. There is a mud mountain inside that fills the entire area where one is supposed to stand. It smells as if it's never been emptied, and the only recent users seem to be me and the flies. You have to stand with your feet at an angle to climb over the mud mountain and reach the actual toilet, no toilet paper, mud caked on the walls. At least I hope it's mud.

When I return, everybody is back working and I return to my station. The next run through by the tractor, I ask them to stop so I can get a drink of water that is bungee cord strapped to the trailer. There are clean, disposable cups next to the Gatorade cooler. Again, another UFW/ALRB requirement for worker safety. Again, I am probably the first worker to ever drink the shit. The water tastes like salt and dirt, and it seems hotter than the air temperature itself. Now I know why the tractor crew (definitely a step up in the hierarchy of job tasks) looked at me as if I was *loco* when I requested a drink.

> The rest of the day tends to blur. The heat . . . waves radiating off the rows that remind me of the National Geographic stock representation of the Serengeti Plains. Repetition, repetition, repetition. One begins to feel like a machine after awhile but this reminds me of all repetitive task jobs I've had (cleaning toilets and polishing the 2,047 cherry wood seats/brass name plates at CU–Boulder's Macky Auditorium, inspecting metal rods for scratches—quality assurance—at an RV accessory factory, mass mailings for Ray-O-Vac, and the list goes on). Being outdoors adds another layer of crap to deal with (dust, dehydration, work hazards). Well, tomorrow will be better. At least, I won't have to start from scratch and I'll have the picking process down (again, so much for unskilled labor). I am surprised how quickly blisters form though, let's hope they harden soon. In addition, my hands have a white stench to them that I assume is the pesticide residue that still clings to the vines even after the punishing rains.

The job tasks of the current labor process are not markedly different from the Bracero Program era. In terms of the crops, the tasks of planting, watering, thinning, weeding, and picking are much the same. Then, the packing process is also similar across crops as it requires sorting, boxing, stacking, and finally shipping. The work hazards are similar, which explains why agriculture consistently ranks as one of the most dangerous occupations in the United States (construction and mining competed with agriculture during the program's duration but today, construction is the sole industry that is consistently more deadly than agricultural labor). The arduous nature of the work, the constant exposure to pesticides, farm machinery and implement hazards, and difficult working conditions are all major contributors to work-related accidents and injuries.

The post-UFW advances and current regulations to protect workers often serve as merely window dressing. My experiences in the field were that the mandated improvements were well marked (signs about pesticides in Spanish and English for instance) but most often one would find not-so-potable water that has never been touched, portable potties that have never been cleaned, and the constant residue of pesticides in fields where the rules of spraying and entry were obeyed. Mandated breaks and working hours, though often defined by state law, more often than not are still dependent upon the crop cycle and available labor pool. The incentive is to get most of the highly perishable product to the market in the narrow window of opportunity that nature gives. The major change I did identify was a return to the families in the fields. Though the Bracero Program placed a premium on young, unattached male workers, the current labor force tends to rely on a family wage and each contributing family member who is able to is providing their labor.

Direct grower-worker relations were irrelevant in the fields I worked in because I never saw the owner of the land. Every aspect of production was dictated by the farm labor contractor. Whether one found work, what rows one would work in, when breaks would be taken (in actuality, if one received a half-hour break for lunch, it was fortunate), how much one would be paid, and whether one would be paid by piece or hourly rates were all decisions made by the FLC. The other facet of the labor process that stood out was the heavy role and presence of surveillance. I avoided the original FLC that gave me my first job as it was readily apparent to the other workers that I had arrived with him, I was given pruning tools by him, and for most of the work day nobody but the female crew boss ever talked to me. Her inquiry was more about whether I was sent to spy on them and their productivity, and my stated role as researcher seemed adequate enough to just avoid me for the rest of the day. It was through lower level contacts that I found subsequent work. Days of exhaustion that I didn't replicate back-to-back but I felt enough after an eight- to ten-hour day to realize that this was extremely hard work—more difficult than my years spent as a janitor, quality assurance peon, electrician's apprentice, or working in my dad's warehouse. The arduous nature of "unskilled" agribusiness labor, coupled with the constant surveillance, makes it quite apparent to me why migrant parents do not want their children working in the fields, why it's a subject deemed not worth talking about, and why only those who seem to have precious few options are the folks who opt in as farm laborers.

ARCHIVAL ETHNOGRAPHY APPROACH[4]

There is a not so old adage, popularized by high school sports coaches across the United States, that "there's no 'I' in team." The idea being that teams are only successful when players are self-less, individuals dutifully perform whatever role is assigned to them, and a single player never puts their own glory or ego before that of the collective entity. The literal interpretation is strictly syllabic given that team is spelled without an "i." When thinking of the historical formation of ethnography as a method of analysis, a comparable saying that there is "no I in ethnography" may very well summarize the vast majority of ethnological and cultural anthropological research. In the historical development of the two disciplines, the author took the role of the imperial, distanced interpreter of all actions and thus presumed the thoughts of the natives while assuming the evolutionary superior position. He presumed that his own interpretations were in fact the only real or true versions of why the inferior natives did what they did. Thanks to Margaret Mead, Frans Boaz, Ruth Benedict, Horace Miner, and Ralph Linton to name a few, cultural relativism (that a culture should be judged according to its own standards, and never to assume that the culture from which you come from is automatically superior to all others) dislodged the evolutionary tinge from the body of anthropological research.

To take on the imperial eye of the anthropologist, it was not until what has been termed the "postmodern turn" or critical/experimental ethnography intervention that we got a sense of the partiality of how an ethnographer interprets their worlds of investigation and a stronger sense of how the "I" in fact shapes the selection of material that is presented, the types of questions to ask, the rituals and performances to study, or in other words how the entire research act is shaped by the investigator themselves. The work of Geertz, Clifford, Marcus, Rabinow, Behar, and in Chicano anthropology Rosaldo, Foley, Flores, and Limon have fundamentally challenged the truth claims of ethnographic investigations and the inherently biased (partial) subject position of the ethnographer.

In some ways, the introspective turn has paralyzed the field of anthropology and too many contemporary ethnographies read in the mode of "enough about you, let's talk about me."[5] Striking out by attempting to avoid the Charybdis of reflexivity to the point of self-narcissism and the Scylla of ethnographer as imperialist that currently plagues ethnographic methods, my method of presentation relies on my own personal subjectivities, but I also am attempting to share other people's stories, stories that are much more fascinating and relevant than mine. The dilemmas posed by new ethnography are best summarized by Doug Foley and Renato Rosaldo.

> There is currently considerable debate over what an ethnographic study really is. Some still think of ethnographies as objective scientific studies. Others, like me, have lost faith in this grand ideal. I now think of ethnographies more as personal encounters. I make no claims that the tale I am about to spin is absolutely true. I have worked hard to make it more fact than fiction, but as in all so-called factual books, I am characterizing people as I see them. I am also reporting the events and stories that I found most interesting and revealing. Others might put a very different face on these people and events (Foley 1995, viii–ix).

> All interpretations are provisional; they are made by positioned subjects who are prepared to know certain things and not others. Even when knowledgeable, sensitive, fluent in the language, and able to move easily in an alien cultural world, good ethnographers still have their limits, and their analyses always are incomplete. . . . Throughout, I have stressed, first, that the social analyst is a positioned subject, not a blank slate, and second, that the objects of social analysis are also analyzing subjects whose perceptions must be taken nearly as seriously as "we" take our own (Rosaldo 1993, 8, 207).

What makes ethnographic investigations so relevant is not simply the ethnographer but it is good to know what their subject position is going in so one has a basis for determining how well the author knows the people they are writing about. In addition, the role of filter by ethnographers can never be underestimated, but we often find the words of researched come through most clearly when they say things the researcher never anticipated. It is really the obligation of the ethnographer to learn how to listen and push themselves to the limits of their partial perspectives.

What we often get is an anthropology of anthropology that does a great job of identifying and criticizing the anthropologist's role in setting the field. I think the questioning of classical ethnography provides a much better picture of the extent to which ethnographies are reflective of anthropology more so than those who are under investigation. The best example that comes to my mind is the photograph of Boas and George Hunt holding a dark sheet to cover up the "modern" background/backyard of fences and bourgeois houses with back porches with an American Indian woman in the foreground rocking a "primitive" cradle made of tree branches and a cord tied to her foot (in Clifford 1988, 186). Often, the way that anthropologists constructed the native had much more to do with the colonialist aspects of how the colonizer viewed the colonized than how the colonized viewed themselves. But why we still do ethnography is we have a lot to learn from other people, particularly those that are most marginalized in our society.

For instance, Foley's *Learning Capitalist Culture* is a relevant ethnography for one overriding reason: though the actors change and the micro-locales are important for setting the context of how high school performances are shaped by the enactment of race, class, and gender roles, the reality is that Paul Willis' lads[6] don't seem that much different in their expressive counter-school culture practices than Foley's Chicano vatos. And just as importantly, I felt like I was reading about my late 1980s high school in Northglenn, Colorado, when I read about how youth interacted in 1970s Pearsall, Texas. In fact, since I have used this book in my "Introduction to Sociology" course since 1997, Northtown High School sure seems a hell of a lot like high schools in Janesville, Wisconsin; San Diego, California; Denver, Colorado; Fort Wayne, Indiana; Ithaca, New York; and Portland, Oregon. I dated Tara, I hung out with the stoners who blew off school, and though the rural context is important—Anglo-Mexicano relations are context specific and duly important—the reality is that competition, a rigid class reproduction system, gender patriarchy, and nasty racial relations are alive and well in nearly every U.S. micro-locale. I was keenly interested in how those micro-locales were recollected in Braceros' life stories.

Life stories are the accounts of a person's own lived experiences as orally communicated by that person. Life histories are life stories and the supplementary materials to the person's own story like written documents, other biographies, and other sources of history (Bertaux 1981, 7). This approach enables respondents in marginalized positions to tell the stories about important events that have shaped their lives. Additionally, the intersubjectivity of all sources of history can be critically explored by focusing on the formal characteristics of each textual source. The potential applications of the approach are varied but it is suited for both the study of lived social relations and the subjective recollections of those relations. Life histories can be used "not only to study the subjective side of social life, but also to understand whole sets of socio-structural relationships such as processes of migration" (Bertaux 1990, 167).

Seventeen life stories of former Braceros were collected. I initially chose to conduct interviews in California because it was the state that received the vast majority of Braceros. Research was conducted in Fresno County as it is the most productive agricultural county in the nation and it is heavily dependent upon migrant labor. Also, it has a metropolitan center where there are opportunities, albeit very limited, for farm workers to improve their economic condition by seeking employment beyond farm labor.

Additionally, oral interviews were conducted with people who had a connection with the program. Bus drivers/crew bosses, postal workers who processed money orders, food suppliers, state government housing inspectors, and Mexican-American activists were asked about their views on the program and the living conditions of former Braceros. The majority of these ancillary interviews were conducted in the San Luis Valley of Southern Colorado. The valley was one of three regions in Colorado that heavily employed Bracero labor and is truly unique in its local history. The valley represents the far northern frontier of Spanish colonization from the New Mexico region. The headwaters of the Rio Grande flow from the valley and the river has enabled agricultural production since pre-Spanish conquest.

More recent research was conducted on the U.S.–Mexico border by then research assistant Sergio Chavez. He collected life stories of five former Braceros from all over Mexico who eventually settled in the border region. All of the respondents were contacted through the burgeoning social movement of former Braceros who are congregating and sharing their experiences on a weekly basis in the border cities, Tlaxcala, and Mexico City, Federal District.

The research, which was dependent upon oral sources, was coupled with other historical sources on the program: secondary literature, government commission and state agency reports, university extension reports, and primary research conducted during its operation by Mexican-American scholar-labor activist Ernesto Galarza. All of these materials together constitute the elements, or as Bertaux refers to them as "life stories and the supplementary materials," of the life history approach.

The issue of statistical representativeness (i.e., using procedures for the purpose of generalizing from sample to population) is not a direct aim of this study but it should be addressed to explain the process of selecting former Bracero workers. Bertaux (1981, 37) states that a sample of life histories should be representative at the sociological level, that is, at the level of socio-structural relations. In qualitative research, one must specify the theoretical relevance of the group one chooses to study. In the previous research on the Bracero Program, workers' experiences tend to be either deemed irrelevant or (when documented with ethnographic research) they tend to be reduced to the salient characteristics that comprise "the typical Bracero." It has followed an epistemological reasoning that attempts to generalize individual biographies to a statistical notion of representativeness or typicality while retaining notions of the objectivity of both the researcher and the data in "discovering" the average Bracero.

Gaining access to the migrant farmworker community is an extremely difficult endeavor for most social scientists. Language barriers for non-Spanish speakers, arranging entry to labor camps owned by growers, and a high degree of skepticism on the part of migrants of anyone viewed as an authority figure associated with the U.S. government (and by extension, *la migra* or ICE/INS) all serve as potential obstacles for the researcher. In my case, initial entry was provided by a source in the migrant service community (Rural Legal Aid). My initial plan when research began was to conduct studies in three regions (California, Colorado, and Northern Mexico) but I sincerely underestimated the amount of time and attention needed to gain access and develop the degree of trust necessary to conduct interviews in a setting that facilitated "open" dialogue between respondents and the interviewer. The time lapse between the U.S. and Mexico components of the study is a direct result. In the following sections, I discuss more fully the limits of this "open" dialogue but potential sources of blocking information in the interviews were my limited command of Spanish (in particular, the fact that my Spanish is "learned" as one of my translators immediately identified), the status of myself and the interviewers as Chicano/as who were born and raised in the United States, my status as an outsider to the Fresno farmworker community, the presence of videotape equipment, and the types of sensitive questions I was asking. Research conducted in Mexico dealt with these barriers as the research was conducted by a graduate student who grew up as a farmworker, who had better communication skills in Spanish with the farmworker community, and who was a son of Mexican immigrants, yet still had significant issues in securing the trust of former Braceros.

To better understand the internal dynamics of the interview situation, I collected life stories by varying the way data-gathering was conducted. The interviews with twelve former Braceros were conducted in the following formats: myself and a translator talking with one Bracero at a time (4), one Bracero interviewing another Bracero while I passively observed (1), myself without a translator talking with two Braceros (2), and a group discussion with former workers (4) and female relatives where I passively observed. Most of the interviews in Mexico were conducted during weekend gatherings of former Braceros and their families in a public park. Interviews were also videotaped but most often conducted in an one-on-one format. All of these interviews were conducted in Spanish. Another translator, a native speaker who grew up in the farmworker community, was hired to capture the subtle differences in linguistic styles. Translations and transcriptions were completed by Alicia Swords after extensive language training and field research in Southern Mexico. Interviews with another female relative and those affiliated with the program in Colorado were conducted in English and utilized one-on-one interview formats.[7]

The topics of the life stories were determined first by the respondent and then followed up by a set of questions that attended to the theoretical issues of concern. In line with the life history approach, my intention was to make my first question as open as possible (Anderson and Jack 1991, Casey 1993). I asked: "Tell me about your life while you were working as a Bracero." Ideally, this would facilitate the story-teller to take control of the interview situation and talk freely (Bertaux 1981, 39). In reality, the question was more perplexing than thought-provoking and was usually met with the response: "What would you like me to talk about?" I read this as a hint toward the power dynamics within the interview relationship.

A series of questions to investigate the reproduction of class relations, resistance to the racial and class privilege, and cultural adaptation were subsequently asked to attend to the theoretically relevant issues of concern. These questions included information about the jobs they took upon arriving in the United States, job mobility (both laterally and vertically), character of work and tasks involved, economic position of children and other important family members, geographic locations of work, reasons for migration, occupations in Mexico, racial/ethnic composition of fellow workers and managers, experiences with Anglo communities, migration history, time-period and duration of stays in the United States, and cultural practices (religious worship, holiday observances, Spanish/English fluency, dietary preferences, intermarriage, and interpersonal relationships). These questions did not follow a set interview schedule but were introduced in a more dialogic fashion. Each issue was dealt with in every interview but exact questions depended upon each interview situation.

The very form of the story depends a great deal on the social locations of those telling the story. Whether the stories originate from the distinct experiences of women (Leydesdorff et al. 1996), specific localities in working-class Italy (Passerini 1987; Portelli 1991), or the particular media of U.S. popular culture (Lipsitz 1990), our memories of individual experiences have an important affinity with our race, class, and gender locations. There are certain significant events in the lives of members who constitute a community and are indelibly marked on the collective conscience. Investigating the way we remember, as it applies to the Braceros' life stories, gives us insight into the sense-making mechanisms of lived experiences. But I think it would be incorrect to overstate this correspondence. Instead, I return to Hall's theory of articulation that "enables us to think how an ideology empowers people, enabling them to begin to make some sense or intelligibility of their historical situation, without reducing those forms of intelligibility to their socio-economic or class location or social position" (Hall 1986b, 53).

The next section is an analysis of the formal aspects of the life stories that I collected during the course of the study. The similar patterns of story-telling shape the content of what is remembered, what is forgotten, and what is silenced during the interview. By examining the sources of the determination of meaning in terms of both the interview context and the social locations of those involved in the research act, the relationship between memory and experience is further explored within and beyond the confines of each individual interview. Finally, I will look at different components of historical memory as it pertains to the citizens of Mexico, the United States, and those border-crossers who live between both worlds.

NARRATIVE AND FORM

Rarely do practitioners of the life history method attend to the formal aspects of the life stories they collect. But these narratives are perfectly suited for a close examination of the formal characteristics necessary to answer the questions: How is the story told? Is the story line consistent or contradictory? What are the conventions relied upon in the re-telling of one's life story? From these questions, I narrowed my focus on the analysis of form to the chronological story lines indicative of most of the life stories I collected. In addition, I examined how the Braceros viewed their experiences and the subjective evaluations they used to describe their life and times during the Bracero Program. Finally, I will discuss the dominant trope invoked, that of being "lucky," to explain the overwhelmingly positive subjective evaluations by the former Braceros.

When considering the formal characteristics of the life stories collected for this study, I initially relied upon the prior publications and unpublished repositories of Mexican immigrant oral histories. Manuel Gamio (1971a, 1971b) was the first to collect the life stories of Mexican immigrants in the United States. What makes his studies problematic, in terms of analyzing the formal properties of his interviews, is the incomplete nature of the published life stories and the heavy reliance upon a set interview schedule. But in terms of the motivations for migrating, Gamio's respondents assist in mapping the general rationales for Mexican immigration to the United States. But as a whole, Gamio's life stories fit a pattern more often seen in the structured format (set-interview schedule) than the more open-ended approach that I attempted to employ.

Ernesto Galarza undertook the most extensive study of Mexican Braceros throughout the duration of the program's existence. Rather than documenting the life stories of his respondents, Galarza focused more on documenting their treatment by U.S. growers. His field notes consist of Galarza's impressions of his respondents like the "worker mentalities stuck in 'Porfinismo', deserve to be poor, no leadership or group techniques" (Galarza Papers, "Field Notes,1952–1957," Box 3, Folder 1). Complete interview transcripts are not available nor are there many direct quotes from Braceros in the field notes. From this record, it is impossible to reconstruct the life stories of individual Braceros to complete a formal analysis of the interview contexts.

It is the work of Maria Herrera-Sobek (1979) that provides the initial basis for the analysis of the forms the life stories take. Her monograph, *The Bracero Experience: Elitelore versus Folklore*, enables us to investigate the conventions of story-telling, interviewer-interviewee relations, and social locations of respondents. The form of the life stories collected for this study resembled the life stories presented in *The Bracero Experience* in one significant way. Each of the respondents I interviewed in groups of two or singularly presented the details of their lives as Braceros in, more or less, the same narrative form.[8] In answering the question: "What was your life like living as a Bracero?," the story followed a chronological line, in the fashion of the states they worked in, when they were contracted, and which crops they were employed in. The details were mostly descriptive in terms of "in 1957, I worked in sugar beets in Utah." The form of the stories held a strong family resemblance with the composite Bracero depicted as "Pedro's Story" in Herrera-Sobek's account of Mexican immigrant folklore. The discussion follows a chronological line with sometimes an interesting anecdote interspersed throughout the time-based recollection. But it is impossible for me to say that the form the life stories take are the same since Herrera-Sobek's is a combination of sixteen respondents worked into one representative story that is guided by the author's editorial hand. Even though her respondents all resided in the same *pueblo* in Michoacan, Mexico and temporarily migrated to Montana, Texas, Michigan, California, Arkansas, Nebraska, Colorado, and Mississippi from the time period of 1947–1963, the experiences in the United States were seemingly similar enough to Herrera-Sobek to warrant the composite sketch of one Bracero's story as representative of all (Herrera-Sobek 1979, 42).

Even with this limitation of reducing multiple stories into one, there was another feature of the formal aspects of the life stories that coincided with Pedro's story. What both Herrera-Sobek and I heard from the Braceros was the overwhelmingly positive evaluation of the Mexican immigrants' experiences in the United States.

> Well, we travelled day and night. We were all very happy when we arrived at Libes [Libby] Montana. It was there, yes it was there that the interpreter tells us, "You men are from Mexico," he says, "how are you doing there?"
> "Well, quite all right, Señor," he answered.
> "Are you happy?" he asked.
> "Yes, sure!" we answered.
> "Well, you will be even more happy to know that over there, in the last car, there are some of your countrywomen waiting for you. They have come to greet you!" he told us (Herrera-Sobek 1979, 44).

Herrera-Sobek's composite Bracero then goes on to explain that the women were in fact nurses who innoculated them for communicable diseases and the negative reaction to the immunization caused a number of them to become extremely ill.

The majority of respondents I interviewed did not express a negative evaluation of their time spent in the program. The consistent answer I got when Braceros were asked if they were mistreated by growers and crew bosses was basically an emphatic no.

> RM: Did you ever have difficulties or problems with Anglo growers?
>
> Don Liberio: Oh no . . . no, no, no, no.

A less emphatic response was given by Antonio de Guanajuato:

> The rancher would pick us up and take us where the work would be and when the work was done then the rancher would take us back [to the association's labor camp]. Each rancher was distinct and some were good and some were bad. I was lucky, I . . . with a good rancher. He was a German. He saw that I didn't have nice clothes and he gave me good clothes. Army clothes. So I put it on because he gave it to me. And if I had known to speak English, I would have requested to stay with him but I didn't know. And I still don't know nothing (Life Story of Don Antonio 1997).

The majority of respondents, with the lone exception of Don Antonio's experience with the German grower in Texas, could not talk about their experiences with growers because they rarely, if ever, met those who owned the land they toiled on. It was the immediate supervisor, the farm labor contractor (FLC) or the crew boss, who was always of Mexican descent, that the Braceos directly interacted with.

As noted above, the Braceros I spoke with did not have any relations, positive or negative, with growers because they simply did not come into contact with them. In the Galarza Papers, there is ample documentation of the complete disregard for the Braceros as anything but hired hands. According to one of Galarza's respondents, who was working for the San Joaquin Farm Production Association, "we have no names—we are known by numbers" (Galarza Papers 3:1). During the time that potential Braceros were participating in the recruitment and contracting processes (in Mexico and U.S. border towns, respectively), they were handled by their number. In effect, batch-handling necessitates a de-individualization of participants and elicits the emotion of feeling like a number.

If Braceros seemed to exhibit dissatisfied attitudes, there certainly would be a strong basis for this belief. If the characterization that Hancock (see chapter 2) put forward had a stronger basis in workers' experiences, it might be more of a dilemma to explain why "the printed reaction to the Bracero Program is unfavorable." But Hancock never questions to whom the Braceros appear satisfied. As a FLC and medical assistant, he had a great deal to say in terms of who was contracted and who was allowed to work. Why would the Braceros complain to him? Why jeopardize their future dealings in the United States by presenting anything but a favorable disposition toward the entire experience as a contracted laborer?

One possible source of similarity between Hancock's positive characterization of the Program as he saw it and the positive evaluations by respondents I spoke with is the power dynamics present in both studies. I have already addressed Hancock's position of power, but it is my social location as a representative of a state-sanctioned public university, an outsider to the community in which my respondents reside, and a fifth-generation Chicano born and raised in the United States who doesn't speak Spanish fluently that may have elicited the positive subjective evaluation of the past experiences of former Braceros.

A common trope utilized by Braceros for explaining why their experiences were so positive is that their particular circumstances were attributed to luck. Herrera-Sobek (1979, 45) addresses the issue of "luck" in the details of the composite Bracero's life story:

> The farmer was responsible for the workers and all the time they were there. It was lucky for us that we got a very nice farmer. He took eight men. We were all from Huecorio [Michoacan]. We worked hoeing beets. Since none of us knew that type of work, the *patron* went to show us how we should do it. He told us how we should stand so that our backs would not hurt so much. Heck, our backs hurt anyway. By evening time we could not straighten ourselves! And how everybody laughed! Yes, there was so much laughter and teasing. We were all laughing and poking fun with each other.

The "luck" of finding a nice farmer is discussed in the same breadth as the mention of the grower's control over laborers and the nature of back-breaking work. Every former Bracero I interviewed expressed that their specific experiences during the program were bearable because they too were extremely lucky. *"Tengo suerte"* was probably the most common phrase expressed by the respondents. The good relations that Don Antonio had with his German grower were attributed to the luck of happening upon a good-natured farmer. When Jorge Colima was asked if he was mistreated, he replied: "I have no reason to say this, or that, I will simply tell the truth. I've always had good luck, I don't know why. I always had work, and the people have always treated me well. I can't say that I've been treated bad." This theme of it being a matter of luck, even in terms of whether one found work, was also explicitly identified in another interview. "It was the luck of the draw if you found work" (Interview with Jose Michoacan).

Yet, within this form of the content, the Braceros I spoke with also detailed a labor process controlled via the principal means of coercion, a life in the United States almost totally segregated from all other non-Braceros, and labor camp conditions that combined the despotic regime of work (even into most non-work related activities) with total social isolation. The conditions they recollect, though never characterized as malicious or even undeserved, closely aligns with the findings of the authoritative source on the program, Ernesto Galarza, who conducted his research while the program was in operation. "There were discontents caused by underemployment, unsatisfactory earnings, deductions from wages, poor food, excessive charges, improper records, substandard housing, unnecessary exposure to hazards and occasional physical mistreatment" (Galarza 1964, 183–84).

THE SOURCES OF MEANING DETERMINATIONS

The inevitable question is why? Why do the Braceros speak favorably of their time spent under contract only to contradict themselves in the process of recollecting the details of their lived experiences? Possible explanations abound but a set of clues as to the nature of the meaning determinations coupled with the research act significantly narrow the range of possible explanations (see Table A2.1). From the prior discussions on the relationship between memories and experiences, the role that the respondents' and interviewer's social locations play in mediating those relations is paramount. In addition, the interview context is extremely important to understanding how the wording of questions shape the possible range of responses and other similar issues.

Sedimentation

The most simplistic way of dealing with the relationship is to posit a direct correspondence between people's memories and their past experiences. The early people's history tradition and in particular, the early work of Paul Thompson (1978), exemplify this method of explanation. Phenomenological discussions of the relationship use the term "sedimentation" to posit a direct link between experiences and memories (see Berger and Luckmann 1966,

		The Source of Meaning Construction:	
		Past Experiences	Present Social Location
Negotiation of Meaning as it Relates to the Interview Context:	Endogenous	Dialogical Research Act	Strategic Manipulation
	Exogenous	Sedimentation	Imposed Definitions From Above

Table A2.1. Meaning Determinations

69). There is no mediating factor in the subjective recollection of past experiences since this approach would posit that memories are in fact direct, or true, copies of past events.

In the present study, it would be difficult to reconcile the contradictory memories of the same experiences as recollected by former Braceros. If one takes the Braceros' words at face value, one has a positive evaluation of their experiences during the program. But one also has to reconcile this with the respondents' detailed explanations that contradict this evaluation: workers cheated out of wages, served rancid food, housed in everything from tents to barns, and forced to live a life of isolation usually reserved to those members of society labelled criminals or mentally unfit for society. Nonetheless, their detailed responses to specific questions about the program rarely, if ever, received the treatment guaranteed to the workers in their standard work contract. In addition, the Braceros interviewed in Mexico presumably were part of the same program that the Fresno Braceros were and the former's detailed recollections of the processing centers definitely attest to some humiliating experiences.

The contradiction between the positive subjective evaluations and the negative treatment recollected by the Braceros makes the view untenable that memories are the direct sediments of past events. It becomes untenable to equate memories with experiences because the memories contradict themselves in terms of the evaluation of experiences and the details of those experiences. If the positive evaluations about life as a contract laborer were coupled with recollections about only positive experiences, one would have a direct correspondence between memories and experiences. But the details of recollected experiences and secondary sources on the Bracero Program belie such a correspondence and a more complicated framework for analysis must be consulted in order to account for this discordance.

The Dialogical Research Act

A second way of dealing with the determination of meaning is to limit the scope of explanation to factors internal to the interview situation. As Eliasoph (1990) notes about the interview context, speech only makes sense in its particular social context. Though Eliasoph is particularly interested in public opinion polls or political attitude surveys, the case is general enough to make the point about any research act. Public opinion polls give us measures of what people think when asked their opinion in a poll. The polls, or any other type of interview, are not true representations of an attitude that people carry around with them irrespective of particular times, places, or situations. What we have after the interview is not a pristine set of facts that neutrally await rigorous analysis, but an intersubjectively constructed conversation—a dialogical research act—that has everything to do with the types of questions the researcher asks, how the interviewee perceives the interviewer, and the ability of both to speak a common language.

To account for the contradictory memories of the Braceros, the focus would not be on past experiences that may influence those memories, but on the interview situation as an experience in and of itself. The experiences under investigation would be limited to the research act as the way of explaining contradictory findings that must reside in the interviewer-respondent interactions. The answer to the question, "Tell me about your life while you were working as a Bracero," either took the form of the chronological story line (e.g., "I worked in cotton in Texas in 1958") or it was countered by the respondent's question, "What would you prefer me to talk about?" In the process of retelling their life story, in reference to the first question, the subjective evaluations of their experiences during the Bracero Program was overwhelmingly positive. But the details belied this characterization when I asked specific questions about housing, wages, deductions, food, job tasks, migration process, recruitment, and processing. All of these questions were asked in a way that divorced the Braceros' living conditions from the direct culpability of growers, FLC's, or crew bosses. According to the dialogical research act's approach to determining the source of meaning constructions, the responses are shaped according to how the question is asked, what is being asked, and who is doing the asking.

The interview context was purposively varied in this study, though not as greatly as the author had intended, in order to determine the extent to which the interviewer-interviewee relationship affected the recollection of past experiences (see Table 5.1 for interview contexts). Again, the form of the life stories most often followed a chronological pattern with the lone exception of the group interview. Rather than the group interview format facilitating a domination-free communicative context, it basically allowed two respondents to control the interview situation according to their own interests.

When the two were interrupted, the other Braceros were able to talk about their life stories and the chronological pattern once again resumed. The interesting component of the group interview is that it included two daughters and one sister of former Braceros. The females' responses were more issue-oriented (talk centered around pay, food, separation from families, and other related topics), often because they were not told a great deal about the program by their fathers or brother. The little tidbits they picked up only provided a partial depiction because the former Braceros' experiences were often details not discussed with their offspring. It seems that the negative memories were deemed best left forgotten. Unfortunately, the interview context, in and of itself, does not allow one to specify the process whereby details are forgotten. The interviews conducted in Colorado with those associated with the program were often more harsh in their condemnation of grower practices and much more forthright on the issue of racism.

The ability to speak a common language with my respondents consists not only of the level of comprehension of Spanish, since the former Braceros I interviewed in California were monolingual Spanish speakers, but also my ability to talk about the Bracero Program in a way that resonates with their memories and experiences. At issue was how well I was able to capture their past experiences in terms of the phrasing of questions and the content of what issues I raised. The differences in responses from the first, open-ended question and the more focused questions on specific aspects of the program attests to the importance of narrowing the topics of mutual interest and application. My limited command of Spanish was dealt with in two ways: (1) I conducted most interviews with the assistance of a translator/interviewer, and (2) I also employed a translator/transcriber to transform the Spanish words of the Braceros into the most commonly spoken English text. The translator/interviewers were both born and raised in the Fresno area in addition to being prominent Mexican-American activists in the area. The first translator/transcriber, employed for the project, was a local resident who grew up in the farmworker community and was much more familiar with the nuances and subtleties of farmworker discursive styles. Subsequent transcribers provided an important accuracy check for the original translations by myself and the translator/interviewers.

All of these factors certainly influenced the types of answers elicited in the research act, but there are two serious problems with treating the interview context as autonomous and *the* source of meaning determinations in and of itself. First, there must be something more going on than the internal dynamics of the research act because the memories of Braceros' experiences show similarities in what they said (as well as similar gaps or silences on particular issues). These commonalities occurred, in what was presented as the content and non-content of the Braceros' experiences during the program, regardless of where the research was conducted, what language the inter-

Table 5.1. Interview Context of Bracero Life Stories and Supplementary Interviews

Translator Present? Y(es)/N(o)	*Person(s) Interviewed*	*Language Spoken*	*Location: City, Room Type*
1. Y	Don Antonio	Spanish	Fresno, Conference Room, Seated at Table
2. Y	Don Liberio	Spanish	"" "" ""
3. Y	Don Jorge	Spanish	"" "" ""
4. Y	Don Francisco, Jorge	Spanish	"" "" ""
5. N	Don Pablo	Bilingual	"" "" ""
6. N	Don Roberto, Don Daniel	Spanish	Fresno, Classroom, Seated in Student Desks
7. Y[1]	Don Jose, Emilio, Hector, Nicolas/2 Daughters & 1 Sister	Spanish	"" "" ""
8. Y	Don Pablo & Naturalization Class	Spanish	Fresno, Conference Room, Seated at Table
9. N	Daughter of Bracero	English	Fresno, Off-site Location
10. N	Don Crecencio	Spanish	Baja, CA, Outdoor Public Park
11. N	Don Lupe	Spanish	"" "" ""
12. N	Don Ramon	Spanish	"" "" ""
13. N	Don Andre	Spanish	"" "" ""
14. N	Don Baldomero	Spanish	"" "" ""
15. N	Señor Freemont	English	San Luis Valley (SLV) Retirement Community Center
16. N	Señor Allen	English	"" "" ""
17. N	Señor Palmas	English	SLV, Owner's Restaurant
18. N	Señor Paulo	English	SLV, Phone Interview
19. N	Anonymous	English	SLV, Phone Interview

20-30. N	Various Interviews: Former Residents, Migrant Service Providers, Chicano Activists	English	Fresno/Colorado, Phone & Face-to-Face Interviews in Office Settings

1. Interviews seven and eight were conducted with a different translator/interviewer than interviews one through four to determine how this component affected the research act.

views were conducted in, or even in areas outside the interview context such as where the Braceros were contracted to work.

Second, the specifics internal to the interview context are important but they do not give enough of a basis for determining what people remember, how they remember it, and in the process what is forgotten. The types of questions asked certainly shaped the answers received but even when I asked about issues not raised by the Braceros, they were noticeably silent or brief about certain unsalient aspects of the program. Discussions about the mandatory medical exam or exactly how much the amount of deductions consisted of were extremely abbreviated or non-existent during the first wave of interviews. A different social context and time frame (the Mexico border during the Bracero social justice movement) also meant that the medical exam was at the forefront of Braceros' recollections. Quite simply, there are forces beyond the research act that are influencing what is remembered, what is forgotten, and how the respondent responds to questions. Viewing the respondent as a strategic manipulator of what he or she presents in the interview avoids one problematic aspect in the relationship between memories and experiences by focusing on how those memories are presented.

Strategic Manipulation

The third explanation for the determination of meaning is also concerned with factors endogenous to the interview situation but focuses on how the various identities that comprise the current social locations of those involved determine the construction of meaning. Not unlike Goffman's (1959) performative self as detailed in *The Presentation of Self in Everyday Life* and postmodern accounts of identities as performances, the position that interviewees are active in the selection of memories of experiences would attribute the positive subjective evaluation of the Bracero Program to one of three sources: the social location of the respondent, the author, or the interviewer/translator. The interviewee is viewed as a strategic manipulator of the presentation of their memories and focuses on how certain experiences are invoked or interpreted in such a way as to conform to the set of role expectations specific to the interview situation. The social location of the interviewer is also extremely relevant since respondents craft their answers based upon what they believe the interviewer wants to hear. In the strategic manipulation approach, the power relations embedded in the research act elicit a performative act that includes a selective presentation of past events that the respondent perceives the interviewer wants to hear. In this study, the present social locations of the translator/interviewers are also relevant.

In terms of the present social locations of the respondents, each of the Braceros interviewed still considered themselves agricultural workers. Though the majority (five of those interviewed) were forced to retire due to poor health, the occupations at the time of the interviews were painter, McDonald's employee, crew boss, and field workers (three). The only Bracero I interviewed—the painter—who moved completely out of agricultural labor was also the only respondent who noted that he did not work in agriculture in Mexico. His father was a leathersmith who made sandals, saddles, and other goods. At the time I interviewed the McDonald's employee, he stated that he was not working and it was only through other sources that I found out his occupation. All of the respondents stated that they did not speak nor comprehend English. In addition, they all considered themselves Mexican even though they were all presently living in the United States.

The interviews in Mexico were conducted with four respondents who were creative entreprenuers (they all patched together work in the informal sector). The only railroad-era Bracero interviewed was working full-time as a construction worker, owned his home, and was paid 200 pesos per week. The respondents in Mexico had varied work histories in both Mexico and the United States, but most found jobs in Mexican industries other than agriculture though all of their employment in the United States was in agriculture (with the exception of Don Baldomero who worked in Pennsylvania on the railroad). All respondents spoke Spanish exclusively and were Mexican citizens.

Given these circumstances, the strategic manipulation approach would focus on how these current social locations shape the details presented in the depiction of the Braceros' life stories. For instance, the crew boss who argued from his present social location that his experiences during the Bracero Program were defined by how well he was treated by *his* crew boss attests to what information is selectively presented through the filters of his current social location. In addition, the authoritative status of the author as a state university representative could also impact what answers are induced. The guarantee of anonymity in an informed consent form does not necessarily assure respondents that their answers will not have an impact on them once the interviews are made public as part of a published research study. There are plenty of plausible reasons why respondents are fearful of the intentions of researchers. It is the place of the researcher to determine why respondents are intimidated or fearful if this situation actually arises.

During the course of the present study, the interviews were videotaped for the purpose of analysis. The reaction to the video camera was not visibly noticeable since most respondents did not look directly into the lens. The camera was always positioned outside the direct sight lines of both the respondent and interviewers. However, it is not necessarily presumable that the content of what was said was not influenced by the presence of videotape equipment. But a person who is visibly uncomfortable in front of the camera (e.g., darting eyes, averting the camera when looking directly at it, extravagant performative gestures) would often exhibit verbal cues as to one's nervousness (e.g., stammering speech patterns, exceedingly quiet or loud vocal tone). Neither sets of clues were exhibited by the Braceros interviewed.

Another component that might have factored into the presentation was my status as an outsider to the Fresno area, Anglo appearance, and general lack of Spanish-speaking abilities. In effect, the responses I received have been along the lines of "tell the *gabacho o pocho* what he wants to hear" because the Braceros may have developed a particular communicative competence in answering those perceived as Anglos in a deferential, strictly positive manner. As the postal worker in Colorado explained the way Braceros acted in public:

> The sad commentary there is that the majority of them, they were suspicious, mistrusting, and I think that was an inherent thing that they had always been put upon. They were not really made welcome into these areas. So they were always real cautious. They didn't want to make any waves. They tried to stay out of the way . . . because they were afraid they might be sent home. It would be contrary for why they were here in the first place (Interview with Señor Freemont).

The final social location relevant to how the determination of meaning was shaped within the interview contexts were those of the translator/interviewers. Both interviewers were active in the Mexican-American community of the Fresno area. One interviewer was female and one was male. The political views of both were very well known to the former Braceros and their views were not necessarily congruent. Particularly concerning women's issues within Mexican culture, the respondents expressed positions that ran counter to both the female interviewer's and my sensibilities. Discussions of culture, family, gender, religion, identity, and race might have been avoided or answered in a way that conformed to the beliefs of the interviewer/translators.

This position is certainly plausible but a series of counter-responses belied what either I or the interviewers had expected. A discussion about why Don Francisco would not allow his daughters to migrate from Mexico because "the United States is no place for women" introduced notions of patriarchal family structures. But the female interviewer explained how strict she was in the raising of her daughter that closely allied with the respondent. In most of the interviews, the positive evaluation of the Bracero Program was accompanied by a set of details that would run contrary to the conflict-free portrayal of past events. It becomes very difficult to ascertain if the respondents are actively manipulating their life stories by solely examining the interview situation. Unfortunately, this study was not able to gather information from respondents outside the interview situation. It is these non-interview contexts that need to be studied in order to determine if manipulation is an appropriate characterization and if it only applies to the research act. If the respondents act the same in other settings (work, home, church, etc.) and retell their life stories in the same manner, then the strategic manipulation model would not necessarily apply to the dynamics internal to the interview context.

The strategic manipulation perspective would posit that respondents would give the type of answers that they perceive the interviewer wants to hear. This would certainly account for why the respondents spoke of the program favorably if the Braceros believed that a U.S. state-university representative wanted to hear positive evaluations. But it is still difficult to reconcile the negative details of the program that would align with a completely different set of perceived expectations. The position that the Braceros entered the interview situation as strategic manipulators of the re-telling of past events is only verifiable if conversations occur beyond the research act. Interviewer-respondent relations, especially if the interviewer is deemed an outsider, make these conversations very difficult to perform. Ultimately, there is a more historically attuned and verifiable explanation for the determination of meaning in the life stories of Braceros.

Imposed Definitions from Above

The final explanation for meaning determinations also focuses on the social location of the interviewee but views the social relations that developed outside the interview situation to be found in the way people remember. The role expectations that serve as the source of memory construction are imposed from above in a set of power relations where the group in charge of the dominated sub-group defines how they are to think, feel, and act regarding the situations at hand.

The approach is discussed in post-colonial theory as a theory of the colonized mind or the inability of the subjects of imperialism (the subaltern) to conceive of their existence in a way outside of their colonizer's definitions (Memmi 1965, Spivak 1988). Another example of this type of explanation should already be familiar. Erving Goffman (1961), in his delineation of the total institution, stated the way inmates conceive of their self-identities is rooted not in the sense of one's true self, but is an artifact of the institutional arrangements between staff and inmates where the latter impose definitions of situations from above. Goffman's "analysis portrays the [total] institution as destructive to individual autonomy in yet more subtle ways, for the person loses . . . the right to independent *thoughts* and *actions*" (Watson 1980, 183). It would be extremely difficult to disagree with the characterization that independent and autonomous *actions* are lost to the requisites of the total institution. But the claim that one's *thoughts* are also controlled or managed requires a closer inspection as to the degree of control. To explain why the former Braceros refrain from condemning their oppressors during an interview, we must look further into the institutional dynamics of the program and the relations among growers, their intermediaries, and workers. It requires a close examination of the circumstances that would demand of workers to evaluate their experiences positively even though they recognize that they were treated much worse than domestic workers. It would explain why the Bracero Program was viewed favorably even though the rights guaranteed to them on the written contract were consistently violated.

The way the self is relayed to others is through interaction and embedded within the stories people tell about their past experiences. But in the case of Braceros, their participation in the total institution of the labor camp resulted in their obligation to meet the role expectations of themselves as content, docile, and thankful for the opportunity to have worked and lived in the United States. If, as Goffman (1961, 7) states, the subordinate members of the total institution feel "inferior, weak, blameworthy, and guilty," the addition of the Braceros' life stories to Goffman is that workers carry this set of role expectations well beyond the initial confines of the total institution (in particular, the labor camp). They certainly recognize how they were mistreated but these subjective feelings of somehow they might have deserved this treatment is best explained by the institutional arrangements that they were inserted into as a result of their inferior social location in the Anglo grower-Mexican worker relationship. It is the making of the Bracero total institution that connects the theoretical articulation of race and class in shaping the past, lived experiences of former Braceros.

NOTES

1. The question was designed to conform with the oral history traditions of people's history, *testimonio*, life story, and life history methods that all share a commitment to highlighting the voices often silenced in power relations. Due to the long-standing relationship between migration studies and life (hi)story methods, I limit my discussion to the latter as it elucidates what I am referring to as archival ethnography.

2. Contemporary mainstream approaches in the sociology of immigration have been apprehensive about the use of "soft" qualitative methods as a source of scientific knowledge. The dominant trope in the field is generalizability so accordingly, qualitative methods are designed to emulate this goal or abandoned altogether in favor of survey methods and statistical replicability.

3. Cuadraz, Gloria Holguin, Christine Marin, Belen Soto Moreno, and Jose Leyba. *Mexican Americans and Litchfield Park: an Oral History Project.* Hayden Chicano Research Collection, Arizona State University Libraries, 2005–2007.

4. I define archival ethnography as an interative process that catalogs what has sedimented into official archives in relation to the lived experiences of those marginalized communities that often do not locate their voice in the historical record. I appreciate the definition offered by Gracy (2004, 337) that "archival ethnography is a form of naturalistic inquiry which positions the researcher within an archival environment to gain the cultural perspective of those responsible for the creation, collection, care, and use of records." But in addition to the internal process, I note the important proviso that it is equally relevant to locate excluded voices and cultures beyond the archival environment and make them part of the official archival record. The point is not only to get the field into the archive but also to get the archive into the field.

5. I would love to take credit for this quip but credit goes to Mike Apple and his expressed concern with the similar postmodern turn, toward a seemingly "possessive individualism," in critical education studies (see Apple 1997, 127 *op. cit.*).

6. Paul Willis (1977) *Learning to Labor* began much of the critical ethnography movement in education, sociology, and cultural studies so his analysis of counter-school culture, as exemplified by the lads' words and behaviors, really set the benchmark for how ethnographers can learn how to listen, even if they tend to be completely non self-reflexive in the process.

7. In all, I intensively interviewed three daughters and one sister of former Braceros. In terms of those affiliated with the program, I interviewed one bus driver/crew boss, one postal worker, one food supplier, one state government housing inspector, and three Mexican-American activists with close ties to the program.

8. The group interview I conducted followed a different format due to two respondents who dominated the conversation. Don Emilio's agenda was to make sure I knew that he worked hard and deserved every cent earned. He initially had a difficult time getting contracted due to an operation he had on his back and was injured on the job picking oranges in California. Don Jose focused more on how well he was taken care of by his crew boss and how the crew boss tended to the Braceros' every need. What I later found out was that Don Jose was employed at the time as a crew boss. When the other respondents spoke without interruption, they tended to follow the same chronological story line that respondents did in the one-on-one interview context.

Appendix III

The Standard Work Contract

THE STANDARD WORK CONTRACT AND ACCOMPANYING DOCUMENTS STANDARD BRACERO WORK CONTRACT

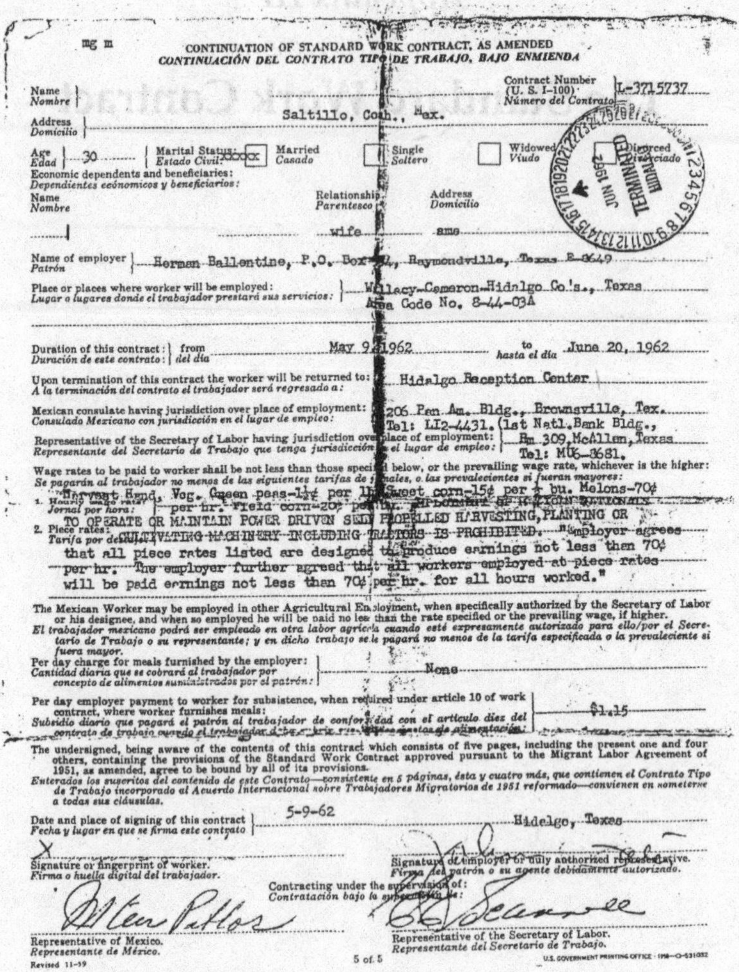

mg m

CONTINUATION OF STANDARD WORK CONTRACT, AS AMENDED
CONTINUACIÓN DEL CONTRATO TIPO DE TRABAJO, BAJO ENMIENDA

Name / *Nombre*

Contract Number (U. S. I-100) / *Número del Contrato* L-3715737

Address / *Domicilio* Saltillo, Coah., Mex.

Age / *Edad* 30 | Marital Status / *Estado Civil* [X] Married / *Casado* [ ] Single / *Soltero* [ ] Widowed / *Viudo* [ ] Divorced / *Divorciado*

Economic dependents and beneficiaries: / *Dependientes económicos y beneficiarios:*

Name / *Nombre* | Relationship / *Parentesco* wife | Address / *Domicilio* same

TERMINATED HIDALGO JUN 1962

Name of employer / *Patrón* Herman Ballentine, P.O. Box 42, Raymondville, Texas E-8649

Place or places where worker will be employed: / *Lugar o lugares donde el trabajador prestará sus servicios:* Willacy-Cameron-Hidalgo Co's., Texas Area Code No. 8-44-03A

Duration of this contract: from / *Duración de este contrato: del día* May 9, 1962 to / *hasta el día* June 20, 1962

Upon termination of this contract the worker will be returned to: / *A la terminación del contrato el trabajador será regresado a:* Hidalgo Reception Center

Mexican consulate having jurisdiction over place of employment: / *Consulado Mexicano con jurisdicción en el lugar de empleo:* 206 Pan Am. Bldg., Brownsville, Tex. Tel: LI2-4431.

Representative of the Secretary of Labor having jurisdiction over place of employment: / *Representante del Secretario de Trabajo que tenga jurisdicción en el lugar de empleo:* (1st Natl. Bank Bldg., Rm 309, McAllen, Texas Tel: MU6-3681.

Wage rates to be paid to worker shall be not less than those specified below, or the prevailing wage rate, whichever is the higher:
Se pagarán al trabajador no menos de las siguientes tarifas de jornales, o las prevalecientes si fueran mayores:

1. Hourly wage rate: / *Jornal por hora:*
2. Piece rates: / *Tarifa por destajo:*

Harvest Hand, Veg. Green peas-1½¢ per lb. Sweet corn-15¢ per ½ bu. Melons-70¢ per hr. Field corn-20¢ per hr. EMPLOYMENT OF MEXICAN NATIONALS TO OPERATE OR MAINTAIN POWER DRIVEN SELF PROPELLED HARVESTING, PLANTING OR CULTIVATING MACHINERY INCLUDING TRACTORS IS PROHIBITED. "Employer agrees that all piece rates listed are designed to produce earnings not less than 70¢ per hr. The employer further agreed that all workers employed at piece rates will be paid earnings not less than 70¢ per hr. for all hours worked."

The Mexican Worker may be employed in other Agricultural Employment, when specifically authorized by the Secretary of Labor or his designee, and when so employed he will be paid no less than the rate specified or the prevailing wage, if higher.
El trabajador mexicano podrá ser empleado en otra labor agrícola cuando esté expresamente autorizado para ello/por el Secretario de Trabajo o su representante; y en dicho trabajo se le pagará no menos de la tarifa especificada o la prevaleciente si fuera mayor.

Per day charge for meals furnished by the employer: / *Cantidad diaria que se cobrará al trabajador por concepto de alimentos suministrados por el patrón:* None

Per day employer payment to worker for subsistence, when required under article 10 of work contract, where worker furnishes meals: / *Subsidio diario que pagará el patrón al trabajador de conformidad con el artículo diez del contrato de trabajo cuando el trabajador deba cubrir sus propios gastos de alimentación:* $1.15

The undersigned, being aware of the contents of this contract which consists of five pages, including the present one and four others, containing the provisions of the Standard Work Contract approved pursuant to the Migrant Labor Agreement of 1951, as amended, agree to be bound by all of its provisions.
Enterados los suscritos del contenido de este Contrato—consistente en 5 páginas, ésta y cuatro más, que contienen el Contrato Tipo de Trabajo incorporado al Acuerdo Internacional sobre Trabajadores Migratorios de 1951 reformado—convienen en someterse a todas sus cláusulas.

Date and place of signing of this contract / *Fecha y lugar en que se firma este contrato* 5-9-62 Hidalgo, Texas

X
Signature or fingerprint of worker. / *Firma o huella digital del trabajador.*

Signature of employer or duly authorized representative. / *Firma del patrón o su agente debidamente autorizado.*

Contracting under the supervision of: / *Contratación bajo la supervisión de:*

Representative of Mexico. / *Representante de México.*

Representative of the Secretary of Labor. / *Representante del Secretario de Trabajo.*

Revised 11-59

5 of 5

U.S. GOVERNMENT PRINTING OFFICE

Figure 5.2. Texas Rio Grande Legal Aid, Personal Correspondence, on file with author, July 1998. Used by permission of TRLA.

OFFICIAL SEAL CERTIFYING MEXICAN MUNICIPAL APPROVAL OF WORKER ELIGIBILITY

EL C. LIC. LUIS VILLA[illegible] PEÑA, OFICIAL MAYOR-
DE LA SECRETARIA [illegible] DE GOBIERNO DEL ESTADO INDE
PENDIENTE, LIBRE Y SOBERANO DE COAHUILA DE ZARAGOZA,

CERTIFICA: Que el C. [illegible] Eulalio Gutiérrez T.,
es Presidente del R. Ayunt[illegible] del Municipio de -
esta Capital, suya la firma [illegible]ntico el sello con
que autoriza el presente documento.

SUFRAGIO [illegible] NO REELECCION.

ESTADO DE COAHUILA DE ZARAGOZA
PODER EJECUTIVO
SECRETARIA GENERAL DE GOBIERNO

Figure 5.3. Texas Rio Grande Legal Aid, Personal Correspondence, on file with author, July 1998. Used by permission of TRLA.

OFFICIAL LETTER CERTIFYING MEXICAN MUNICIPAL APPROVAL OF WORKER ELIGIBILITY

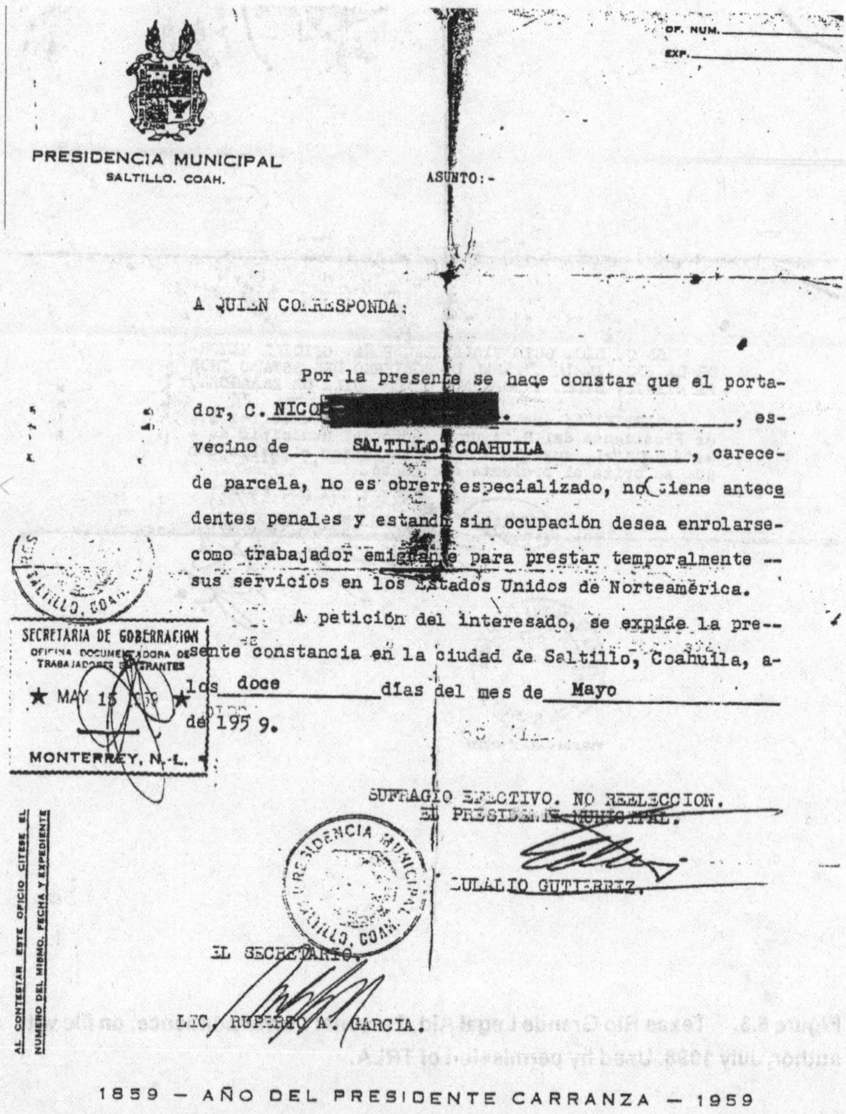

PRESIDENCIA MUNICIPAL
SALTILLO. COAH.

OF. NUM.
EXP.

ASUNTO:-

A QUIEN CORRESPONDA:

Por la presente se hace constar que el portador, C. [redacted], es-vecino de SALTILLO, COAHUILA, carece de parcela, no es obrero especializado, no tiene antecedentes penales y estando sin ocupación desea enrolarse como trabajador emigrante para prestar temporalmente sus servicios en los Estados Unidos de Norteamérica.

A petición del interesado, se expide la presente constancia en la ciudad de Saltillo, Coahuila, a los doce días del mes de Mayo de 1959.

SECRETARIA DE GOBERNACION
OFICINA DOCUMENTADORA DE TRABAJADORES EMIGRANTES
★ MAY 15 1959 ★
MONTERREY, N.-L.

SUFRAGIO EFECTIVO. NO REELECCION.
EL PRESIDENTE MUNICIPAL.

EULALIO GUTIERREZ.

PRESIDENCIA MUNICIPAL SALTILLO, COAH.

EL SECRETARIO.

LIC. RUPERTO A. GARCIA.

AL CONTESTAR ESTE OFICIO CITESE EL NUMERO DEL MISMO, FECHA Y EXPEDIENTE

1859 — AÑO DEL PRESIDENTE CARRANZA — 1959

Figure 5.4. Texas Rio Grande Legal Aid, Personal Correspondence, on file with author, July 1998. Used by permission of TRLA.

U.S. GROWER RECOMMENDATION LETTER FOR RECONTRACTING PURPOSES

143

LANGSTON & LANGSTON
ENTERPRISES
ROUTE ONE
BLYTHEVILLE, ARKANSAS

Nov. 14, 1958

Re: [redacted]

TO WHOM IT MAY CONCERN:

This will introduce and recommend the above Mexican National who has been employed by me during this cotton picking season. He is a good worker, sober, industrious and cooperative.

I hereby recommend him to anyone that is need of labor.

Respectfully,

Charles C. Langston

Figure 5.5. Texas Rio Grande Legal Aid, Personal Correspondence, on file with author, July 1998. Used by permission of TRLA.

Appendix IV

Original Bracero Agreement of 1942

Agreement of August 4, 1942

For the Temporary Migration of Mexican Agricultural Workers to the United States as Revised on April 26, 1943, by an Exchange of Notes Between the American Embassy at Mexico City and the Mexican Ministry for Foreign Affairs

General Provisions

1. It is understood that Mexicans contracting to work in the United States shall not be engaged in any military service.
2. Mexicans entering the United States as result of this understanding shall not suffer discriminatory acts of any kind in accordance with the Executive Order No. 8802 issued at the White House June 25, 1941.
3. Mexicans entering the United States under this understanding shall enjoy the guarantees of transportation, living expenses and repatriation established in Article 29 of the Mexican Federal Labor Law as follows:

   Article 29.- All contracts entered into by Mexican workers for lending their services outside their country shall be made in writing, legalized by the municipal authorities of the locality where entered into and vised by the Consul of the country where their services are being used. Furthermore, such contract shall contain, as a requisite of validity of same, the following stipulations, without which the contract is invalid.

   Transportation and subsistence expenses for the worker, and his family, if such is the case, and all other expenses which originate from point of origin to border points and compliance of immigration requirements, or for any other similar concept, shall be paid exclusively by the employer or the contractual parties.

The worker shall be paid in full the salary agreed upon, from which no deduction shall be made in any amount for any of the concepts mentioned in the above sub-paragraph.

The employer or contractor shall issue a bond or constitute a deposit in cash in the Bank of Workers, or in the absence of same, in the Bank of Mexico, to the entire satisfaction of the respective labor authorities, for a sum equal to repatriation costs of the worker and his family, and those originated by transportation to point of origin.

Once the employer established proof of having covered such expenses or the refusal of the worker to return to his country, and that he does not owe the worker any sum covering salary or indemnization to which he might have a right, the labor authorities shall authorize the return of the deposit or the cancellation of the bond issued.

It is specifically understood that the provisions of Section III of Article 29 above-mentioned shall not apply to the Government of the United States notwithstanding the inclusion of this section in the agreement, in view of the obligations assumed by the United States government under Transportation (a) and (c) of this agreement.

4. Mexicans entering the United States under this understanding shall not be employed to displace other workers, or for the purpose of reducing rates of pay previously established.

In order to implement the application of the general Principles mentioned above the following specific clauses are established:

(When the word "employer" is used hereinafter it shall be understood to mean the Farm Security Administration of the Department of Agriculture of the United States of America; the word "sub-employer" shall mean the owner or operator of the farm or farms in the United States on which the Mexican will be employed; the word "worker" hereinafter used shall refer to the Mexican Farm laborer entering the United States under this understanding.)

Contracts

a. Contracts will be made between the employer and the worker under the supervision of the Mexican Government. (Contracts must be written in Spanish.)
b. The employer shall enter into a contract with the sub- employer, with a view to proper observance of the principles embodied in this understanding.

Admission

a. The Mexican health authorities will, at the place whence the worker comes, see that he meets the necessary physical conditions.

Transportation

a. All transportation and living expenses from the place of origin to destination, and return, as well as expenses incurred in the fulfillment of any requirements of a migratory nature shall be met by the Employer.
b. Personal belongings of the workers up to a maximum of 35 kilos per person shall be transported at the expense of the Employer.
c. In accord with the intent of Article 29 of Mexican Federal Labor Law, quoted under General Provisions (3) above, it is expected that the employer will collect all or part of the cost accuring under (a) and (b) of Transportation from the sub- employer.

Wages and Employment

a. (1)Wages to be paid the worker shall be the same as those paid for similar work to other agricultural laborers under the same conditions within the same area, in the respective regions of destination. Piece rates shall be so set as to enable the worker of average ability to earn the prevailing wage. In any case wages for piece work or hourly work will not be less than 30 cents per hour.
b. (2)On the basis of prior authorization from the Mexican Government salaries lower than those established in the previous clause may be paid those emigrants admitted into the United States as members of the family of the worker under contract and who, when they are in the field, are able also to become agricultural laborers but who, by their condition of age or sex, cannot carry out the average amount of ordinary work.

c. The worker shall be exclusively employed as an agricultural laborer for which he has been engaged ; any change from such type of employment or any change of locality shall be made with the express approval of the worker and with the authority of the Mexican Government.

d. There shall be considered illegal any collection by reason of commission or for any other concept demanded of the worker.

e. Work of minors under 14 years shall be strictly prohibit, and they shall have the same schooling opportunities as those enjoyed by children of other agricultural laborers.

f. Workers domiciled in the migratory labor camps or at any other place of employment under this understanding shall be free to obtain articles for their personal consumption, or that of their families, wherever it is most convenient for them.

g. The Mexican workers will be furnished without cost to them with hygienic lodgings, adequate to the physical conditions of the region of a type used by a common laborer of the region and the medical and sanitary services enjoyed also without cost to them will be identical with those furnished to the other agricultural workers in the regions where they may lend their services.

h. Workers admitted under this understanding shall enjoy as regards occupational diseases and accidents the same guarantees enjoyed by other agricultural workers under United States legislation.

i. Groups of workers admitted under this understanding shall elect their own representatives to deal with the Employer, but it is understood that all such representatives shall be working members of the group.

The Mexican Consuls, assisted the Mexican Labor Inspectors, recognized as such by the Employer will take all possible measures of protection in the interest of the Mexican workers in all questions affecting them, within their corresponding jurisdiction, and will have free access to the places of work of the Mexican workers, The Employer will observe that the sub- employer grants all facilities to the Mexican Government for the compliance of all the clauses in this contract.

j. For such time as they are unemployed under a period equal to 75% of the period (exclusive of Sundays) for which the workers have been contracted they shall receive a subsistence allowance at the rate of $3.00 per day.

Should the cost of living rise this will be a matter for reconsideration.

The master contracts for workers submitted to the Mexican government shall contain definite provisions for computation of subsistence and payments under the understanding.

k. The term of the contract shall be made in accordance with the authorities of the respective countries.

l. At the expiration of the contract under this understanding, and if the same is not renewed, the authorities of the United States shall consider illegal, from an immigration point of view, the continued stay of the worker in the territory of the United States, exception made of cases of physical impossibility.

Savings Fund

a. The respective agencies of the Government of the United States shall be responsible for the safekeeping of the sums contributed by the Mexican workers toward the formation of their Rural Savings Fund, until such sums are transferred to the Wells Fargo Bank and Union Trust Company of San Francisco for the account of the Bank of Mexico, S.A., which will transfer such amounts to the Mexican Agricultural Credit Bank. This last shall assume responsibility for the deposit, for the safekeeping and for the application, or in the absence of these, for the return of such amounts.
b. The Mexican Government through the Banco de Crédito Agrícola will take care of the security of the savings of the workers to be used for payment of the agricultural implements, which may be made available to the Banco de Crédito Agrícola in accordance with exportation permits for shipment to Mexico with the understanding that the Farm Security Administration will recommend priority treatment for such implements.

Numbers

As it is impossible to determine at this time the number of workers who may be needed in the United States for agricultural labor employment, the employer shall advise the Mexican Government from time to time as to the number needed. The Government of Mexico shall determine in each case the number of workers who may leave the country without detriment to its national economy.

General Considerations

It is understood that, with reference to the departure from Mexico of Mexican workers, who are not farm laborers, there shall govern in understandings reached by agencies to the respective Governments the same fundamentals principles which have been applied here to the departure of farm labor.

It is understood that the employers will cooperate with such other agencies of the Government of the United States in carrying this understanding into effect whose authority under the laws of the United States are such as to contribute to the effectuation of the understandings.

Either Government shall have the right to renounce this understanding, given appropriate notification to the other Government 90 days in advance.

This understanding may be formalized by an exchange of notes between the Ministry of Foreign Affairs of the Republic of Mexico and the Embassy of the United States of America in Mexico.[1]

NOTE

1. The original agreement was formalized the 23th of July of 1942. Months later, the agreement was modified. This is the final version, released on April 26, 1943. The original agreement was signed by representatives from both countries. From México, Ernesto Hidalgo, representative of the Foreign Affairs Ministry and Abraham J. Navas, Esq., representative of the Ministry of Labor. From United States: Joseph F. McGurk, Counsel of the American Embassy in México, John Walker, Deputy Administrator of the Farm Security Administration, United States Department of Agriculture (USDA), and David Mecker, Deputy Director of War Farming Operations also from the USDA.

Appendix V

Braceros from Mexican State of Origin, 1942–1946 and 1951–1964

	1942- August 1946		1951-1964	
	Total Number	Percent of Total	Total Number	Percent of Total
Aguascalientes	8137	2.52%	80970	1.89%
Baja California	0	0.00%	21078	0.49%
Campeche	723	0.22%	1256	0.03%
Coahuila	3466	1.07%	191074	4.47%
Colima	0	0.00%	12190	0.28%
Chiapas	330	0.10%	1473	0.03%
Chihuahua	5203	1.61%	434938	10.17%
Federal District	144401	44.67%	44431	1.04%
Durango	8818	2.73%	386260	9.03%
Guanajuato	23829	7.37%	567514	13.27%
Guerrero	6793	2.10%	133821	3.13%
Hidalgo	5544	1.72%	33712	0.79%
Jalisco	7258	2.25%	465396	10.88%
Mexico	3235	1.00%	79288	1.85%
Michoacan	32082	9.93%	463811	10.84%
Morelos	2743	0.85%	38376	0.90%
Nayarit	0	0.00%	46660	1.09%
Nuevo Leon	0	0.00%	185311	4.33%
Oaxaca	10766	3.33%	126453	2.96%
Puebla	3382	1.05%	63381	1.48%
Queretaro	3598	1.11%	50853	1.19%
Quintana Roo	0	0.00%	75	0.00%
San Luis Potosi	6440	1.99%	211703	4.95%
Sinaloa	0	0.00%	42546	0.99%
Sonora	0	0.00%	44527	1.04%
Tabasco	5813	1.80%	16032	0.37%
Tamaulipas	5883	1.82%	56652	1.32%
Tlaxcala	3504	1.08%	29430	0.69%
Veracruz	6659	2.06%	10802	0.25%
Yucatan	261	0.08%	47285	1.11%
Zacatecas	24364	7.54%	390061	9.12%
Total	323232		4277359	

Figure 5.6. Created by author, adapted from Mexico Federal Government, Secretaria del Trabajo y Prevision Social (1946) and Garcia (1980).

Bibliography

PUBLISHED MONOGRAPHS, ARTICLES, AND BOOK CHAPTERS

Alarcón, Rafael. "Skilled Immigrants and *Cereberos*: Foreign-Born Engineers and Scientists in the High Technology Industry of Silicon Valley." In *Immigration Research for a New Century: Multidisciplinary Perspectives*, edited by Nancy Foner, Rubén Rumbaut, and Steven J. Gold, 301-321. New York: Russell Sage Foundation, 2000.

Althusser, Louis. *For Marx*. London: Allen Lane, 1969.

———. *Reading Capital*. New York: New Left Books, 1970.

Anderson, Henry Pope. *The Bracero Program in California*. New York: Arno Press, 1976 [1961].

Anderson, Kathryn and Dana C. Jack. "Learning to Listen: Interview Techniques and Analysis." In *Women's Words: The Feminist Practice of Oral History*, edited by Sherna B. Gluck and Daphne Patai, 11-26. New York: Routledge, 1991.

Apple, Michael W. "Consuming the Other: Whiteness, Education, and Cheap French Fries." In *Off White: Readings on Race, Power, and Society*, edited by Michelle Fine et al. New York: Routledge Press, 1997.

Bach, Robert L. "Mexican Immigration and U.S. Immigration Reforms in the 1960's." *Kapitalistate* 7 (1978): 63-80.

Bentham, Jeremy. *The Panopticon Readings*. New York: Verso, 1995.

Berger, Peter and Thomas Luckmann. *The Social Construction of Reality*. New York: Anchor Books, 1966.

Bertaux, Daniel ed. *Biography and Society: The Life History Approach in the Social Sciences*. Berverly Hills, CA: Sage Publications, 1981.

———. "Stories as Clues to Sociological Understanding: the Bakers of Paris." In *Our Common History*, edited by Paul Thompson, 92-108. New York: Humanities Press, 1982.

———. "Oral History Approaches to an International Social Movement." In *Comparative Methodology: Theory and Practice in International Social Research*, edited by Else Oyen, 151-171. Newbury Park, CA: Sage Studies in International Sociology (40), 1990.

Blassingame, John.W. *The Slave Community: Plantation Life in the Antebellum South, Second Edition*. New York: Oxford University Press, 1979.

Blight, David C. *Passages to Freedom: The Underground Railroad in History and Memory*. Washington, DC: Smithsonian Books, 2006.

Bonilla-Silva, Eduardo. *White Supremacy and Racism in the Post-Civil Rights Era*. Boulder, CO: Lynne Rienner, 2001.

———. *Racism without Racists: Color-Blind Racism and the Persistence of Racial Inequality in America, Fourth Edition*. Lanham, MD: Rowman and Littlefield, 2014.

Bourdieu, Pierre. "The Social Space and the Genesis of Groups." *Theory and Society* 14 (1985): 723-744.

Braswell, M., Dillingham, S. and Jr., R.M. *Prison Violence in America*. Cincinnati, OH: Anderson Publishing Co., 1985.

Braverman, Harry. *Labor and Monopoly Capital*. New York: Monthly Review Press, 1974.

Brissett, Dennis and Charles Edgley. *Life as Theater: A Dramturgical Sourcebook*. New York: Aldine de Gruyter, 1994.

Broyles-Gonzalez, Yolanda. 1994. *El Teatro Campesino: Theater in the Chicano Movement*. Austin: University of Texas Press, 1994.

Burawoy, Michael. "The Functions and Reproduction of Migrant Labor: Comparative Material from Southern Africa and the United States." *American Journal of Sociology* 81 (1976): 1050-1087.

———. *Manufacturing Consent: Changes in the Labor Process Under Monopoly Capital*. Chicago: University of Chicago Press, 1979.

———. *The Politics of Production*. New York: Verso Press, 1985.

Bustos, Sergio. "Braceros Seeking Release of Funds." *Arizona Republic*, Phoenix, AZ. 2002.

Calavita, Kitty. *Inside the State: The Bracero Program, Immigration and the I.N.S.* New York: Routledge, 1992.

Cardoso, Lawrence. *Mexican Emigration to the United States, 1897-1931: Socio-Economic Patterns*. Tucson: University of Arizona Press, 1980.

Casey, Kathleen. *I Answer With My Life: Life Histories of Women Teachers Working for Social Change*. New York: Routledge, 1993.

Chesler, Phyllis. *Women and Madness, 25th Anniversary Edition*. New York: Four Walls Eight Windows, 1997.

Clifford, James. *The Predicament of Culture*. Cambridge: Harvard University Press, 1988.

Cobas, José A., Jorge Duany, and Joe R. Feagin eds. *How the United States Racializes Latinos: White Hegemony and its Consequences*. Boulder, CO: Paradigm, 2009.

Cohen, Deborah. "Caught in the Middle: The Mexican State's Relationship with the US and Its Own Citizen-Workers, 1942-1958." *Journal of American Ethnic History* 20 (2001): 110-32.

———. *Braceros: Migrant Citizens and Transnational Subjects in the Postwar United States and Mexico*. Chapel Hill: University of North Carolina Press, 2011.

Collins, Randall. *Four Sociological Traditions*. New York: Oxford University Press, 1994.

Copp, Nelson Gage. *"Wetbacks" and braceros: Mexican migrant laborers and American immigration policy, 1930-1960*. San Francisco: R and E Research Associates, 1971.

Craig, Richard B. *The Bracero Program: Interest Groups and Foreign Policy*. Austin: University of Texas Press, 1971.

De Certeau, Michel. *The Practice of Everyday Life*. Berkeley: University of California Press, 1984, 2002.

Delgado, Richard and Vicky Palacios. "Mexican Americans as a Legally Cognizable Class under Rule 23 and the Equal Protection Clause." *Notre Dame Lawyer* 50 (1975). Accessed November 9, 2015. http://ssrn.com/abstract=2104282.

Deutsch, Sarah. *No Separate Refuge: Culture, Class and Gender in an Anglo-Hispanic Frontier in the American Southwest, 1880-1940*. New York: Oxford University Press, 1987.

Driscoll, Barbara. *The Tracks North*. Austin: University of Texas Press, 1999.

Driscoll de Alvarado, Barbara. "The 10% Solution: Bracero Program Savings Account Controversy." *ReVista: Harvard Review of Latin America* (2003). Accessed March 1, 2008. http://www.drclas.harvard.edu/revista/articles/view/307.

DuBois, W.E.B. "The Telented Tenth." In *The Future of the Race*, edited by Henry Louis Gates and Cornel West. New York: Alfred Knopf, 1996 [1948].

Durand, Jorge. *Más Allá De La Línea: Patrones Migratorios Entre México y Estados Unidos*. México, DF: Consejo Nacional para la Cultura y las Artes, 1994.

Eliasoph, Nina. "Political Culture and the Presentation of a Political Self: A Study of the Public Sphere in the Spirit of Erving Goffman." *Theory and Society* 19 (1990): 465-494.

Elkins, Stanley M. *Slavery: A Problem in American Institutional and Intellectual Life*. Chicago: University of Chicago Press, 1959.
Feagin, Joe R. *Systemic Racism: A Theory of Oppression*. New York: Routledge, 2006.
———. *The White Racial Frame: Centuries of Racial Framing and Counter-Framing*. New York: Routledge, 2010.
Fields, Barbara. "Slavery, Race, and Ideology in the United States of America." *New Left Review* 181 (1991): 95-118.
Fiske, John. *Reading the Popular*. Boston: Unwin Hyman, 1989a.
———. *Television Culture*. New York: Routledge, 1989b.
———. *Power Plays Power Works*. New York: Verso, 1993.
Foley, Douglas E. *Learning Capitalist Culture: Deep in the Heart of* Tejas. Philadelphia: University of Pennsylvania Press, 1990.
———. *Learning Capitalist Culture: Deep in the Heart of* Tejas, Second Edition. Philadelphia: University of Pennsylvania Press, 2010.
———. *The Heartland Chronicles*. Philadelphia: University of Pennsylvania Press, 1995.
Foley, Neil. *The White Scourge*. Austin: University of Texas Press, 1997.
Foucault, Michel. *Power/Knowledge*. New York: Pantheon, 1980.
———. *The Foucault Reader*. Edited by Paul Rabinow. New York: Pantheon. 1984.
———. *The History of Sexuality: An Introduction, Volume 1*. New York: Vintage Books, 1990 [1978].
———. *Discipline and Punish: The Birth of the Prison*. New York: Vintage Books, 1995 [1977].
———. *Madness and Civilization*. New York: Routledge, 2001 [1965].
Frankenberg, Ruth. *White Women, Race Matters: The Social Construction of Whiteness*. Minneapolis: University of Minnesota Press, 1995.
Galarza, Ernesto. *Strangers in Our Fields: Based on a Report Regarding Compliance with the Contractual, Legal, and Civil Rights of Mexican Agricultural Contract Labor in the United States*, 2nd ed. Washington, DC: United States Section, Joint United States-Mexico Trade Union Committee, 1956.
———. *Merchants of Labor: The Mexican Bracero History*. Santa Barbara, CA: McNally and Loftin, 1964.
———. *Tragedy at Chualar*. Santa Barbara, CA: McNally and Loftin, 1977.
Gamboa, Erasmo. *Mexican Labor and World War II : Braceros in the Pacific Northwest, 1942-1947*. Austin: University of Texas Press, 1990. Reprinted Seattle: University of Washington Press, 2000.
Gamio, Manuel. *Mexican Immigration to the United States*. Chicago: University of Chicago Press, 1971a [1950, 1930].
———. *The Mexican Immigrant: His Life Story*. New York: Arno Press, 1971b [1931].
García, Juan Ramon. *Operation Wetback : The Mass Deportation of Mexican Undocumented Workers in 1954*. Westport, CT: Greenwood Press, 1980.
García y Griego, Manuel. "The Importation of Mexican Contract Laborers to the United States, 1942-1964." In *The Border That Joins: Mexican Migrants and US Responsibility,* edited by Peter Brown and Henry Shue, 49-98. Totowa, NJ: Rowman and Littlefield, 1983. Reprinted in *Between Two Worlds: Mexican Immigrants in the United States*, edited by David Gutiérrez, 45-76. Wilmington, DE: Scholarly Resources, Inc, 1996.
Gaventa, John. *Power and Powerlessness: Quiescence and Rebellion in an Appalachian Valley*. Urbana: University of Illinois Press, 1980.
Goffman, Erving. *The Presentation of Self in Everyday Life*. New York: Anchor Books, 1959.
———. *Asylums: Essays on the Social Situation of Mental Patients and Other Inmates*. New York: Anchor Books, 1961.
———. *Relations in Public*. New York: Basic Books, 1971.
Goldberg, David Theo. *Anatomy of Racism*. Minneapolis: University of Minnesota Press, 1990.
———. *Racist Culture*. Cambridge: Blackwell Publishers, 1993.
Goméz, Laura. *Manifest Destinies: The Making of the Mexican American Race*. New York: NYU Press, 2007.

Gonzalez, Gilbert G. *Guestworkers or Colonized Labor? Mexican Labor Migration to the United States*. Boulder, CO: Paradigm Publishers, 2006.

Gould, Stephen Jay. *The Mismeasure of Man*. New York: W.W. Norton & Co, 1996.

Gracy, Karen F. "Documenting Communities of Practice: Making the Case for Archival Ethnography." *Archival Science* 4 (2004): 335-365.

Griswold del Castillo, Richard and Garcia, Richard A. *César Chávez A Triumph of Spirit*. Norman: University of Oklahoma Press, 1995.

Grossberg, Lawrence. *Bringing It All Back Home: Essays on Cultural Studies*. Durham, NC: Duke University Press, 1997.

Grove, Wayne A. "The Mexican Farm Labor Program, 1942-1964: Government-Administered Labor Market Insurance." *Agricultural History* 70 (1996): 302-20.

Gutiérrez, David G. *Walls and Mirrors: Mexican Americans, Mexican Immigrants, and the Politics of Ethnicity*. Berkeley: University of California Press, 1995.

Habermas, Jurgen. *The Postnational Constellation: Political Essays*. Boston: MIT Press, 2001.

Hadley, Eleanor. "A Critical Analysis of the Wetback Problem." *Law and Contemporary Problems* 21 (1956): 334-357.

Hall, Stuart. "Race, Articulation and Societies Structured in Dominance." In *Sociological Theories: Race and Colonialism*, 305-345. United Kingdom: UNESCO, 1980.

———. "Gramsci's Relevance for the Study of Race and Ethnicity." *Journal of Communication Inquiry* 10 (1986a): 5-27.

———. "On Postmodernism and Articulation: An Interview with Stuart Hall," edited by Lawrence Grossberg. *Journal of Communication Inquiry* 10 (1986b): 45-60.

———. "Cultural Studies: Two Paradigms." In *Media, Culture, and Society: A Critical Reader*, edited by Richard Collins, 33-48. Beverly Hills, CA: Sage Publications, 1986c.

———. "Race, Culture, and Communications: Looking Backward and Forward at Cultural Studies." *Rethinking Marxism* 5 (1992): 10-18.

Hall, Stuart and Tony Jefferson. 1976. *Resistance Through Rituals*. Working Papers in Cultural Studies, University of Birmingham: CCCS. 1976.

Hall, Stuart, et al. *Policing the Crisis: Mugging, the State, and Law and Order*. New York: Holmes & Meier, 1978.

Hanrahan, Jennifer. "Braceros Seek Justice," *San Diego Union-Tribune*, September 26 (A1): 1999.

Hawley, Ellis. "The Politics of the Mexican Labor Issue, 1950-1965." *Agricultural History* 40 (1966): 157-176.

Hellman, Judith Adler. *Mexican Lives*. New York: New Press, 1994.

Herrera-Sobek, Maria. *The Bracero Experience: Elitelore versus Folklore*. Los Angeles: UCLA Latin American Center Publications, 1979.

Hoggart, Richard. *The Uses of Literacy*. Fair Lawn, NJ: Essential Books, 1957.

Horkheimer, Max and Theodor Adorno. *The Dialectic of Enlightenment*. New York: Herder and Herder, 1972.

Jones, Robert C. *Mexican War Workers in the U.S.: The Mexican-U.S. Manpower Recruiting Program and its Operation*. Washington, DC: Pan American Union, 1945.

Kirstein, Peter N. *Anglo Over Bracero: A History of the Mexican Worker in the United States from Roosevelt to Nixon*. San Francisco: R and E Research Associates, 1977.

Kiser, George C. and Martha W. Kiser eds. *Mexican Workers in the United States*. Albuquerque: University of New Mexico Press, 1979.

Kong, Deborah. "Former Mexican Guest Workers Call for Wells Fargo Boycott." *La Prensa*. Toledo, OH. September 4, 2002. Accessed July 12, 2016.

La Gente. "Ex braceros no encuentran documentos para reclamar dinero," November 26, 2008. Accessed July 10, 2015 at http://www.radiolaprimerisima.com/noticias/inmigrantes/42393.

Leydesdorff, Selma, Luisa Passerini and Paul Thompson, eds. "Gender and Memory." In *International Yearbook of Oral History and Life Stories*. Vol. 4. New York: Oxford University Press, 1996.

Lipsitz, George. *Time Passages: Collective Memory in American Culture*. Minneapolis: University of Minnesota Press, 1990.

———. *The Possessive Investment in Whiteness: How White People Profit from Identity Politics*. Philadelphia: Temple University Press, 1998.

———. *American Studies in a Moment of Danger*. Minneapolis: University of Minnesota Press, 2001.

———. *The Possessive Investment in Whiteness: How White People Profit from Identity Politics, Revised and Expanded Edition*. Philadelphia: Temple University Press, 2006.

———. *How Racism Takes Place*. Philadelphia: Temple University Press, 2011.

López, Ian Haney. *White By Law: The Legal Construction of Race*. New York: NYU Press, 2006.

López, Paul, ed. ¿Que Fronteras? *Mexican Braceros and a Re-examination of the Legacy of Migration*. Dubuque, IA: Kendall Hunt, 2010.

López, Paul. "Mexican Braceros and Social Capital (1942-1964): Personal Accounts, Family Accounts, and Just Accounts." In ¿Que Fronteras? *Mexican Braceros and a Re-examination of the Legacy of Migration*, edited by Paul López, 179-195. Dubuque, IA: Kendall Hunt, 2010.

Lopez Tushar, Olibama. *People of El Valle: A History of the Spanish Colonials in the San Luis Valley*. Pueblo, CO: El Escritorio Press, 1992.

Martinez, George A. "The Legal Construction of Race: Mexican-Americans and Whiteness." *Harvard Latino Law Review* 2 (1997): 321-47. Accessed November 9, 2015. http://latcrit.org/media/medialibrary/2013/09/lcigmartinez.pdf.

Martinez, Valerie. "The Braceros of the South Plains and Trans Pecos Regions, 1949-1964." In ¿Que Fronteras? *Mexican Braceros and a Re-examination of the Legacy of Migration*, edited by Paul López, 161-178. Dubuque, IA: Kendall Hunt, 2010.

Marx, Karl. *Capital, Volume I*. New York: Penguin Books, 1976.

Massey, Douglas, et al. *Return to Aztlan*. Berkeley: University of California Press, 1987.

Massey, Douglas and Xiang Liang. "The Long-term Consequences of a Temporary Worker Program: The U.S. Bracero Experience." *Population Research and Policy Review* 8 (1989): 199-226.

Matsuda, Mari. "Looking to the Bottom: Critical Legal Studies and Reparations." In *Critical Race Theory: The Key Writings that Formed the Movement,* edited by Kimberle Crenshaw et al., 63-79. New York: New Press, 1995.

Matthiessen, Peter. *Sal Si Puedes: Cesar Chavez and the New American Revolution*. New York: Random House, 1969, 2000.

McWilliams, Carey. *North From Mexico*. New York: Praeger, 1990 [1948].

Memmi, Albert. *The Colonizer and the Colinized*. New York: Orion Press, 1965.

Mills, C. Wright. *The Sociological Imagination*. New York: Oxford University Press, 1959.

Mitchell, Don. *They Saved Our Crops: Labor, Landscape, and the Struggle over Industrial Farming in Bracero-Era California*. Athens: University of Georgia Press, 2012.

Mize, Ronald L. "The Persistence of Workplace Identities: Living the Effects of the Bracero Total Institution." In *Immigrant Life in the US: Multidisciplinary Perspectives*, edited by Donna R. Gabaccia and Colin W. Leach, 155-175. New York: Routledge, 2004.

———. "Reparations for Mexican Braceros? Lessons Learned from Japanese and African American Attempts at Redress." *Cleveland State Law Review, LatCrit VIII Symposium Issue* 52 (2005): 273-295.

———. "Power (In)-Action: State and Agribusiness in the Making of the Bracero Total Institution." *Berkeley Journal of Sociology* 50 (2006a): 76-119.

———. "Mexican Contract Workers and the U.S. Capitalist Agricultural Labor Process: The Formative Era, 1942-1964." *Rural Sociology* 71 (2006b): 85-107.

———. "Critically Interrogating the Elusive Sign: The 'New' Race Theories and a Plausible Alternative for Understanding Cultural Racializations of Latino/a Identities." *Latino Studies* 11 (2013): 341-365.

Montejano, David. *Anglos and Mexicans in the Making of Texas*. Austin, TX: University of Texas Press, 1987.

Murray, Douglas. "The Abolition of El Cortito." In *Social Problems*. Reprinted in *Down to Earth Sociology,* edited by James Henslin. New York: Free Press, 1982.

Ngai, Mae. *Impossible Subjects: Illegal Aliens and the Making of Modern America*. Princeton, NJ: Princeton University Press, 2005.

Omi, Michael and Howard Winant. "On The Theoretical Concept of Race." In *Race, Identity, and Representation in Education*, edited by Cameron McCarthy and Warren Crichlow, 3-10. New York: Routledge, 1993.

———. *Racial Formation in the United States: From the 1960s to the 1990s*. Second Edition. New York: Routledge, 1994.

———. *Racial Formation in the United States: From the 1960s to the 1990s*. Third Edition. New York: Routledge, 2014.

Oregon State College. *Extension Service Records* (RG111), SG2, Folder 10, 1943.

Oregon State College. *Fighters in the Field: A Story of the 1943–1946 Oregon Emergency Farm Labor Program*. Extension Circular 492. Corvallis, OR. 1947.

Oregon State College Extension Service. "Farm Labor News Notes." Oregon State University Libraries Special Collections and Archives, August 6, 1945.

Passerini, Luisa. *Fascism in Popular Memory*. New York: Cambridge University Press, 1987.

Peck, Gunther. *Reinventing Free Labor: Padrones and Immigrant Workers in the North American West, 1880-1930*. Boston: Cambridge University Press, 2000.

Peña, Devon G. *The Terror of the Machine: Technology, Work, Gender, and Ecology on the U.S.-Mexico Border*. Austin: University of Texas Press, 1997.

Portelli, Alessandro. *The Death of Luigi Trastulli and Other Stories: Form and Meaning in Oral History*. Albany: SUNY Press, 1991.

Rosaldo, Renato. *Culture and Truth: The Remaking of Social Analysis*. Boston: Beacon Press, 1993.

Rosas, Ana Elizabeth. Abrazando el Espíritu: *Bracero Families Confront the U.S.-Mexico Border*. Berkeley: University of California Press, 2014.

Sanchez, George I. *Forgotten Americans*. Albuquerque, NM: C. Horn, 1967.

Sanchez, George J. *Becoming Mexican American*. New York: Oxford University Press, 1993.

Scott, James C. *Domination and the Arts of Resistance: Hidden Transcripts*. New Haven, CT: Yale University Press, 1990.

Scruggs, Otey M. "Evolution of the Mexican Farm Labor Agreement of 1942." *Agricultural History* 34 (1960): 140-9.

———. "The Bracero Program under the Farm Security Administration, 1942-1943." *Labor History* 3 (1962): 149-168.

———. *Braceros, "Wetbacks," and the Farm Labor Problem: Mexican Agricultural Labor in the United States*. New York: Garland Publishers, 1988 [1942].

Shimabukuro, Robert Sadamu. *Born in Seattle: The Campaign for Japanese American Redress*. Seattle: University of Washington Press, 2003.

Smith, James. "Ex-Migrants Sought for Class-Action." *Los Angeles Times*, Los Angeles, CA. March 15, 2001.

Spivak, Gayatri Chakrovorty. "Can the Subaltern Speak?" In *Marxism and the Interpretation of Culture*, edited by Cary Nelson and Lawrence Grossberg. Urbana: University of Illinois Press, 1988.

Takaki, Ronald. *A Different Mirror*. Boston: Little, Brown, and Company, 1994.

Thomas, Robert J. *Citizenship, Gender, and Work: Social Organization of Industrial Agriculture*. Berkeley: University of California Press, 1985.

Thomas, W.I. and Florian Znaniecki. *The Polish Peasant in Europe and America: Five Volumes*. New York: Alfred Knopf, 1984 [1918-1920].

Thompson, E.P. *The Making of the English Working Class*. New York: Pantheon, 1968.

Thompson, Paul. *The Voice of the Past: Oral History*. New York: Oxford University Press, 1978.

Trujillo, Luis M. *Diccionario del Español del Valle de San Luis de Colorado y del Norte de Nuevo México*. Alamosa, CO: O & V Print, 1983.

Turner, Ronny E. and Charles Edgley. "From Witchcraft to Drugcraft: Biochemistry as Mythology." *Social Science Journal* 20 (1983): 1-12.

Wall, Stephen. "Bracero Laborers Seeking Wages." *Inland Valley Daily Bulletin*. Accessed March 10, 2008. http://www.dailybulletin.com/ci_8423564.

Watson, Catherine. "The Presentation of Self and the New Institutional Inmate." In *Life as Theater: A Dramaturgical Sourcebook*, edited by D. Brissett and C. Edgley. New York: Aldine de Gruyter, 1994 [1980].
Weber, Devra. *Dark Sweat, White Gold: California Farm Workers, Cotton, and the New Deal*. Berkeley: University of California Press, 1994.
Wells, Miriam J. *Strawberry Fields: Politics, Class, and Work in California Agriculture*. Ithaca, NY: Cornell University Press, 1996.
Williams, Raymond. *Culture and Society, 1780-1950*. New York: Harper and Row, 1958.
———. *The Long Revolution*. New York: Oxford University Press, 1961.
———. *The Politics of Modernism: Against the New Conformists*. New York: Verso, 1989.
Willis, Paul. *Learning to Labor: How Working Class Kids Get Working Class Jobs*. New York: Columbia University Press, 1977.
———. "Shop Floor Culture, Masculinity and the Wage Form." *Working Papers in Cultural Studies*. CCCS, 1979.
———. *Common Culture*. Boulder, CO: Westview Press, 1990.

GOVERNMENT DOCUMENTS, UNPUBLISHED SOURCES, LIFE STORIES, AND INTERVIEWS

Anderson, Henry Pope. *Fields of Bondage*. Berkeley, CA: Mimeographed, 1963.
Colorado Agricultural Experiment Station. "Annual Report." Ft. Collins, 1958.
Crisler, Carney C. "The Mexican Bracero Program with Special Reference to Colorado." Master's thesis, University of Denver, 1968.
Cuadraz, Gloria Holguin, Christine Marin, Belen Soto Moreno, and Jose Leyba. *Mexican Americans and Litchfield Park: an Oral History Project.* Hayden Chicano Research Collection, Arizona State University Libraries, 2005-2007.
Direccion de Prevision Social. *Los Braceros*. Cuidad Mexico: Secretaria del Trabajo y Prevision Social, Direccion de Prevision Social, 1946.
Driscoll, Barbara A. "The Railroad Bracero Program of World War II." Ph.D. diss., University of Notre Dame, 1980.
Ernesto Galarza Papers. Department of Special Collections, Stanford University Libraries, Stanford, California.
García y Griego, Manuel. "The Importation of Mexican Contract Laborers to the United States, 1942-1964: Antecedents, Operation, and Legacy." La Jolla, CA: Program in United States-Mexican Studies, University of California, San Diego, 1980.
Hancock, Richard Humphris. *The Role of the Bracero in the Economic and Cultural Dynamics of Mexico: A Case Study of Chihuahua*. Stanford, CA: Hispanic American Society, 1959.
Johnson Gonzalez, Bill and Mireya Loza eds. "Opening the Archive: Documenting the Bracero Program." *Dialogo*. Forthcoming 2016.
Lessard, David Richard. "Agrarianism and Nationalism: Mexico and the Bracero Program." Ph.D. diss., Tulane University, 1984.
Lyon, Richard Martin. "The Legal Status of American and Mexican Migratory Farm Labor." Ph.D. diss., Cornell University, 1954.
McCain, Johnny Mac. *Contract Labor as a Factor in United States-Mexican Relations, 1942-1947*. Austin, TX: s.n., 1981.
Mize, Ronald L. "Court Affidavit Filed on Behalf of Plaintiff," *Jimenez de la Torre v. U.S. Federal Government, Republic of Mexico, Wells Fargo Bank, Banco de Mexico, Banco de Credito Rural*. 2002.
Mize, Ronald L. "The Invisible Workers: Articulations of Race and Class in the Life Histories of Braceros." Ph.D. diss., University of Wisconsin Madison, 2000.
Murrow, Edward R. "Harvest of Shame." *CBS Reports*. Directed by Fred W. Friendly. 1960. New York: CBS News Productions/Columbia Broadcasting System (CBS), 2005.
Rasmussen, Wayne. *A History of the Emergency Farm Labor Supply Program. 43-7 Ag. Monograph 13*. Washington, DC: U.S. Department of Agriculture, Bureau of Agricultural Economics, 1951.

U.S. President's Commission on Migratory Labor. Migratory Labor in American Agriculture. Washington, DC: U.S. Government Printing Office, 1951.

Wisconsin Administrative Register. "Migrant Labor Chapter DWD 301-2004." Accessed July 21, 2005. http://www.legis.state.wi.us/rsb/code/dwd/dwd301.pdf.

Yamamoto, Eric. "TransAfrica Forum: The Case For Black Reparations – Transcript." Accessed July 10, 2015. http://www.mdcbowen.org/p2/rap/transafrica_transcript.htm.

INTERVIEWS

Group Interview with Naturalization Class Group, 1997. Fresno, California.

Interview with Anonymous Bracero. 1997. Alamosa, Colorado.

Interview with Anonymous Daughter of Bracero, 1997. Fresno, California.

Interview with Anonymous Daughter of Bracero, 1998. Fresno, California.

Interview with Anonymous Sister of Bracero, 1997. Fresno, California.

Interview with Dolores Chihuahua. 1997, Fresno, California

Interview with Don Jose

Interview with Doña Isabel. 1997. San Luis Valley.

Interview with Mr. Allen, Former Colorado State Housing Inspector, Colorado Department of Health. 1997. Alamosa, Colorado.

Interview with Señor Freemont, Fomer Postal Worker. 1997. Alamosa, Colorado.

Interview with Señor Palmas, Former Food Provider. 1997. Alamosa, Colorado.

Phone Interview with Señor Paulo, Former Bus Driver and FLC. 1997. Alamosa, Colorado.

The Life Story of Don Andres. 2005. Mexico.

The Life Story of Don Antoñio. 1997. Fresno, California.

The Life Story of Don Baldomero. 2005. Mexico.

The Life Story of Don Crecencio. 2005. Mexico.

The Life Story of Don Daniel. 1997. Fresno, California.

The Life Story of Don Francisco. 1997. Fresno, California.

The Life Story of Don Hector. 1997. Fresno, California.

The Life Story of Don Jorge. 1997. Fresno, California.

The Life Story of Don Jose. 1997. Fresno, California.

The Life Story of Don Liberio. 1997. Fresno, California.

The Life Story of Don Lupe. 2005. Mexico.

The Life Story of Don Nicolas. 1997. Fresno, California.

The Life Story of Don Pablo. 1997. Fresno, California.

The Life Story of Don Ramon. 2005. Mexico.

The Life Story of Don Roberto. 1997. Fresno, California.

The Life Story of Emilio. 1997. Fresno, California.

Various Interviews with former residents, migrant service providers, Chicano activists. 1996-1998. San Luis Valley, Colorado. Denver, Colorado. Central Valley, California.

Index

About the Author

Ronald L. Mize is associate professor of language, culture, and society at Oregon State University. He previously taught sociology, Latino studies, and ethnic studies at Humboldt State University, Cornell University, University of Saint Francis–Fort Wayne, CSU–San Marcos, UC–San Diego, Southwestern College, Colorado State University and the University of Wisconsin–Rock County. Trained as a journalist at the University of Colorado Boulder, he went on to study Sociology at Colorado State University (M.A.) and the University of Wisconsin–Madison (Ph.D.). He focuses on the historical origins of racial, class, and gender oppression in the lives of Mexicano/as residing in the United States. Due to the reliance on Mexican labor in the rural industries of agriculture, mining, and railroad construction, his historical research explores the intersectional formations of Anglo-Chicano-Latino relations as they relate to these sectors of rural spaces and the economy. He investigates the degree to which contemporary immigrant labor is informed by the history of Mexican incorporation into the rural United States. He examines the underlying assumptions about nation, race, identity, gender and class in how the public forms opinions about immigration and he aspires to carve out a new paradigm for understanding both the political economy and culture of immigration as well as their interconnections. Mize is the author of over fifty scholarly publications, including *Consuming Mexican Labor: From the Bracero Program to NAFTA* (2010, University of Toronto Press) and *Latino Immigrants in the United States* (2012, Polity Press).

CPSIA information can be obtained
at www.ICGtesting.com
Printed in the USA
LVHW101350120222
710993LV00008B/628

9 781498 517805